Lord Singh of Wimbledon CBE is an internationally recognised journalist and broadcaster and frequent commentator on social and religious issues. He is widely regarded as both the secular and religious voice of the British Sikh community. In 1989 he became the first non-Christian to be awarded the UK Templeton Prize 'for the furtherance of spiritual and ethical understanding'.

Indarjit was named by *The Independent*, a leading British newspaper, as one of 50 people who have made a major contribution to world peace. In 2011 he was made an Independent Peer in the House of Lords.

Dedications

To my mother, Kundan Kaur, to whom I owe much for her humour and compassion for (almost) all, regardless of race or religion, and to my father, Dr Diwan Singh, for his example of living true to his principles despite the difficulties and challenges he faced.

Indarjit Singh
(Lord Singh of Wimbledon)

THOUGHTS
ON POLITICS & SOCIETY
Broadcast on BBC Radio 4

AUSTIN MACAULEY PUBLISHERS™
LONDON · CAMBRIDGE · NEW YORK · SHARJAH

Copyright © Indarjit Singh 2023

The right of Indarjit Singh to be identified as author of this work has been asserted by the author in accordance with sections 77 and 78 of the Copyright, Designs and Patents Act 1988.

All rights reserved. No part of this publication may be reproduced, stored in a retrieval system, or transmitted in any form or by any means, electronic, mechanical, photocopying, recording, or otherwise, without the prior permission of the publishers.

Any person who commits any unauthorised act in relation to this publication may be liable to criminal prosecution and civil claims for damages.

A CIP catalogue record for this title is available from the British Library.

ISBN 9781398432840 (Paperback)
ISBN 9781398432864 (ePub e-book)
ISBN 9781398432857 (Hardback)

www.austinmacauley.com

First Published 2023
Austin Macauley Publishers Ltd®
1 Canada Square
Canary Wharf
London
E14 5AA

Acknowledgements

My wife Kanwaljit and daughters Mona and Rema for their encouragement and ideas, and grandchildren Simran, Pavan, Harleen, Tavleen and Devan for their affection and unending inspiration.

THOUGHTS AND REFELCTIONS ON CURRENT EVENTS 1984-2019
BBC RADIO 4 TODAY PROGRAMME

About the author

The Today Programme on BBC Radio 4 includes a reflective live three minutes slot called 'Thought for the Day'. Initially this was provided almost entirely by Christians, with an occasional contribution by a Jewish Rabbi. In the autumn of 1983, the BBC decided to make it a bit more inclusive with occasional contributions from other faiths and a Hindu, Muslim and I were invited to broadcast in One World Week. It was recorded – they didn't fully trust us!

Doing 'Thought for Day' (TFTD) over some 35 years was interesting and enjoyable. It also had both its serious and hilarious moments. In the mid-eighties, the Indian government labelled Sikhs as terrorists to justify the Indian army attack on the Golden Temple on one of the holiest days in the Sikh calendar. The talented and affable Producer Brian Redhead latched onto this as I came in to do a TFTD and asked me 'where's your bomb? I replied, I didn't want to bring it into the studio and left it outside an office marked Director General. We laughed, but I had the last laugh when Brian went on air and inadvertently referred to a British terrorist, instead of tourist, missing in France.

Initial wariness about a Sikh broadcasting in a predominantly Christian religious slot, quickly turned to appreciation. In 1989 I was the first non-Christian to be awarded the UK Templeton Prize for the Furtherance of Spiritual and Ethical Understanding, and in 1991, the BBC and Council of Christians and Jews presented me with a Gold Medallion for Services to Broadcasting. In January 2005 I was short-listed in a BBC competition for Radio 4 listeners to choose a person who they felt could make a significant contribution in the House of Lords. I ended up coming second to Bob Geldof.

Some talks led to wider public debate, particularly one on the construction of a giant Ferriss Wheel near Parliament to celebrate the Millennium. My comment, that there were better ways of celebrating the birth of Jesus Christ, was widely appreciated and I received letters of appreciation from the Archbishop of Canterbury and Buckingham Palace, I was also asked to be a member of the Lambeth Group which helped establish a Faith Zone at the Millennium Dome in Greenwich.

My appointment as an independent peer in the House of Lords coincided with a less welcoming attitude to Sikh teachings by the new Senior Producer who even tried to dissuade me from talking about Guru Nanak, the founder of the Sikh Faith, and a later Guru who gave his life in support of right to freedom of belief for people of all religions.

My decision to leave the slot after 35 years made headline news in the Times. James Purnell, BBC Director of Radio also wrote to me saying:

'I have no doubt that your contribution over many years is deeply appreciated by the Radio 4 audience as a voice of wisdom in these intolerant times'

There was however no assurance that the discriminatory treatment of key Sikh teachings would be tackled, and I left the slot with some enduring friendships and many good memories. The one I cherish the most was being introduced by the British Ambassador, at an interfaith conference in Estonia. as 'the man who brought Guru Nanak to the breakfast tables of Britain'.

My First Thought for the Day
The Lift is Full

The talk below is a light reflection on irrational prejudice that is widely used for teaching in schools:

I once worked for a large civil engineering company on the seventh floor of an eight-story building. At the end of the day we would leave our desks and make our way to the lifts, and as the doors opened, a curious sight would meet our eyes. Those already in the lift, who belonged to the Overseas Section of the same company and felt themselves superior to us Home Civil Engineers, would stick out their stomachs a little to give the impression that the lift was a little fuller than it was. Anyway, we would ignore their less than cordial invitation, and pile in. The lift door would close and, in the short space of time it took to reach the floor below, those in before us would step back a little and make genuine efforts to make their fellow Civil Engineers feel at home.

Now, the floors below ours contained a lower order of society, truly inferior people—civil servants—to be precise. People who did nothing but sit around all day drinking tea and creating mountains of useless paperwork. It's odd how we get these prejudices. Now that I'm in local government and a public servant myself, I know how untrue these can be!

Naturally, we would stick out our stomachs to prevent those lazy bureaucrats getting into *our* lift. But, crazed with non-stop tea drinking, they would get in nonetheless. And, by the time the lift reached the ground floor, we had forgotten our, by then, seemingly petty differences, and as fellow workers, we'd leave the lift and make our way home.

I think my little story tells us a lot about human nature. It's rare for anyone getting into a lift or train or entering a new country, to be made welcome by those already there. But soon, the newcomer and the original inhabitants assume a near common identity, and perversely, strengthen this in joint hostility to further newcomers, or simply foreigners in general.

These false notions of national or racial superiority were fairly harmless in earlier times. But after the holocaust against the Jews, and with the social and political changes of recent decades, coupled with our new-found scientific ability to destroy all life on our planet, such behaviour carried to extremes, can lead to major conflict.

Guru Gobind Singh, the tenth Guru of the Sikhs, speaking some 300 years ago to an Indian society bitterly divided by caste and religion, stated: 'Recognize the oneness of the whole human race'. It is a message of even greater relevance today. In this very special anniversary of One World Week, celebrating the fortieth anniversary of the founding of the United Nations Organisation, we would do well to reflect on the enlightened teachings of the Gurus, who, in stressing the equality of all human being – men and women; their emphasis on social and religious tolerance and their brave and forthright attack on all notions of caste, class or racial superiority, gave us not only a forerunner of the UN Declaration of Human Rights, the key, not only to sanity and survival in the world today, but also an understanding that different cultures and different ways of life are not barriers between people, but gateways to a fuller understanding and enrichment of life itself.

14 November 1985

The Need for Balance Between the Material and Spiritual

Guru Nanak, the founder of Sikhism, whose birth anniversary we are celebrating this week, always laid great stress on a life carefully balanced between the spiritual and material.

The story is told that once on his travels, he visited a remote Himalayan region where, in following the commonly accepted ideal of renunciation, a number of saints and holy men had retreated from the corruption and wickedness of worldly life, to seek contemplative self-improvement. Arrogant and feeling superior, they asked Guru Nanak 'how goes the world below?'

'The world below is suffering,' replied Guru Nanak, critically, 'and how can it be otherwise when those who claim moral and spiritual insight, desert those in need of guidance'.

The wise Guru was equally critical of the blind pursuit of material wealth. The story goes that he once met a very rich merchant called Dunni Chand, who was very proud of his wealth and possessions. Guru Nanak quietly gave the rich man a needle and asked for it to be returned to him in the next world. 'How can I take a needle into the next world,' began the old miser, and then he stopped as he realized the truth of the Guru's message.

I sometimes feel that much of the discord in the world today stems from this failure to realise that life has both spiritual and material dimensions, and that if we neglect either of these it will be to our ultimate regret.

All too often in the past, religion has taught spiritual improvement, while countenancing disease, suffering and injustice. Now the pendulum has swung the other way and we are taught by clever advertising that happiness is related to the number or size of our material possessions. Get instant happiness now, on easy terms!

Take a plant into an inert atmosphere, give it as much food as you like, and it will not flourish. Nor can a plant grow on air and sunshine alone. Similarly, society fed on materialism alone cannot flourish and today, particularly in the industrialized world, we are choking ourselves with material comforts.

Are spiritual happiness, material possessions and social obligations mutually exclusive? Guru Nanak taught they were not. Indeed, all are necessary in leading a properly balanced life.

Guru Nanak taught his followers to consider the ideal of a lotus flower which, while having its roots in muddy water, still flowers beautifully above it.

Similarly, he taught we should live a full life in society, working constantly for its improvement and yet, always being above its meanness and pettiness.

It would make for a happier and more contented world, if we were to heed his sane advice.

15 November 1985

Obsession with Personal Wellbeing

This week's rains, floods and chill winds, blamed on Hurricane Charlie, mark for many of us the end of what is laughingly called the summer holiday season. The prospect before us is a long break-free haul to Christmas.

This habit of holidays has become so engrained in us that, this year, not having been able to get away, I feel jaded and edgy – like a holiday addict without his annual fix. Having experienced this ultimate deprivation, I can't help wondering how our parents' generation managed when the annual holiday was far less common.

The greater wonder is, that despite longer hours and more arduous conditions, not only did they manage, but they also seemed to find greater contentment in what they did. They seemed to have less of the frustrations and tensions that have now become a part of everyday life, and paradoxically, such tensions seem to have increased with the increase in leisure time.

The truth is that we divide our lives into work – a time for martyred suffering, and leisure – a time to enjoy the ritual of ice-creams and candy floss, or, plastic food from plastic trays in romantic trips abroad.

Our search for artificial enjoyment or happiness outside our daily round, reminds me of the story of the king who, though he ate and drank heavily and slept soundly, was convinced that he was sick. He summoned the best physicians in the land. None could cure him, until, one, wiser than the rest, advised that he would be totally cured if he slept one night in the shirt of a completely happy man. He sent out his servants to find such a shirt and such a man, but it proved no easy task and the king began to look to the well-being of his subjects and forgot his supposed sickness.

Guru Nanak gave similar advice when asked the secret of total happiness. He advised that the possession of a grain of mustard seed from a home that had known no sorrow, would guarantee lasting happiness. Of course, such a home could not be found, and, as with the king, it was the search itself that gave the clue to true contentment. Sorrow and joy do not exist in isolation but are inextricably entwined in our daily lives.

The Guru, elaborating on this formula for contentment through positive living, emphasised three essentials. Namely, meditate on God – that is not to sit vacantly in impossible positions, but simply to remember and constantly focus on the realities of life; to work earnestly and honestly at our daily tasks and, most importantly, share our earnings with the less fortunate. He taught that the secret of true happiness lay not outside our ordinary working lives, but within. Not in trying to get away from it all, but in looking within. A little reflection on this message, might just help us make it to the Christmas break.

22 April 1986

Perspective and the Wider Picture

When I was a little boy, the greatest delight of my life was the weekly comic. I'd readily identify with an athlete called Wilson – reputedly hundreds of years old – who could run a mile in three minutes! There were other heroes too, particularly detectives.

The important thing about these comics was that it was easy to recognize both hero and villain. The anarchist trying to blow-up the world, carried a round black object, conveniently labelled 'bomb'. The burglar inevitably wore a black and white stripped jersey and carried a bag marked 'swag'. Heroes would chuckle; villains sneered!

The more I look at newspapers today, the more I am reminded about those comics. Word pictures, like 'Iron Lady' or 'Mad Dog of the Middle East', are used to convey images designed to channel our thoughts and mould our attitudes, and worst of all, destroy our capacity for independent moral judgment. It is a situation made worse by a reluctance to listen to true religious guidance. For it is religion that gives, or should give, moral guidance and perspective to both individuals and society. The events of the past week have underlined for many of us, that not only are we now living in a complex and violent world, but also, in a dangerous moral vacuum.

The situation is very similar to that found by Guru Nanak in India 500 years ago. Hindus and Muslims were then locked in violent conflict, with each claiming to be the one true faith – Guru Nanak courageously urged that they look beyond labels. Different religions he taught, were merely different paths to the same goal and no one religion had a monopoly of truth.

Though the problems of conflicting ideologies are similar, the implications of the moral vacuum we find today, are far more hazardous. I know it jars a little to talk about cricket after the recent battering in the West Indies, but I can best, explain myself with a cricketing analogy. The pitch, human society, is basically the same. The batsmen and the bowlers -those in positions of power, and those that oppose them, are basically the same in their competence – or lack of it. But today, the pace of scientific change has, like overnight rain on an uncovered cricket pitch, has made conflict today virtually unplayable. The slightest error of judgment can lead to world disaster. It is then, even more important that we look carefully, beyond the catchy headlines and the attitude-begging word pictures, to the reality of the world today – especially to the social and political injustice on which violence so easily thrives.

24 April 1986

Baisakhi: Looking Beyond Doing No One No Harm

It is no surprise to most of us to be told that this April has so far been one of the coldest since records were first kept. Spring seems to have completely eluded us. But it's not so everywhere. In India, they do have a spring, with the colourful festival of Basakhi heralding the start of the Indian New Year.

It was on Basakhi day in 1699, that Guru Gobind Singh, the tenth Guru, asked Sikhs to drop their old Hindu caste names and take, in the case of male Sikhs, the common name Singh (literally – lion) – not to cause total confusion, as some schoolteachers in places like Southall or Birmingham believe, but simply to emphasize a common brotherhood and the absence of caste. At the same time women were given the common name or title 'Kaur' – literally 'princess' to emphasize their dignity and complete equality.

On the same day as he gave Sikhs the names Singh and Kaur, he also gave a set of guiding principles which remain strikingly relevant today. Perhaps the most dominant creed of our times is the constantly echoed 'it doesn't matter what we do as long as it does no one any harm'. It is a creed of outwardly compelling reasonableness, heavy with emphasis on personal freedom and yet it is hollow and totally negative within.

The smug assertion 'I've never done anyone any harm', however, sounds less impressive when we recall that countless plants, stones and rocks could boast a similar achievement. What a way of looking at things! What a legacy for future generations. Compare this 'lotus eaters' creed with Guru Gobind Singh's famous prayer which begins: -

Lord may I never refrain
From doing positive good
The Guru taught that a life not spent in doing positive good, in assisting the less fortunate, was a life wasted.

There is an English verse by Charles Mackay which neatly echoes this teaching of the Guru: -

You have no enemies you say?
Alas my friend, the boast is poor.
He who has mingled in the fray
Of duty, that the brave endure,
Must have made foes. If you have none,
Small is the work that you have done,
You've hit no traitor on the hip,
You've dashed no cup from perjured lip,
You've never turned the wrong to right,
You've been a coward in the fight.

History tells us that the Guru did 'mingle in the fray of duty' in an age of incredible cruelty. He lost his four sons in his struggle for a more just society, but he never became despondent. In this he gave us the principle of 'chardi kala' – optimism under all circumstances; surely a teaching highly relevant to us all today.

19 May 1987

Manifestos

With all the media discussion, and the publication later this morning of the remaining manifestos, I'm sure you'll all agree, the election campaign is well and truly on! Each manifesto offers its own mix of enticements – jobs, homes and consumer goods. References to freedom, justice and equality are also thrown in – like decorations on a political cake – and the choice before us is to decide which cake seems the most promising.

At the time of Guru Nanak, religious too, forgetting the teachings of their founders, also behaved like rival political parties, each with its own manifesto, a total contempt for the manifestos of others, and a politician-like-faith that salvation was just around the corner. The only difference was that the rewards promised were not of this world but the next – with the usual slogan now completely inverted, to have now, pay later.

In Guru Nanak's time, the religious leaders taught that those who gave them food and money were, in effect, giving it to their ancestors in heaven. And, unbelievably, they got away with it. The Guru found that religion had been reduced to pilgrimages, penances, and rituals – all aimed at collecting bonus points for the next world – to the utter neglect of this one. No wonder people turned away from religion, or what passed for religion, to the pursuit of the equally false mirage of happiness through material possessions.

Somewhere along the road, we seem to have missed out on the possibility of finding true contentment in a balance between the material and the spiritual. Perhaps, we can find this if we go back to the actual teachings of the great religious leaders rather than the campaigning zeal of their followers. Jesus Christ, for example, taught that man shall not live by bread alone. He taught the importance of the material, but emphasized there was more, much more to life than mere material existence. Similarly, Guru Nanak taught three dimensions of life – prayer – the spiritual dimension, earning by own effort, the material dimension and sharing our good fortune with others – social responsibility.

Perhaps, their manifestos, blurred by time and discarded by many, contain something of relevance to society today.

19 May 1987

Launch of the Inter Faith Network UK

Last week, while attending a meeting for the public launch next month of the Inter Faith Network, a major new initiative in interfaith dialogue, I took out my diary to agree a date for another short meeting this week to complete our preparations and came down to earth with a start. Penciled in for this week for today and tomorrow were: 'A' level Biology and 'A' level Chemistry Practical. The dreaded exam season was on us again! Fortunately, it was not me taking the exams but my daughter. I had taken the precaution of marking the dates in my diary to ensure that I was on my best and most tactful behaviour. For of all exams it is 'O' and 'A' levels with their links to career and job that are perhaps the most trying, not only on students themselves, but on the entire family.

Like other parents, I too have tried to do my bit to help with revision and looking at science a second-time around. I have been struck by two thoughts. Firstly, the pompous wording of so-called scientific laws and secondly their simple relevance to ordinary, everyday life.

Take for example Newton's First Law of Motion – 'All bodies continue in their state of rest or uniform motion in a straight line unless acted on by a force'. This being loosely translated into non-exam language means 'Things don't happen unless they are made to happen'.

Nothing clever or earth shattering about that, you might say. But Sir Isaac Newtown concluded that the apple fell because it was made to fall – by a force. He termed this force 'gravity' and went on to calculate the effect of this force on bodies in motion. And from his observations, we have gone on to the wonders of space travel.

I couldn't help thinking of Newton's Law – things don't happen unless they are made to happen – as we continued to plan for the official launch of the Inter Faith Network. Interfaith dialogue, like peace is unexciting. Most people are for it in a passive sort of way, and yet, dialogue and understanding, so important to today's multi-racial society, won't take place unless it is made to happen. Ignorance and prejudice will not disappear on their own accord. This is true anywhere but particularly so in Britain where culture and tradition combine to produce an infuriating politeness in which any discussion of religion, personal politics, or anything else of relevance, is considered unseemly.

Inter Faith groups throughout the UK have, for a number of years, been working quietly to remove the ignorance on which prejudice thrives. Any network linking this effort must be a good thing.

22 June 1987

Guru Arjan's Martyrdom: Looking Beyond Personal Grief to the Needs of Others

In the first week of June, nearly 500 years ago, Guru Arjan Dev, the fifth Guru of the Sikhs and founder of Darbar Sahib the famous Golden Temple at Amritsar, was cruelly tortured to death in the searing heat of an Indian June.

His crime, grave in the India of his day, was that he taught religious tolerance. He taught that no one religion had a monopoly of truth. For this he was martyred, and his followers persecuted. In keeping with the Guru's teachings, Sikhs mark the anniversary of his suffering, not by any demonstration of bitterness, but simply by setting up roadside stalls wherever practicable to serve cool refreshing drinks to passers-by. Sikhs remember the thirst and suffering of Guru Arjan Dev by looking to the thirst and suffering of others, whatever their creed.

As a Sikh brought up in Britain, I was very impressed and moved on my first visit to India by the sight of these stalls and the free distribution of chilled limewater and soft drinks. It seemed so positive.

I was therefore delighted when a few days ago, a Sikh philanthropist in this country, phoned me to say that he wanted to do something similar in London: to give away 20,000 soft drinks in one of London's major parks to mark the anniversary of the Guru's martyrdom, which this year falls on the last day of this month.

He asked if I would help him get the necessary permission. As well as being right in itself, I felt his gesture would give a positive lead to young Sikhs, whose bitterness over the Indian Army invasion of the Golden Temple and the resultant loss of many innocent lives, has sometimes led to some un-Sikh-like behaviour.

I readily agreed to my friend's request and contacted the Department of the Environment for permission to give away the free drinks in Hyde Park. The response was cold and negative. Hyde Park is a Royal Park. We cannot allow such things in a 'Royal Park'. Undaunted, I tried a non-Royal Park; Battersea Park. It seemed hopeful at first. A diary was consulted. 'We have a major event on Saturday 30th May'. I said that this was for Sunday 31st May.

'No, we can't have two major events in the same weekend'.

I tried to stand my ground. 'This is not an event that has to be organized; simply the giving of cool drinks to whoever happens to be passing. The voice at the other end of the phone became more suspicious and firm. 'I'm sorry we cannot give permission – how do we know that others won't try to do the same thing'.

I had no answer to that. I had never contemplated the likely effect of copycat attempts to promote love and concern for others. It could lead to destabilization – perhaps to the end of society as we know it.

29 June 1987

Unity through a shared dislike of Others

Once when returning from a motoring holiday in France, my family and I found ourselves in a horrendous traffic jam some fifteen miles from Paris. The traffic had ground to a complete halt, and I got out of the car to stretch my legs.

Almost immediately, a well-dressed American got out of his car, came up to me and began to complain bitterly about the traffic and French incompetence and how he had to be at an important dinner engagement in half an hour. And then another person came running up to us, saying in the broadest of Birmingham accents, 'It's all right, I'm British!'

His, 'it's all right', didn't mean that he was a traffic engineer with a magical solution to traffic jams. It meant, that he too was English-speaking. So, there we were: an American, a Sikh with turban and beard, and an Englishman – all with a sense of common unity based on language which importantly, strengthened by our common, though totally irrational irritation at French traffic management, and at the French in general!

My story illustrates an unknown law of human behaviour, Indarjit's law. Simply stated, it is 'that 'when two or more people find sufficient in common to call themselves us, they will immediately look for a them to hate'.

It is a law that applies over the whole range of human behaviour, from criticism of French traffic jams to more serious racial and national prejudices. This urge to divide ourselves into mutually hostile groups, and to strengthen our sense of identity by looking to the faults in others, is found everywhere – in politics, religion, even in the arts and in science. We certainly saw a lot of it in the recent General Election.

In Guru Nanak's day, it was religion rather than party politics that separated people into warring factions. Not only were there bitter divisions between Hindus and Muslims, but also between the many factions or holy orders within Hinduism itself.

In a country badly divided and stratified by religious difference, Guru Nanak in his very first sermon taught that 'in God's eyes, there was neither Hindus nor Muslims, only Man'.

To the numerous Hindu holy orders, proud and snug in their emphasis on difference, he taught: 'let belief in the oneness of all humanity be the creed of your holy order'. These sentiments are of continuing relevance to the world of today – in which new political dogmas have added to the old-fashioned divisions created by religious bigotry. They are also of relevance to our country today, where the highlighting of political difference in the Election Campaign, should now give way to an emphasis on unity and mutual tolerance.

10 August 1987

Fortieth Anniversary of Partition of India – the Fallacy of Irreconcilable Difference

The weekend saw the fortieth anniversary of the ending of the Raj and the transfer of power to the new governments of India, Pakistan and Sri Lanka. The British departure from India marked the end of two centuries of an extraordinary era of colourful pageantry and splendor, of genuine social reform and brazen economic exploitation.

Forty years ago, there were two views of Indian independence. One, fashionable in Britain, was that it was all a sell-out to agitators and extremists, like Nehru and Gandhi, and that Indians were incapable of ruling themselves. A second view, widely prevalent in the sub-continent, was that, now the people controlled their own destiny, all would be unity, peace and prosperity.

We have, in the ensuing years, seen the partial break-up of Pakistan and the birth of Bangladesh – with even these smaller nations experiencing tension and dissent. Severe ethnic conflict has almost torn Sri Lanka apart, and India has restless Sikh, Muslim and Gurkha minorities. The search for unity, based on common identity, has, as in many other areas of the globe, proved all too elusive.

Many blame religions for these divisions in our human family. And, in a sense they are right in the religions, or more accurately, people that claim allegiance to different religions, all too often emphasize difference and blur our common humanity. Guru Nanak drew attention to this when he taught: -

Na koi Hindu, Na koi Mussalman – that in God's eyes there are neither Hindus nor Muslims – only human beings. That God is not interested in labels but in truly religious behaviour.

The difference between religion and the misuse of religion is important. One can take hold of a Bible, or other holy book, and hit someone hard enough on the head with it kill them, but are the contents of that holy book in any way to blame?

Today there is an urgent need for both those that aspire to lead, and those that use religious books as offensive weapons, to pause, open and look at the contents of those books. They may well find pointers to that all too elusive unity between different segments of our human family.

17 August 1987

A 200th Anniversary of the Founding of the MCC

The 200th anniversary of the founding of the MCC is an appropriate time to reflect on the impact of a game that many regard almost as a religion. The phrase, 'it's not cricket' has become a part of the English language to mean 'it's not fair or just!' 'To play a straight bat', is 'to be cautiously correct and unwavering!'

I don't know if it's this ethical dimension to cricket or what, but the game does have the rare ability to bring out the best in human beings. I remember an ogre of an art teacher at school who, not recognizing my latent – sadly, still latent – Picasso-like genius, used to revel in sarcasm with remarks like 'Which way up?' or 'What is it?' when viewing my efforts at art. But even he used to turn miraculously human on the cricket field. 'Cricket', he said, was his religion.

I wouldn't go quite that far, but I must admit to constantly finding similarities between cricket and the game of life. The length of our life-innings is unpredictable, and it is for each of us to make the best of it, both for ourselves and our team – our family, friends and others with whom we share common aspirations. While we come and go and make our mark, or lose our chances, as individuals, it is in the team – in sharing our life with others – that we begin to lose some of our selfishness and look beyond ourselves to a concern for others.

The idea of team, or putting others before self, is an essential aspect of Sikhism, Guru Nanak, while emphasizing the need for personal improvement, stressed that this is counter-productive and negative if pursued in isolation and selfishness – as was common among so-called holy people in the India of his day. A truly religious person he taught was not one who merely crossed the peril-filled ocean of life himself, or herself, but one who also helped others to do so. The Guru continually stressed the importance of '*Sadh Sangat*', or team effort, in helping others and working for the betterment of society.

The description of something as 'my religion' is surely used to indicate a degree of commitment; a degree of commitment that ironically is often missing in the practice of religion. Today religious influence in peace-making and building a better social order is conspicuous by its absence. It's almost as if the leaders of religions, finding the modern world too complex, the wicket too difficult, have retreated from the field, when true religion is so badly needed.

If religion is to have real meaning in the world of today, it must show cricket-like commitment, return to the field of ordinary human activity and help us face, what Shakespeare might have termed – 'the bumpers and bouncers' of everyday life.

24 August 1987

Death of a prominent Nazi leader and Racism today

This summer, through the trial of Klaus Barbie and the death of Rudolph Hess, we have seen fleeting reminders of the evil of racism – the belief that one group of humans are inherently superior to others.

Racism also crept back into the news last week with the controversy over the City of Birmingham's Racism Awareness Course. What upset people was an Asian lecturer's vigorous denunciation of 'whites' being, as it were, "genetically endowed' with racism – from which non-whites, he maintained, were immune! Could this gentleman have forgotten the expulsion of Asians from East Africa, or be unaware of the evil of caste in India? But these are asides; surely the real criticism of such courses is that, by linking behavioural attitudes to colour, they give credence to Hitler's discredited theories of visibly different races with different aptitudes and aspirations.

Such notions have been shown to be absurd by geneticists and other scientists. Centuries earlier, religions recognized the dangers of such claims to difference and superiority. The poet Kabir, whose writings are included in the Sikh holy scriptures, ridiculing the notion of race or caste, inquired of the Brahmins – the supposedly higher caste: -

If blood flows in my veins
Does milk flow in yours?

Guru Nanak taught us that we should look to the inner light within, rather than to false notions of race, colour or caste.

Anyone who has suffered discrimination in employment or other walks of life simply because they look different, and I believe there are few newcomers to these, or other shores who have not, will readily appreciate the bitterness which this engenders. But this bitterness can all too easily warp our response into equally foolish prejudices and generalizations!

We need to be clear that what we are seeking is not equality between different races – there are no different races – but between members of one human family from different geographic, social or religious backgrounds. The difference is important and was emphasized by Guru Gobind Singh, the 10th Guru of the Sikhs, some 300 years ago when he wrote of conflict between religions:

God is in the Hindu worship, as he is in the Muslim prayer
We all pray to the same one God.

31 August 1987

Volcanic Eruption in the Cameroons

One factor that I find puzzling in the news of the tragic loss of life in the volcanic eruption in the Cameroon, is that news of the disaster, which apparently occurred in the middle of last week, took so long to reach us. This, in a world which prides itself on its technical progress, underlines the tremendous disparity in both communications and scientific advance in different parts of the globe – and the extremes of vulnerability to natural disasters.

It is, unfortunately, almost human nature to regard suffering in distant and remote parts, compared to that nearer home, as a lesser disaster, and it takes the dedicated skills of television cameramen – as in the case of the worsening famine in southern Sudan – to wrench us from our apathy and drive home to us that sense of global unity taught by Guru Gobind Singh, who wrote:

'Recognize the oneness of the whole human race'

The sad truth is that despite such teachings, and despite the growing evidence of our own eyes in our increasing trips abroad, we often fail to see foreigners as members of our own human family. Although, this latest disaster is what we call a natural calamity, there are strong parallels between it and the human tragedy at Chernobyl a few months back. The Chernobyl accident too was distant – at least at first. It was only when the huge radioactive dust-cloud began to drift our way that we recognized the tragedy not as a Russian disaster, but a global one. The drifting radioactive cloud gave John Donne's words about no man being an island, a starker truth.

Most of the deaths in the Cameroon have also been caused by a lethal cloud. This time of poisonous gas, which though not radioactive, and without long-term effects on others, is to the families of those involved equally cruel in its consequences.

Though there is no danger of wider contamination, there is a very real danger that this relative blessing itself may blunt the speed and magnitude of our response to this major human tragedy. It is only right that, despite differences in language, colour and customs, we look on those suffering in Cameroon, as our own brothers and sisters and help them accordingly. For, as the Guru wrote:

'*Ek pita ekas ke hum barah*'
'There is one father and we are all his children'

5 September 1987

Travel explodes the Myth of Difference

We learnt in this programme last week that tourism was the fastest growing industry in the world. I'm not a bit surprised. An industry with the wit and genius to make capital out of natural disasters like the Grand Canyon, civil engineering fiascos, like the leaning Tower of Pisa, or monuments to man's vanity and folly, like the Pyramids of Egypt – is bound to be successful.

I fell into this tourist trap while attending a conference in the United States last year. It was a particularly grueling timetable with endless late-night seminars and, at the end of it, totally exhausting. I found myself with some five hours to see Washington before flying on home.

Guidebook in hand and cameras on shoulder, I boarded the tourist bus that took us on a 3-hour tour of the city. Eyes half-closed through lack of sleep, I dutifully clicked away on my camera, not realizing at the time that the film wasn't properly loaded and that not one of my shots could see the light of day. Determined to get my $9 worth and report back to the family on all the wonders I had seen, I fought an almost losing battle with sleep.

The young guide had all the facts at his fingertips. The relative alignment of the White House, the Pentagon and the Washington Memorial, the number of steps on the Memorial, its floor area, in hectares, square meters, square feet, and the geometric properties of the Obelisk.

Starved of sleep, I grumpily began to ask myself what did those things matter? How important was it to know the exact number of steps to the top, or that there was a delay between commencement and completion? Then, in my half-awake state, I saw more clearly that I had ever seen before, that what the guide, like all guides was trying to do, was establish the uniqueness of the visit – whereas the real wonder of foreign travel is the discovery, that despite differences in language, or culture, or false pride in shape or size of building, we are all very much alike the world over.

12 August 1987

A Valuable Return on Investment

Whichever way I turn, I keep coming across the phrase, 'return on investment'. Yesterday's colour supplements were full of little else but calls for us to part with cash and obtain a unique return on investment. The words, 'return on investment', have almost become a modern 'mantra', that's repeated again and again, to remind us of the supremacy of money in our daily lives. It's a cry that's become increasingly strident. But it's not new.

It was very much the same in Guru Nanak's time. The Guru's father was a small-time businessman who made his living buying merchandise and selling it at a profit. He was very keen that his son should follow in his footsteps. When Nanak was about fifteen, his father decided to put him to the test. He gave Nanak some money and told him to go away and invest it profitably.

Guru Nanak duly set off towards town. On the way he met some poor people who clearly had not eaten for several days. The Guru went to the nearest market and bought fruit, vegetables, bread and milk and gave the poor unfortunates their first meal for many days. He noticed that their clothes were torn and that they were shivering in the winter cold, so he bought them warm clothes. Soon, all his money was gone.

Nanak was pleased; what better investment than feeding the poor and hungry! But when he returned home, his irate father, expecting a more tangible return on capital, took quite a different view! He had expected Nanak to bring home goods for the shop which could then be sold at a profit. He was appalled by Nanak's lack of business sense.

The young Nanak had been equally appalled by the indifference of the people around him to the obvious suffering of the poor and saw the opportunity to, not only alleviate this suffering in a small way, but also to emphasize our basic human responsibility to look to the needs of others.

This simple story is one that Sikhs tell their children to provide balance against the other Sikh injunction that requires us to earn and live by our own efforts – for it's far too easy to become single-minded and selfish in our devotion to a career or in running a business.

The Guru's teaching was simple and uncompromising – money amassed for its own sake is worse than valueless. The only true return on capital is its use to help others – clearly a thought that provides balance and direction in today's over-commercialized times!

8 February 1988

Restructuring and the Need to Build From the Bottom Up

Reorganization, or restructuring, are very much vogue words in the Britain of today, and rightly so, for it's all too easy for those that provide goods and services to become set in their ways, and insensitive to the changing patterns of demand. Unfortunately, reorganization frequently becomes a panic measure – a tinkering with the management structure to give the reassurance of 'under new management' – while, in reality, changing little.

I'd like to illustrate this with a quote, not from some disgruntled civil servant, but from a Roman soldier called Petronius who lived in the first century AD. He wrote: -

'We trained very hard, but it seemed to me that every time we began to form into teams, we were reorganized!". Petronius continues: -

'We tend to meet every new situation by reorganizing – and a wonderful method it can be for creating the illusion of progress while producing inefficiency and demoralization!'

The Roman soldier's misgivings would clearly strike a responsive chord in many who have suffered some of the reorganizations of recent years!

Guru Nanak, in the India of 500 years ago, also had problems with restructuring. The trouble, as he saw it, was that society was structured from the top down! At the top were the Brahmins, those born into the priestly class who were supposed to be in direct communion with God, and were to be fed, clothed and revered by the others! At the bottom of the pile were the lower castes who had to serve those above. Religion for the majority consisted in accepting this hierarchy of injustice as God's will!

Guru Nanak was critical of this supposedly religious society rooted, as he saw it, in inequality, suffering and injustice. Perversely, he took the heretical view; that we should build from the bottom upwards, with emphasis on sound foundations. To this end, he taught the oneness of humanity, the absurdity of distinctions of birth, caste or race; the equality of women, and the need for tolerance and respect for other ways of life – all in his view, essential aspects of religion.

I think Guru Nanak's teaching – that we define and adhere to basic core values of ethics and morality in our attempt to restructure society – also provides guidance in other fields. Take, for example, those engaged in the mammoth task of sorting out problems in the Health Service. They can start at the top and improve the efficiency of the management structure – or they can, like Guru Nanak, start at the bottom, and define minimum socially-acceptable standards of care and provision! In the same way, we can all use the richness of our religious teachings to guard us and guide us from the shallow and superficial, to the positive and lasting!

15 February 1988

Multi-tasking

The words 'Thought for the day', are frequently used as a panic time-check; a reminder that we need to rush off to work, or bundle children out of the house for school.

To help us cope with the morning rush, we generally try to do several things at the same time, rather than one after the other – such as putting on the kettle, popping a slice of bread in the toaster and pressing a shirt while we wait.

This approach to saving time by doing as many things as possible in parallel, rather than in unnecessary sequence, is the basis of an important planning technique with the impressive sounding name of 'critical path analysis', that's widely used in the construction industry to minimize delay.

It's years since I had anything to do with the construction industry, but I was suddenly reminded of this discipline while listening to the Home Secretary, Douglas Hurd's, remarks on 'Today', a week or so ago, in which he said that 'Now we've got the economy under control, we should turn to other areas of concern'.

He was, of course, referring to the increasing violence among the young – even away from deprived inner-city areas. But I wonder about the apparent suggestion that concern on social issues should follow that on the economy, or whether there should be a sequence at all.

It's so easy to think of life as a series of mutually exclusive activities. We do it all the time. For much of the year we work and then we have holidays and we enjoy, and in this way, we condition ourselves into thinking of life as discrete phases of enjoyment and work.

It's very much the same with religion. By having a set day or set times of the day for prayer, we divorce religion and the richness of religious influence from our daily lives. It was even worse in the India of Guru Nanak's day, when life itself was divided into a learning stage, an earning stage and a final religious stage.

The Guru was critical of this fractured approach to living and taught the necessity of living life to the full: that is, looking to our material needs and our social obligations at one and the same time while being immersed in, and guided by, religious teaching.

The Guru responded to the usual criticism of how we can find time for religion in our busy lives, with a beautiful verse contained in our holy book – the Guru Granth Sahib: -

Young girls bring pitchers
To fill them at the city well
And talk and laugh as they carry them
But keep their minds on the pitchers
When the child is asleep in the cradle

*The mother is busy inside and outside the house
But she keeps her mind on the child.*

Life is too short and precious to put spiritual direction, care and compassion on some backburner, when we can so easily make them vital aspects of everyday life!

23 August 1988

Terrorism in Northern Ireland

The uniform reaction of shock and horror over the blowing up of the army bus in Northern Ireland, reinforced by yesterday's murder of a Naval Officer, gives added impulse to calls for internment, tougher policing and suspension of legal safeguards for those accused of terrorist offences.

While it's right to pursue those responsible for the recent outrages and bring them to justice, there is a danger of overreaction leading to accusations of repression that strengthen the very hand of terrorism. We need to ask ourselves, is the long-term interest of Northern Ireland best safeguarded by seeking to eradicate the individual terrorist, or by concentrating greater effort on the environment in which it thrives?

A simple analogy might be helpful. When we seek to buy a house, we ask for an expert's report on signs of rot or insect damage. Sometimes urgent action is recommended to destroy infestation – the terrorists in the woodwork, but we are also advised that the long-term remedy is to look to adequate ventilation and damp-proofing. Similarly, action against individual terrorists might well be necessary, but open and objective examination of the environment of suspicion and supposed injustice from which terrorism draws its strength, is of far greater long-term importance. The real battle in Northern Ireland is for the minds and hearts of its inhabitants. A battle in which the IRA seeks to make its point through the use of the bullet and the bomb.

The Sikh view on the use of force, was put by Guru Gobind Singh, the tenth Guru. He taught that violence can only be justified if three conditions are fulfilled: -

Firstly, it must be directed against tyranny and injustice.

Secondly, all peaceful means of securing redress must first be tried.

And lastly, there should be no consideration of personal gain.

Interestingly, this is a view very similar to that expressed at the recent conference of Anglican Bishops.

It clearly stems from this view, that the way forward in the fight against terrorism in Northern Ireland is for the Government to: -

- expose fallacies or address causes of oppression and injustice:
- show that there are democratic methods of voicing dissent against official policies; and
- show the terrorists for what they really are – self-seekers trying to gain power through killing and intimidation.

Terrorism in Northern Ireland is a parasitic infection that lives and thrives in an atmosphere of alleged oppression and injustice. It is best destroyed by destroying the fears and suspicions that sustain it.

30 August 1988

Language in Religion and Politics

We all know that human body is composed of millions and millions of tiny cells, each a complete life system in itself, and yet part of a greater whole. Similarly, language is composed of hundreds of thousands of words, each precise in their meaning that in combination convey the complexity of thought, emotion or fact, or at least that's how it ought to be. All too often, however, language is used not to elucidate, but to shroud understanding.

Nowhere has this been more evident than in the field of religion. In the India of Guru Nanak, religious power was in the hands of the Brahmins, a priestly class that preserved their power asserting that they, and only they, were capable of interpreting religion. They were so successful in their aim, that for the majority of people, religion consisted not only of penances and meaningless rituals, but also to the giving of food and money to the priestly class.

One of the main techniques used by these priests to preserve their monopoly, was to make the language of religion so complicated as to be beyond the comprehension of ordinary men and women. The language employed was Sanskrit, a language not understood by most people. Religious texts contained such complex disciplines and practices, as to be virtually unintelligible to the priests themselves.

Guru Nanak boldly challenged this deliberate shrouding of the essence of true religion.

In a memorable passage, written in the language of the day, he observed: -

There are many dogmas, many systems, many modes to fetter the mind,

He reminded people of the need to look beyond the details of teachings and writings to actually living the guidance given.
Truth is high,
But higher still is truthful living.

The Guru taught, we should look beyond the fog of religious dogmas, not only to an understanding of religious truth, but more importantly, to living a life of truth, of service to God through service to his creation.

Today, we too are plagued by the misuse of language. Going back to the human body, just as cancerous cells can combine to destroy the proper functioning of the human body, innocent words are frequently used in cancerous combination to destroy meaning and convert it into near-empty rhetoric. This is particularly true in the field of politics where words like: justice, equality, civilization and tolerance are frequently used to play on emotion and prejudice. In the coming months of Party Conferences, we too will need to look beyond the rhetoric to the reality of what we are told and how it relates to truthful living.

1 September 1987

Dangers of Tunnel Vision

One of the hardest parts of doing a live broadcast is getting to the right place at the right time, and I find it is well worth my while to take a taxi from my home near Wimbledon to the studio in Central London.

The different routes taken by these taxis are a constant source of wonder. Sometimes the journey is over Putney Bridge or via Hammersmith; another driver will prefer the backstreets of Southfields and Wandsworth Bridge. Sometimes it's via Clapham and Battersea. The number of different routes seem endless! What is important is that each of the drivers is always totally convinced that his particular route is unquestionably the best! Equally important is the fact that, in reality, the actual journey time is nearly always much the same.

Followers of different religions have for centuries been single-minded in their belief that their particular route was the one and only way and were openly contemptuous and actively hostile to followers of other faiths. It was right, reasonable and religious to seek to convert the 'unbelievers' and 'heathens' to the one true way.

Guru Nanak was appalled by such bigotry. He taught that God was not interested in religious labels, but in belief and action. He emphasized that no one religion had a monopoly of enlightenment and there were many ways to the same goal of merger in God's truth.

It is not only taxi-drivers that remind us of the fundamentals of life – travel on public transport anywhere is a sermon in itself. This is certainly true here in London for those of us, like myself, who travel on the Underground. Trains marked: 'Charing Cross', turn up at the Bank, and vice versa, giving new meaning to the theories of predestination, while teaching us resilience and adaptability. At my local station there is an indicator board on which changes to times and destinations are made with bewildering frequency, emphasizing the deep uncertainties of life. And then, there is the frequent announcement over the loudhailer that, if you can't get a train to where you want to go, then go somewhere else and change!

Such advice may, at first sight, seem fatuous and irritating, but it is a message of the deepest significance. These lateral-thinkers of the Underground help remind us that we can all too easily develop a tunnel vision approach to life.

It is a message of relevance to the thousands who will be receiving their GCSE results later today. If your grades are not quite those hoped for, don't be deterred, keep trying! There is more than one way – not only to religious fulfillment, but also to educational success.

14 March 1989

Fine Tuning Our Priorities

Today, as if we could forget, is Budget Day. After the confident predictions, there will be the budget itself, and then, the inevitable post-mortems.

The Chancellor, with Paul Daniels-like dexterity, will take money from our one pocket and put it back, more or less, intact in another – deeming the whole performance a good thing. And doubtlessly the Shadow Chancellor, with equal conviction, will describe the proposals as 'an unprincipled imposition on the long-suffering public'.

While there is always argument about how revenue is raised, even greater argument arises over what constitutes a sound use of money – as Guru Nanak found when his father tried to nudge him into the world of business, by giving him a modest sum of money to invest at a profit.

The young Nanak dutifully went off towards the town. On the way he met a group of people huddled together under a tree shivering in the winter cold. They were clearly starving. Without hesitation, the young Guru bought them clothes, blankets and food. Soon all his money was gone. The Guru was happy that he had used the money profitably, but as he returned home, however, he soon found that his irate father had expected a far more tangible return on capital.

In the business world of today, economists use the concept of 'Opportunity Cost' to decide between alternative areas of investment. That is, before deciding on a course of action they consider what else could be done with the money. Guru Nanak must have done just this in placing the welfare of fellow humans above the making of more capital – as an end in itself.

It's fascinating how the teachings of one faith find a resonant echo in another. When Jesus Christ taught that man shall not live by bread alone, he recognized the importance of bread – the material side of life but taught there was more – much more to life – than the pursuit of a mirage of material happiness.

Similarly, Guru Nanak taught the need to live a life carefully balanced between *Naam Japna* the pursuit of spiritual truth, *kirt karna* earning by our own effort and *waand chakna* the sharing of those earnings with the less fortunate.

One hopes that the Chancellor will also find the right balance between material and social need. And, as we queue in post offices or filling stations to beat the budget – if only for a while – we might do well to reflect on our own budget of life. A little fine tuning between our priorities could yield rich returns.

15 March 1989

Harsh Reaction to Salmon Rushdie – Does God Need Protecting?

A sentence of death, broken diplomatic relations and this week's attempt to invoke the blasphemy laws; the Salman Rushdie affair continues to make the headlines and strain our tolerance.

What we are seeing is a new and unchartered phase in race relations, not only in this country but throughout the world. Before, we could coexist, ignorant and often contemptuous of our neighbor's culture. What the fallout from the publication of Satanic Verses has shown is that today, coexistence without understanding is hardly enough.

Interestingly, a similar clash of cultures occurred in the India of Guru Nanak's day. The majority Hindu community had been invaded by the forces of Islam. There was co-existence of a sort but no dialogue – with each faith believing that it was the one true way.

The Guru was acutely concerned about such bigotry and taught that different religions were simply paths to the same goal and that no one religion had a monopoly of truth. It is a message of tolerance that is still highly relevant to us all, whatever our faith.

Today, western culture with its dogma that virtually nothing is sacred, and everything open to question, and Asian culture with its quite different values on reverence and respect, face each other with mutual suspicion and distrust.

While the issue of Mafia-like death threats must be unreservedly condemned, is freedom of speech really absolute? There are libel laws to protect the individual and while I believe it's almost blasphemous to say God needs protecting, what of minority communities struggling for acceptance and understanding?

There is a saying in Sikhism that 'no one can understand another's pain', but having seen a Sikh child sent home from school because he was wearing a turban instead of a cap, and having heard the turban described as '–grotesque-like, something out of a pantomime' I can, I feel, understand the deep sense of hurt in the British Muslim community at what they see as unthinking slurs on the Islamic faith.

The real tragedy of the uproar over Satanic Verses is that it is leading to a hardening of attitudes and a putting up of shutters when we should be looking to that which we hold in common.

Sikh emphasis on one God, for example, is a resonant echo of the same teaching in Islam. Similarly, the Sikh teaching that 'there is an inner light in all, and that light is God', has its beautiful parallel in a line of a Christian hymn 'in all life Thou livest the true life of all'.

It is this sort of dialogue that can lead to the all-important understanding that different cultures are not barriers between people but gateways to a greater understanding and enrichment of life.

16 August 1989

A Deafening Sound

There is a saying in Sikhism that 'We love the gift but forget the giver'. The words are used in a spiritual context, but they are also true of everyday life.

I've long forgotten who it was that gave us a present of a rechargeable electric toothbrush, some ten or twelve years ago. It was never really suited to the sturdy demands of the Singh family – but it did give rise to a most unusual dream. The dream started with isolated reports about a strange and deeply upsetting noise. Doctors blamed stress and prescribed tranquilizers. But without success. The complaint became more widespread not only in this country but also abroad, and soon became the subject of major world concern.

An international conference of scientists was called to consider the situation, and, after days of intensive deliberation, came up with a solution – specially designed earmuffs to filter out the offending noise. It worked at first, but soon people complained that the earmuffs were beginning to lose their protection and that the noise was becoming even more distressing.

In despair, a conference of religious leaders gathered and, after much discussion, concluded that the noise was, in some inexplicable way, nature's reaction to the way in which human beings were treating each other and destroying the environment in the process. I'll never know what happened next. At that moment, I woke up to the noise of the toothbrush holder on charge in the bedroom.

This strange dream occurred many years before the current concern over the environment. Today it's not nature that's making a noise of protest but people all over the world, alarmed by the potentially lethal gap in the ozone layer, the hazards from excess carbon dioxide and other known forms of pollution, too numerous to mention, as well as others still unknown, undoubtedly lurking around the corner waiting to be discovered. It all adds up to the inescapable fact that we humans are proving far too clever and short-sighted for our own good. No doubt scientists will come up with their own earmuff-like solutions, but is there any real alternative to major changes in attitudes and priorities?

A verse from Sikh scriptures reminds us of an important need for a sense of perspective in considering our role and responsibility in God's creation: -

'There are many universes
And hundreds and thousands of worlds
How many vex their hearts to know His limits
But seeking to explore infinity can find no bounds.'

We puny humans need to lose a little of our arrogance and certainty, in just such reflection. Only then can we acquire the humility and wisdom necessary to see the full extent of our lack of vision, an essential first step in preserving the precious gift of our environment for ourselves and our children.

8 August 1989

Balancing the Spiritual and Material

I've always tried to live by the Christian injunction 'Give unto Caesar the things that are Caesar's, and to God the things that are God's'. Caesar, in my case being the Local Authority in which I work.

Normally, it's quite easy to keep the two separate, but I ran into difficulties when I was awarded the UK Templeton Prize for Religion, earlier this summer. A National Daily phoned to say they wished to interview me, preferably in my office at work. I was hesitant. Pushed by the reporter, I agreed to seek guidance.

I carefully broke news of the award to close colleagues. They were kind, though not exactly, ecstatic. One could sense they were asking themselves 'What was someone they'd always assumed to be normal, doing in the unreal world of religion?'. The bureaucracy was even more confused, they'd never had a request for an interview about religion! Eventually, it was agreed that 'There was no overriding objection'.

Why is it that local authorities and public bodies on all sides of the political spectrum, are so uniform in their distrust of religion, rating it below bingo as a force for social uplift? One such authority, with a proud record of enlightened assistance to ethnic minorities, drew the line at anything to do with religion, saying: 'All they do is bowing and chanting'. It's a somewhat unfair judgment, but one widely shared by those outside organized religion.

I feel the reason lies with the reluctance of religions to get involved with issues of everyday concern. It's as if organized religion, finding the challenges of worldly life too complex and daunting, has retreated into a cloistered contemplation of life in the hereafter.

A similar situation existed in the India of Guru Nanak's day. Religion had become reduced to ritual and superstition and a holy person was considered to be one who left family and friends to seek spiritual self-improvement in caves and forests. The Guru was scathing in his criticism of such, opting out of social obligations. The world was suffering cruelty and injustice he said, precisely because such desertion gave free reign to tyrants and evildoers. True religion, he taught, did not consist of seclusion, penances or austerities, but in serving God through service to His creation.

The role of religion is to supply the essential spiritual and moral dimension so necessary for both social justice and spiritual fulfilment, but unless it addresses real concerns, it will continue to be marginalized as 'so much bowing and chanting', of little relevance to everyday life.

9 August 1989

President Gorbachev Heralds in Democracy- and Opposition

The news that President Gorbachev is already having trouble with the Soviet Union's first official opposition for seventy years, leaves me with decidedly mixed feelings. While any move towards greater democracy must be a good thing, my sympathies are very much with the Soviet President struggling to achieve genuine reform.

Mr. Gorbachev will also have to face the added paradox present in all democracies as to what extent should leaders lead, or are they there simply to reflect the views of those that put them in power?

It's not a problem for Sikhs. A leader in the Sikh community is unique in being the one person who does what he or she is told. The reason for our robust lack of deference to those in authority, lies in both Sikhism, with its rejection of all notions of caste or social hierarchy, and in Sikh history with the community's constant opposition to all forms of autocratic rule.

Sikhs like to claim the dubious distinction of being the world's first true democrats. Our gurdwaras are run by democratically elected management committees – naturally, there's an opposition – normally, everyone not on the management committee!

More seriously, Sikhs, throughout their 500-year history, have constantly been involved in the fight to secure democratic rights and fundamental freedoms for people of all communities; a struggle that led to the martyrdom of two of our ten Gurus. Naturally then, we find it a little difficult to accept the suggestion contained in recent commentaries on the French Revolution, that democracy and human rights are peculiarly Western institutions.

There is, however, a more fundamental reason why religion is viewed in negative terms and democracy as a panacea for all ills in society; just as people in Guru Nanak's day believed that ritual immersion in water would lead to spiritual purity; today it is often naively assumed that the ritual placing of pieces of paper in a ballot box is itself a guarantee of human rights and democratic purity.

It's a fallacy that arises out of the constant blurring of the difference between democracy and majority rule – which can be every bit as cruel as the tyranny of the minority. The truth is that the ballot box is only a first small step in the direction of fundamental human rights. The larger step lies in looking to the needs, fears and aspirations of those outside the majority.

It is this wider view of democracy that can move us nearer to Guru Nanak's concept of as just a society as one that recognizes both the worth of an individual and the oneness of our human family.

10 August 1989

Mandatory Daily Collective Worship

The Education Reform Act which comes into force next month has already got off to a bad start. The new Act makes mandatory, daily collective worship which should, and I quote, be 'wholly or mainly of a broadly Christian character'.

Many people of other faiths, rightly or wrongly, see this as a buttressing of the Christian religion and culture at the expense of that of others. Already there is talk of withdrawing children or setting up separate schools. Inevitably there will also be a jockeying by minority communities for maximum coverage of their faith in the remaining balance of collective worship. All in all, it's not the best way to promote interfaith understanding. It's interesting to note that the concern of minority religions to the new requirements, is a mirror image of the concern of the Christian community to the erosion of its religion and culture in multi-faith Britain.

Sikhs find themselves in a curious position in this debate. Guru Nanak taught *'Na koi Hindu, na koi Musalman'*. That is, 'in God's eyes there is neither Hindu or Muslim', and by today's extension, no Christian, Jew or Sikh. God, he taught was not interested in religious labels, but in the actual way in which we live and serve our fellow human beings. Or as Guru Gobind Singh put it: -

God is in the Hindu worship
As God is in the Muslim prayer

Sikhs see different faiths as different paths on a mountain. The paths are not the same. Some seem a little more direct than others. There are also apparent shortcuts which might well prove otherwise. But the paths are not necessarily mutually exclusive, and they often meet at key points or cross areas of common outlook.

What concerns me as a Sikh is that both the new requirements on collective worship and the reaction of minority faiths are as one in neglecting this area of common ground and instead, behaving as if absolutes like God, truth, goodness and justice in one religion or language, were somehow holier than their equivalents in another.

It is to counter this sort of thinking that our Holy Book, the Guru Granth Sahib, contains not only the writings of the Sikh Gurus, but also those of Hindu and Muslim saints where these are in consonance with the thrust of Sikh teachings.

One hopes that commonsense will prevail over the divisive language of the Act, and the accent will be on real dialogue. The exploration of our different faiths will not only lead to a respect for genuine differences but will also highlight the vast expanse of common ground, and the truth that God, Waheguru, Jehovah, or Allah, are different perceptions of the same one ultimate reality.

9 January 1990

Birthday of Guru Gobind Singh

This last week, Sikhs have been celebrating the birthday of Guru Gobind Singh, tenth Guru of the Sikhs. It was he who gave us our distinctive identity and the apparent paradox of a religion, that while teaching the equality of all human beings requires its followers to look distinctive. Gobind Singh, or Gobind Rai, as he was then, was only nine when his father, Tegh Bahadur, the ninth Guru, was publicly beheaded for his courageously supporting the right of another community, the Hindus, to follow their own faith, during a campaign of forced conversion to Islam by the bigoted Moghul rulers. Following the execution, the Sikhs who then had no distinctive appearance, were openly challenged to claim their master's body. Fearing a similar fate to that suffered by the Guru, no one came forward, and the body was eventually removed under cover of darkness.

As the young Gobind grew into manhood, he thought long and hard of how to prevent future lapses of courage among his Sikhs. He chose the harvest festival of 1699 to put the community to the test. While the crowd was celebrating the gathering of the winter crops, the Guru suddenly emerged from a tent, sword in hand and asked if there were any Sikh who was there and prepared to die for his faith.

In the deathly silence that ensued, a Sikh followed the Guru into the tent, and then, to everyone's consternation, the Guru emerged alone sword apparently covered in blood, and asked for another Sikh to come forward. In all, the Guru took five Sikhs in turn into the tent each time coming out alone, sword seemingly covered in blood. The crowd was stilled to silence thinking the Guru had gone mad.

On the fifth occasion, however, to everyone's wonder and joy, the Guru emerged from the tent not alone, but followed by the five Sikhs who were alive and well, now wearing turbans and what were to become other distinctive symbols of the Sikh faith. Symbols that cannot easily be discarded in a moment of weakness.

No one knows what went on in the tent. What we do know is that the discipline and courage of the community had been tested in the most rigorous way possible and that it had come through with flying colours.

The Guru initiated the Sikhs with sweetened water stirred with a sword, as a reminder of the need for both moral strength and sweetness of temperament. From that moment on male Sikhs took the common name Singh, literally 'lion', to denote courage. Similarly, women were given the title Kaur, literally 'princess', to denote a new dignity and equality.

Our symbols are then a uniform to remind us of the egalitarian principles of our faith. As in other faiths, rituals and symbolism can all too easily become surrogates for belief and action. We must constantly remember that their value lies solely in reminding us to live the ideals they represent.

10 January 1990

Fall of Romanian Dictator Nicolae Ceausescu

Shelley's poem 'Ozymandias', describes a traveler in a forgotten land discovering two vast and trunkless legs standing in the desert in a scene of total desolation. He draws our attention to the irony of the words on the pedestal which read: -

My name is Ozymandias, King of Kings
Look on my works ye mighty and despair

It was similar Ozymandias-like arrogance that inspired the Romanian dictator Nicolae Ceausescu to construct a palace of gold and marble opulence, so vast that its rooms had never been properly counted. Today it stands silent and deserted; the province of stray dogs and would-be looters; a monument to extraordinary vanity, and the labyrinth of tunnels and torture rooms beneath, a continuing reminder of man's inhumanity to man.

We pride ourselves as human beings on our ability to learn from the past, on cumulative wisdom. And yet, in this respect, we seem to have learnt nothing. Similar inhumanity amid vulgar opulence in the India of the sixteenth century, led Guru Nanak to declare: -

The age is a knife
Kings are butchers
In this dark night of falsehood
No moon of truth is seen to rise

The Guru realized that for evil to succeed, it only requires the good to remain silent and he was very critical of so-called holy people who, instead of speaking out against injustice, retreated into the wilderness to meditate and seek personal salvation.

The parallel with modern times continues with the tenth Guru, Guru Gobind Singh, being forced to take up arms to defend the weak and oppressed against cruel mercenaries bent on exploitation of the masses. It was a struggle that was to cost him the martyrdom of his four sons.

Today in the West there is a feeling of smugness. It could never happen here. Not to the same extent perhaps. We do have the benefit of the Press, media and other democratic institutions to act as safety valves against arbitrary rule. While few now seek escape from social responsibility in the physical wilderness we do have the widespread philosophy of looking after number one, of not getting involved in the troubles of others, of escape in an inner wilderness.

Guru Gobind Singh taught that such abandonment of social responsibility invites cruelty and oppression. His prayer: 'May I never be deterred in the fight for truth and justice', a sentiment paralleled in the courageous struggle of the East European dissidents, points the way for all people struggling to secure and preserve the sort of freedom we in the West have long since taken for granted.

11 January 1990

Capitalism at Highgate Cemetery

The recent offer of the capitalist government of West Germany to assist in the upkeep of the grave of Karl Marx in Highgate Cemetery, must have had the old gentleman turning in the ground below. As if recent events in Eastern Europe weren't bad enough: if present trends continue, people there will soon be able to enjoy the decidedly mixed blessings of the free market economy, with its survival of the fittest, be they individuals or industries.

I shouldn't really grumble. The free market treats me well. My mail is full of offers of free gifts. The accompanying blurb is always designed to appeal to our vanity in seeing or hearing our own name. 'Dear Mr. Singh, you will be pleased to know Mr. Singh that you Mr. Singh, have been selected to take part in our free prize draw.' What nice people. Even kinder, are the credit card organizations which give us bonus points for free gifts to make us spend more. I might just make a steam iron before the offer closes next month. But I'll have to hurry. The danger in such hurrying, however, is that it reduces thinking time. Perhaps this is deliberate and necessary. Thinking might result in us challenging the assumption that more is better than enough – a philosophy that provides the rationale of a system in which we are encouraged to buy more than we can afford to enable manufacturers to produce more than is required.

We are encouraged and cajoled to believe success or failure in life is to be determined by our 'standard of living' which, in a commentary on the times, is measured in terms of number of cars, fridges or electronic gadgetry. This is not to decry the value of material goods, which can often add substantially to the quality of life. What must be challenged, however, is the unthinking assumption that happiness or contentment is in some way proportional to the number of such possessions.

The Sikh Gurus constantly reminded us that there was also another dimension to life, the spiritual. And that true contentment lies not in extremes but in a life of balance between the spiritual and material.

The fifth Guru, Guru Arjan, emphasized this when he wrote: -

To live by grinding corn
Wearing only a blanket
But having a contended heart
Is better than ruling a Kingdom
Without inner peace

A little over a century ago, Karl Marx reminded us that religion, if it induces indifference to human suffering, is like an opium of the people. Today, we should be careful not to allow unthinking consumerism to become an opiate that desensitizes us to spiritual values and our duty to our fellow humans.

4 July 1990

No Shortcuts to Curing Social Ills

Guru Nanak once observed: *'Jo sahj pakhe, so mitha hoe'*. 'The fruit which ripens slowly, tastes the sweetest'. That is, speed is no substitute for soundness.

I was reminded of this when speaking at a local government conference on 'Religion in today's society'. The conference itself was something of a breakthrough, because local authorities have long treated religion and culture as something of taboo subjects, quite unrelated to everyday life. My talk appeared to be well received, but, from the questions that followed, it soon became clear that there was still a considerable misunderstanding about religion.

'What advice does Sikhism have on the pollution of the environment?' I was asked; 'on the problem of the homeless'; 'what about violence and bad language on television?' Apart from the fact that some of these problems never existed at the time of the Gurus, what concerned me most, was the implicit hope for near-instant solutions to deep-rooted problems.

This quest for instant solutions, is very much the mood of today, and it is, ironically, the very cause of many of our problems. Our blinkered pursuit of instant material happiness through an ever-higher standard of living, has clearly left in its train all manner of social and environmental ills.

In Guru Nanak's day, religious leaders of society, instead of addressing social problems around them would retreat into the wilderness in search of God and contemplation of the hereafter.

The Guru warned against the two extremes of seeking selfish contentment through blindly chasing the mirage of material happiness and equally selfish withdrawal from contamination with society's problems. He taught the importance of balanced living, which Sikhs 'Sahej' – that is, a life of balance rooted in positive concern for others.

I reminded the Conference that the social problems raised by my questioners, though serious – 15,000 homeless by today's news – were natural consequences of wrong priorities and false values, and to moving to sahej or balance, would take an overriding commitment to enlightened social standards for housing, health and social care with similar safeguards for the environment. This might reduce our disposable income but would increase our standard of living in the fullest sense of the word. It's not the instant cosmetic remedy demanded in our impatient times, but, in the Sikh view, it's the only solution that will endure.

5 July 1990

The Tebbit Cricket Test

Today's third Test against New Zealand will inevitably be overshadowed by the football World Cup.

It's bad enough having the Cup Final in late spring, and the start of the new football season in August, now cricket lovers, like myself, find even the middle of summer is no longer sacrosanct.

Cricket is a game rich in moral metaphors – 'play life with a straight bat' – a reminder of correctness of action; 'keep your eye on the ball' – that is, 'don't be diverted from your true objective'. These and similar comparisons, remind me of a verse that describes the all-pervading nature of God through the eyes of a cricketer:

I am the batsman and the bat,
The bowler and the ball
The cricket pitch stumps and all
Sikhism sees God in similar terms
He is the fisherman and the fish
The water and the net

The Sikh Gurus constantly used such everyday occupations and experiences to illustrate universal religious themes – such as the oneness of God, and our common humanity.

'God the one potter has fashioned all the pots
And His light pervades all creation'

Sadly, it is a truth all too often ignored in a more general pandering to petty nationalism, and I am reminded today of the recent discussion over the support of New Commonwealth immigrants for a cricket team, being an indicator of their national loyalty.

Such a comparison however, betrays not only an ignorance of the motives and mechanics of migration, but worse, an ignorance of cricket itself which applauds merit, irrespective of team. When people move from one country to another, they bring with them visible baggage – clothes and personal belongings. They also carry with them invisible baggage – family relationships and friendships with those left behind, a religion and culture, and nostalgic memories of sporting and other heroes that fashioned their youth.

As Guru Nanak puts it in the Sikh prayer, the Japji Sahib: -

Kar Kar Karna Likh Lea Jau

We carry with us the record of our past.

True loyalty is not blind allegiance to a piece of land, or a cricket team or even a religion, but to the memories and values they represent.

If Hindus, Muslims and Sikhs from the sub-continent are true to their religious and cultural values of honest effort, compassion and positive concern for others, they will be infinitely better citizens than if they merely rejoice or commiserate with England at cricket and football.

29 January 1991

Russian Dissident Alexander Solzhenitsyn on Religion

Alexander Solzhenitsyn, the famous Russian dissident, was an early recipient of the Templeton prize for religion. The award was presented to him in 1983, and it recognized a wider view of religion. It is a view that accords with Sikh teaching that religion lies not in rituals or ceremonies, but in the way we conduct ourselves.

In his Guildhall acceptance speech, Solzhenitsyn recalled his childhood, when people, appalled by the suffering in the early years of the revolution, would remark: *'it's all because we've forgotten God'*. He continued: -

'today having witnessed suffering and horror that totally dwarfs that of earlier years, if I am asked to explain why the excesses, I can do no better than repeat those pithy words – it's all because we've forgotten God'

It's useful to look at the suffering in the Middle East in the context of Solzhenitsyn's remarks. The immediate cause of the war is, as we all know, Saddam Hussein's naked aggression against the people of Kuwait. But it was the Soviet Union and the West that supplied him his vast arsenal of sophisticated weaponry, including gas, chemical, and, as we've heard this morning, possible nuclear capability.

When we consider, what seems to me, the utter immorality of the arms trade, and the proven futility of trying to build long-term peace on the shifting sands of political expediency, I cannot but echo Solzhenitsyn's remark – it's all because we've forgotten God. It's not so much forgotten God, as having pushed God out of the equation with the modern mantra 'keep religion out of politics.

Sikh teaching, in common with those of other faiths, insists that the only true peace is God's peace, rooted in justice. Guru Ram Dass, the fourth Guru, warned against factional politics when he said: -

'Some make a pact with
Brother, son and friend,
Others join factions with warlords
For selfish ends.
I have a pact with God.
I rely on Him alone.
All other pacts are for worldly power
That divides man into warring groups.
I am of God's faction.'

A just peace does not necessarily follow a just war. Nor can it come from new permutations of old factional alliances. A truly just and lasting peace can only be secured by unreserved allegiance to godly ideals, such as those so clearly enshrined in the United Nations Charter; – dedicated allegiance that ensures security of abode and religious and cultural freedom for all the people of the Middle East. Never again should we have to say, 'it's all because we've forgotten God'.

30 January 1991

Sikh Teachings on War and the War Against Saddam Hussein in Iraq

There's a district in Delhi called Tis Hazare. It means the 30,000. It marks the area where in 1787, a Sikh general stormed the walled defenses and captured the city.

He had marched from Punjab with a force of 30,000 to protest against the desecration of a Sikh holy site. He summoned the defeated rulers and demanded assurances that a Sikh temple would be built on the holy site. The assurances were readily given. He then astonished both rulers and later historians by leading his victorious army on the long march back to Punjab.

The astonished rulers asked him why he had decided not to keep the fruits of conquest. He replied that Sikh teachings forbade the use of force to acquire even an inch of territory.

The story will come as a surprise to those familiar with the exotic but misleading British-Raj image of Sikhs as 'a martial race'. The correct Sikh response to personal injury or affront is to 'kiss the feet of those that would do you harm'; a teaching remarkably similar to the Christian 'turning of the other cheek'.

However, The Sikh Gurus also taught that when violence or injustice is directed against the weak or disadvantaged, it's the duty of Sikhs to respond. If all other means have been tried and failed in such response, it is legitimate to use force. It's a doctrine that is closely paralleled in the preamble to the United Nations Charter.

The Gurus also taught, and insisted, that, force should never be used for personal gain and should always be tempered with humanity.

There's a story of a Sikh water-carrier brought before the Guru accused of giving aid and comfort to the enemy by supplying their wounded with water. The Guru immediately embraced the accused man, saying 'you have acted like a true Sikh'.

In the heat of the war now being waged against Saddam Hussein, the sight of prisoners being ill-treated, and their use as a human shield which, according to Baghdad, has already resulted in one death, can easily blind us to our objectives. Emotive calls for revenge can all-too-easily lead us down the slippery slope to humiliation and the seeking of political or economic advantage over a beaten people. It's a sure recipe for future conflict.

Guru Nanak warned against this flawed view of justice and wrote: -

'The highest vision of justice
Lies not with man,
Nor with any creature of the Universe,
But with God alone.'

The examples of the Sikh General and the water-carrier are salutary reminders of this higher vision of justice – so necessary in the world of today.

31 January 1991

Thirtieth Anniversary of Founding of Amnesty International

This summer, Sikh commemoration of the martyrdom of Guru Arjan, fifth Guru of the Sikhs, has coincided with the thirtieth anniversary of the founding of Amnesty International – events separated by more than three centuries, and yet linked by a common concern for basic human rights.

Guru Arjan was tortured and martyred for his alleged heresy in preaching that there was more than one path to God. It was he who compiled the Sikh holy book, the Guru Granth Sahib, and true to his teaching, incorporated in it the writings of Hindu and Muslim saints to emphasize that no one religion has a monopoly of truth.

Guru Arjan also founded the Golden Temple in Amritsar, built with its famous four doors to welcome visitors from all directions and remind us that God does not restrict truth and piety to one path or one door. Typically, the Guru asked a member of another faith, Mian Mir, a Muslim, to lay the foundation stone. The Guru's mission was to illuminate our minds with a broader and richer view of religion that emphasized tolerance and respect for the beliefs of others.

The role of Amnesty International has also been one of shedding light, not on man's mind and belief, but on cruel and inhuman behaviour – deliberately shrouded in political darkness.

Earlier, Guru Nanak, referred to such darkness and the abuse of human rights in the India of his day. He observed: -

The age is a knife,
Kings are butchers,
In the dark night of falsehood
No moon of truth is seen to rise.

Strong words, which sadly, still ring true in the latter part of the twentieth century, where, in our civilized world, nearly 100 countries practice cruel and inhuman torture.

Andrei Sakharov, the famous Russian dissident, who himself suffered considerable persecution, made clear that human rights abuses would always continue unless and until we become even-handed in our condemnation of injustice – a timely warning to our tendency to be selectively blind to human rights abuses of 'friendly' powers and trading partners.

Sikh teachings warn us against factions and alliances that lead us to dubious moral compromises: -

'*All such alliances are subject to death and decay,*
All such pacts are for worldly power,
And selfish ends.

I am of the Lord's faction'.

What the Guru was saying was that moral considerations should never be subservient to political expediency. A sentiment essential to the true furtherance of human rights.

3 July 1991

A Global Perspective on Economic Issues

It was Groucho Marx who said that he wouldn't want to be a member of any club that would have him as a member. He was making the point that the most sought-after clubs were characterized by their exclusivity. I know what he meant. Years ago, when I was still playing cricket – a useful leg spinner – though I say so myself – I applied to join the MCC. I'm still waiting!

The India of Guru Nanak's day also contained numerous exclusive groupings; not clubs but religious sects identified by external symbols, including, unbelievably, skinheads and punks complete with spiked hair, all claiming a uniqueness of doctrine.

So numerous were these sects that when Guru Nanak came to a small town inhabited by such people, their leaders sent the Guru a cup full to the brim with milk, to suggest to him that there was no room for yet another sect. Guru Nanak gently placed a jasmine flower on top of the milk and sent it back, indicating that it was often possible to add fragrance and meaning to existing truth. He went on to remind the sects not to be obsessed with petty dogma but to look outwards and make the welfare of the whole human family their common concern.

The World Economic Summit, a grouping of seven of the world's richest and most powerful nations, meeting in London later this month, has also been criticized as inward-looking, an exclusive club lacking concern for the wider world outside. Since the Summits started in 1974, the rich have become richer and the poor progressively poorer.

There's an apparent glimmer of hope that the Group may at long last be looking beyond its narrow horizons in an agenda that includes modest proposals for debt relief and aid to famine areas. But in themselves, these proposals are a very small drop in a very large ocean. It's rather like popping a small sum in the charity envelope pushed through the letterbox. It might make us feel good, but to quote Guru Nanak, on the ritual giving of charity: 'in real terms it's not worth even a grain of sesame seed'.

If the Group of Seven wish to make real progress, they will have to look outwards with a deep commitment to redressing chronic economic imbalances to ensure poorer nations don't always remain so – even if it means an end to their own exclusivity.

4 July 1991

The Break-up of Yugoslavia: Bridge Building Between Communities

Some years ago, in what now seems another incarnation, I found myself in charge of a large mine in the Indian State of Bihar. New government regulations required the provision of a workers' canteen, and true to my egalitarian Sikh principles and Western education, as well as with a sense of power in being the manager of a large enterprise, I saw the requirement as an opportunity to do something about the caste system.

I pompously issued a decree that the canteen would be open to all castes at all times. No one came! On investigation, I found that it was not only the higher castes that took affront, but also the lower castes who saw my dictat as an attack on their religion. Admitting defeat, I staggered the canteen opening hours for different castes, keeping only a couple of hours in which, anyone could use the facilities. It was the busiest time of the day.

The continuing unrest in Yugoslavia that brought this near-forgotten episode back to mind. My experience taught me that the use of power and authority in a high-handed manner can only have the opposite effect to that desired.

There seems to be a general yearning for cultural identity, often seen in demands for greater autonomy -whether it's the Kurds and Shias in Iraq, the Baltic Republics of the USSR or Serbs and Croats in Yugoslavia.

An additional feature, common to these communities, is that they have all suffered from ill-considered political settlements in which they have found themselves truncated and arbitrarily assigned to different national boundaries to which they are expected to show undying loyalty.

What is certain, is that ignoring the very real desire of people to relate to their roots, culture and religion, will provoke similar resentment to that of my clumsy attempt to abolish the caste system in a tiny corner of Bihar. The episode taught me the need to be sensitive to people's beliefs and cultures.

This was very much the approach of Guru Nanak, who criticized the ritual and superstition in society while remaining sensitive to the fundamentals of Hindu and Muslim beliefs. His contribution to resolving the conflict between religions was to show the essential unity of religion by emphasizing common elements that brought both communities together. The measure of his success was that when he died, both Hindus and Muslims claimed him as their religious leader.

It was the historian, George Bruce, who described the Guru as the first bridge-builder between different faiths. It's this bridge-building approach between the different religions and cultural communities in Yugoslavia that is so necessary today.

8 October 1991

Religious Input in Tackling Secular Concerns

In a meeting of the Home Secretary's Committee for Race Relations, I asked the then Registrar General if a question on religion could be added to the 1991 census. I felt it would be helpful to the fair allocation of Local Authority and other resources to have some idea of the size and distribution of minority faiths – particularly in regard to schooling and collective worship.

It was, I thought, a fair question, but sudden hush fell on the meeting and all eyes turned towards me. It was as if I had socially disgraced myself in some way. That instant I knew exactly how Oliver Twist must have felt when he asked for more. 'No, religion is a private affair' came the slap on the wrist reply.

I'll never learn! Forgetting my earlier rebuff, I asked a senior council officer last week why his Authority excluded religious organizations from the grant giving process. They were, after all, a part of the community. His reply was instant, scathing and dismissive. 'Religions do nothing for the community – it's all bowing and chanting'. I used to feel that such comments stemmed from a misunderstanding of religion, particularly of minority faiths, but the furore over Dr Carey's remarks on inner city violence a couple of weeks back, has made me realise the extent to which religion has been marginalized from everyday life. Dr Carey, you'll recall, had simply commented that in preventing future riots we should not 'ignore the reality' of a sense of marginalization in some religious communities in inner city deprivation. The uproar that followed was not so much on what he said, but on his right to bring religion into discussion on social and political issues. As a Sikh, I've always believed that the purpose of religion was to do just that. Guru Nanak taught that religion has a vital part to play in working for a better society.

The Guru's message was simple and direct. Take the ritual and obsession with personal salvation out of religion and keep what's left – that is a higher understanding of justice and compassion – back into human affairs.

I would readily agree with those that argue organized religions don't have a monopoly of higher ethical values, but we live in a world replete with man-made imperfections, injustice and cruelty, and need all the help we can get in trying to move to a saner society. To exclude religion from this process would indeed reduce it to so much bowing and chanting.

9 October 1991

Party Conference: the One Question Politicians Must Address

There was a little cartoon in Monday's Guardian showing a Conference-weary delegate, saying: 'Wake me up when it comes to the standing ovation'. In my innocence I used to believe that these, now mandatory, displays of affection were genuine measures of popularity. Then I read that Stalin used to have standing ovations of more than an hour, with none daring to be the first to sit down. Last year we saw the apparent fickleness of political allegiance, with Margaret Thatcher losing the Party leadership within weeks of receiving a record standing ovation.

The problem then, is to measure the reality behind all the rhetoric and dazzling displays of loyalty. Increasingly the Party Conference season seems like the TV panel game, in which contestants have to decide which of several equally plausible explanations gives the true meaning of an obscure word from the dictionary.

As we look or listen to what's said in the various Party Conferences, we too have to decide the truth between highly conflicting stories.

The Health Service is in excellent health; the Health Service is falling apart! The economy is in the ascendancy with inflation falling; the economy is in a shambles with unemployment spiraling! In the panel game we know that one of the contestants is telling the truth. In the self-praise and selective emphasis coming from the different conference halls, many are left with a feeling that truth is an early casualty in this war of words.

The problem of deciding the truth between conflicting claims is one that exercised the mind of a rich merchant, Makhan Shah whose ship was caught in a fierce storm in the Bay of Bengal. He prayed to God for safe delivery, vowing that he would give fifty gold pieces to the Guru on reaching safety.

The storm duly subsided and, true to his pledge, the merchant went in search of the Guru. To his consternation he found numerous people all claiming to be the one true Guru. Some boasted the greatest following, others miraculous cures and shortcuts to salvation.

It was then that he realized that perhaps he'd been asking the wrong questions. He enquired which of the holy men was best known for his piety and strength of character. All pointed to a distant hut that housed Guru Tegh Bahadur, nineth Guru of the Sikhs.

In assessing the conflicting claims of modern political gurus, it's helpful to look beyond the glitter of the short-term promises and miracle cures, to a different question – 'What will best benefit our children and their children?'

In focusing on the long-term in this way, perhaps we may get our politicians to do the same.

10 October 1991

Minority Rights

It's grotesque, like something out of a pantomime!

That's how, just ten years ago, the head of a Midlands school spoke to a boy who had come to school in a turban for the very first time. In a neighboring school, a head refused a child admission also on the grounds that he was wearing a turban. He agreed it was religious discrimination but argued rightly that the 1976 Race Relations Act covered race, ethnic origin, colour and nationality but not religion.

The Commission for Racial Equality asked if I would help in a test case to try and prove that Sikhs were a race. I advised against this, as Sikhs hold race and caste to be meaningless divisions of our human family. A more attractive alternative was to try to show that Sikhs were an 'ethnic' group within the meaning of the Act; that is, an identifiable group – without the rigid connotations of permanent biological difference associated with the term 'race'.

We lost our action in the County Court, and in the Appeals Court under Lord Denning – who gratuitously compared the Sikhs to hippies and described the CRE as 'an engine of oppression'.

Eventually, the case went to the House of Lords who found that Sikhs were an ethnic group within the meaning of the Race Relations Act and should have its protection.

Yesterday, ten years on, I received a note in the post of a proposal to amend the Act to give protection to all religious groups.

Fine for religions; but what of others suffering discrimination? Sikhs have always campaigned to get wider protection for all groups, including Gypsies, Rastafarians and those of no faith.

In this we have the brave example of Guru Tegh Bahadur, our nineth Guru, who gave his life upholding the rights of others – whatever their creed – and we are duty-bound to follow his enlightened lead.

The Guru taught: *'Maan jithe jaag jith'*, that is, to fight prejudice in all its forms, we must start by fighting the evil within us.

Today, it's fashionable to talk of racists, sexists and so on, in a way that suggests that the rest of us are free of such tendencies. But prejudice is latent within us all, and, given a suitable trigger, all too easily reveals the worst side of human nature – even in the police, the judiciary and others responsible for safeguarding our freedom to live, move and work free from harassment.

We cannot legislate to remove such prejudice but, as the Guru reminded us, all people should be equally protected against its worst excesses.

11 February 1992

The Collapse of the Soviet Union

I find there's nothing like time and distance to help me see things in perspective. In our normal domestic life, we're often too close to family and friends to appreciate their true worth. We often focus only on faults and petty irritations. But go to any airport or railway station and see in the hugs and embraces how time and distance reduce petty imperfections to their true proportions.

One man, who has probably acquired not only a clearer perspective of family and friends, but also of world events, is Colonel Sergei Krikalev. Now, virtually marooned on the space station Mir, this cosmonaut was a hero of the Soviet Union when he left for space, last May. Today, he is almost a forgotten figure, and the Soviet Union is no more.

Orbiting the Earth sixteen times a day, patiently waiting for some unknown bureaucrats to organize his return, he must by now have gained a near God-like perspective to put into focus some of the extraordinary goings-on in his former country: a failed coup; Gorbachev's exits and entrances; the collapse of the Communist Party and of the Soviet Union itself; the rise of ethnic unrest.

From his enforced detachment, and reflections on where, or to whom, his loyalty lies, his thoughts might well echo those in a verse in the Sikh Holy Granth, on the impermanence of any man-made order:

The Guru taught:
All such powers and pacts
Are subject to decay
All such pacts are for worldly power
For worldly power the evil emesh
others in conflict

The Guru taught that ethnic and religious difference bring colour and richness to life. But in this verse, he warns against the all-too-easy exploitation of these differences by foolish power seekers.

From his vantage point on Mir, Sergei Krikalev will no doubt be aware of the rising tide of ethnic and religious conflict – not only in the former Soviet Union, but also in Northern Ireland, the Middle East, India, and many other parts of the globe – and its potential for turning men into warring factions.

While praying for the good colonel's safe and speedy return to the embrace of family and friends, the thought occurs; why waste a still functioning space station?

As the Guru reminded us, 'there are those who for their own ends enmesh others in conflict'. Such people would clearly benefit from a period of 'enforced sense of perspective' – and their distance would probably benefit us all.

12 February 1992

Dangers of Pride in Looking to a Wider Perspective.

Sikhism talks of five deadly sins. One of them is pride. In our daily prayer, the Ardas, which has a similar position in Sikhism to the Lord's prayer in Christianity, we ask for God's blessings to help us to be low in pride and high in our ideals.

I was reminded of the dangers of pride on a recent management course – where the consultants introduced themselves as a 'zero defects' organisation! Now the trouble with such boasts is that they are hard to live up to. On day one of the course, the overhead projector broke down and a group photo failed to come out.

The essential thrust of the course, with its emphasis on improving procedures, was fine, though in my view, marred by a lack of parallel interest in the needs and concerns of those involved.

I find religion and business management have much in common. One is concerned with managing an enterprise in an efficient and effective way; the other with doing much the same sort of thing with our personal lives. Both share the same danger of obsession with skills of the trade, blurring our vision of the reality of what we are trying to achieve.

In Gum Nanak's day, so-called holy people felt themselves above ordinary mortals and not wishing to be contaminated by the crowd, moved to the wilderness to perform austerities and penances to bring them nearer to God.

Gum Nanak was not impressed. He pointed out that their pride had blinded them to the fact that an understanding of God could only be reached through humility and service to those they had so selfishly abandoned.

Similar blinkered vision occurred in some management experiments of the 1930s. In one work study, engineers proudly announced that improved lighting on a factory assembly line had increased output. A shrewd office employee however, persuaded the consultants to go back to dim the lights and see what happened. To their surprise, output continued to rise until it was too dark to see. It wasn't the increase in lighting that had boosted production so much as the increased feeling of those engaged in dull repetitive work that they too were important.

At the end of my recent course, we were each given a heftily inscribed paperweight to remind us that we were graduates of a unique management discipline. Mine reminds me of the need for a little humility and less brashness in what we do. Partly because of the Sikh teaching against pride, but perhaps more because of its garish appearance, my paperweight lies safely tucked away in the back of the office drawer.

13 February 1992

Understanding the Beliefs of Others

The growing debate over interfaith dialogue, reminds me of the day I rushed home from school with the exciting discovery that as a Sikh, I didn't have to attend either assembly or religious knowledge classes.

This meant that I might even be able to catch up with homework for which I was always being chased by teachers. I told my parents the wonderful news. They didn't quite see things my way. 'You'll attend both assembly and divinity classes', they said,- 'learning about the religion of those around you, won't do you any harm.'

I had always found my parents open to reason, and yet here they were being uncharacteristically rigid. Anyway, I soon found myself enjoying the hymn singing and being fascinated by Bible stories. It was some years before I understood the reason for my parent's insistence. They were simply following the teachings of Sikhism.

In his first sermon Guru Nanok declared, *Na Koi Hindu, Na Koi Mussalman'*. That is in God's eyes, there is neither Hindu nor Muslim. And by today's extension, neither Christian, Sikh nor Jew. That God isn't interested in religious labels, but in the way we conduct ourselves.

Sikhism sees different religions as different paths on the same quest for an understanding of truth and reality. Sikhs believe that those different paths are not mutually exclusive; and sometimes they merge to give us a heightened understanding of our own faith. For this reason, the Gurus included writings of both Hindu and Muslim saints in our holy Granth.

I'm not suggesting there aren't problems in interfaith dialogue. I vividly recall feeling angry and uncomfortable in my fifth form year, with the teacher saying, 'the only way to God was through Jesus Christ.' I suggested an amendment. 'Christians believe the only way to God is through Jesus Christ.' This was readily accepted, and peace restored.

To me, the benefit of interfaith dialogue is the excitement of finding what is common between our various faiths and, importantly, learning to respect the difference.

And the differences aren't always what they seem at a distance. In the last few weeks, I've read two learned articles, both of which refer to *Christianity*, *Judaism* and *Islam* as the three monotheistic faiths. What of Sikhism, whose scriptures start with the words 'There is but one God!' Innocent ignorance no doubt. But ignorance is fuel for prejudice.

In yesterday's world, knowledge of other faiths was highly desirable. In today's multicultural society, it is an urgent necessity.

23 June 1992

Guru Arjan's Martyrdom: Inspiration to Look to the Needs of Others

June, the month of Guru Arjan's martyrdom, is a time of quiet reflection for Sikhs. The Guru taught that service to our fellow humans performed from the background of any faith, was far more pleasing to God than all the rituals of formalized religion. For this he was cruelly tortured and put to death. The Guru lived his teachings by establishing orphanages and leper colonies and serving in them himself.

One man who has taken the teachings of Guru Arjan to heart is Bhagat Puran Singh, eighty-eight this month. Puran Singh was a sturdy lad in his teens when, on his way back from a gurdwara in Lahore, he saw a small child shivering in the winter cold. He wondered why the child hadn't gone to the gurdwara for food and shelter. And then he saw the withered leg and smashed skateboard-like-affair that was the little boy's only means of transport. Without hesitation, Puran Singh lifted the little mite onto his shoulders and carried him to food and shelter.

Soon, the lanky figure of Puran Singh, carrying those abandoned by society, to food and warmth, became a familiar sight in Lahore, and later in Amritsar, where he established the Pinglewara, a home for disabled people.

Virtually unknown outside India, the Panglewara has today become the largest such establishment in Northern India and has restored thousands to mainstream life, and where this hasn't been possible, provided others in need with food and shelter.

How a modest man, without means and averse to publicity, has been able to achieve so much, seems a minor miracle. The thousands of rupees required daily come from donations from ordinary Sikhs who see in the work of Puran Singh, an echo of their Guru's teachings.

I had the good fortune to be able to spend a day with this remarkable man some twenty years ago. I found him full of energy, with an almost mischievous sense of humour. He was carrying people from a dormitory into the autumn sunshine, and I offered to help. He agreed. After a couple of hours, I was totally exhausted! He, eyes twinkling at my lack of fitness, was as sprightly as ever.

At a time when news is full of senseless killings – from last week's massacre in the South African township of Boiphatong where even infants and babies were not spared, to yesterday's mortar bombing of those searching for food in Sarajevo – it is well to remark that there are many Puran Singhs of all nationalities and faiths working quietly to preserve the balance of sanity. Their silent contribution, as the Guru taught, beats all the ritual of formal religion, and it is they who give us the right to call ourselves human.

24 June 1992

Commercialization of Sport

For two weeks every year, SW19 becomes the centre of the world, or at least the sporting world. For two weeks we locals have the luxury of our own weather forecast, and the more dubious privilege of paying twice as much for strawberries as anyone else.

It's as a native of SW19 that I'd like to wish all visitors to Wimbledon the best of luck, not with the weather and tennis, so much as with the new one-way traffic system. This nightmare of new lights and roundabouts may make sense on a higher plane of traffic management but leaves many of us lesser mortals practicing the language skills of John McEnroe.

The Sikh Gurus encouraged both sport and physical fitness among their followers. They often compared life itself to a game, that we should play to the full in meeting opportunities and obligations, rather than be silent spectators to evil and injustice.

Guru Nanak reminds us that a life lived positively in this way isn't always easy. he wrote:

'He who would play this game of love should come forward, prepared to lose all.'

Sikh teachings extend this metaphor of life as a game, to the outcome. Win or lose, good fortune or disaster upon disaster, we are taught to accept the result of our endeavors with equanimity, as the will of God.

A reminder of a similar approach to sport greets Wimbledon players as they enter the All England Club. On the wall in the club landing is a verse from Kipling, reminding players meeting with 'triumph or disaster', to treat those 'two imposters' just the same. In practice though, the increasing pressures of commercialization makes such a relaxed and sporting approach almost impossible.

Kitty Godfrey whose death was reported over the weekend, was twice winner of the Wimbledon ladies' singles in the 1920s at a time of far greater sportsmanship and courtesy. But then, with a five-guinea gift voucher as prize, there was far less at stake.

Today the winning lady's prize is £240,000 and the man's an additional £25,000, and it is easy to understand the tensions, grunts and tantrums. Whoever else wins next week, sponsorship and commercialization will more and more dominate not only sport, but all fields of human activity.

There seems to be no getting away from it. To me, to use my earlier analogy, it's as if we're on a busy one-way road system, with a distinct feeling that we're going in the wrong direction but being unable to do anything about it.

Perhaps I should just accept it as the will of God and concentrate on watching the play.

25 June 1992

The Pursuit of Peace in Israel and Palestine

The Labour Party's victory in Israel's general election, and its promise of a greater flexibility towards the Palestinians, makes the possibility of peace a little more likely, but there is still a long way to go. Powerful voices will still argue 'it's our land' and 'we'll never give up an inch of our territory'.

It's an argument that's been heard again and again, all over our strife-torn world since the dawn of history and carries with it the assumption that national boundaries are somehow or other, God given and just, whereas, in reality, most have come about in ungodly conquest.

Another major impediment to peace is perhaps the even more dangerous fallacy, that differences of history, religion or culture, are irreconcilable leading, a mindset that leads to the sort of 'ethnic cleansing' that we've just heard about in Bosnia. It was an argument that fragmented India at the time of Guru Gobind Singh, in a powerful verse he wrote:

'Some call themselves Hindus,
others call themselves Muslims,
Among these are the Shias,
There are the Sunnis also,
And yet man is of one race in all the world.'

It is an ideal found in the prayers of most religions but not always in their practice. The truth is that religion has allowed itself to be exploited by the irreligious, often in religious garbs, as a vehicle for preaching superiority and difference.

The Gurus acknowledged differences of history, religion and culture, and emphasized that these should be respected but they also stressed that these, far from being divisive, actually enriched society. Nor was this mere lip service. For example, the Gurus frequently used Hindu and Muslim themes to illustrate the teachings of Sikhism.

One body that has constantly been working to widen understanding of other faiths in this way, is the Interfaith Network UK, which today celebrates its fifth birthday. In the Network, Christians, Jews, Hindus, Sikhs, Muslims and others, engage in dialogue – not to pretend that all religions are the same, but to understand and respect differences and rejoice in that which we have in common.

My prayer, as we cut the celebratory cake later today, will be that this respect for the culture and aspirations of others, extends beyond academic religious debate to the wider world.

If Yitzsak Rabin and his Palestinian counterpart can look together to the rights and aspirations of all people in that troubled land in a spirit that recognizes a common humanity, they will considerably increase the chance of a real and lasting peace and earn the gratitude of people far beyond their borders.

1 December 1992

Role of Religion in the Pursuit of Racial and Religious Justice

Today is the fiftieth anniversary of the founding of the Council of Christians and Jews. This body came into being in the dark days of the Second World War. Its aim: to stand against the forces of anti-Semitism and racial or religious hatred.

Today, fifty years on, we seem to have learnt nothing! We see racial conflict in the former Soviet Union, ethnic cleansing in what was Yugoslavia and, the now daily, attacks on foreigners in Germany. This is to say nothing of the oppression of minorities in the many parts of the world hidden from our TV screens.

To me as a Sikh, the anniversary has added poignancy for it falls in a week Sikhs commemorate the martyrdom in 1675 of our nineth Guru, Guru Tag Bahedur It was a martyrdom unique in religious history. The Guru, though not a Hindu, gave his life upholding their right to worship in the manner of their choice in the face of fierce Mughal persecution. This systematic killing of Hindus was dwarfed by the holocaust of the 1940's, only by the latter's cold, scientific thoroughness.

Today, few of us can put our hands on our hearts and say, with any degree of conviction, that systematic attacks on minorities will soon be a thing of the past. Or that in fifty years' time the Council of Christians and Jews, or some similar body, won't be expressing parallel concerns, with an even greater sense of urgency.

The martyrdom of the nineth Guru showed that the pursuit of tolerance is not an easy quest: it's a fight against hatred and powerful human instincts of prejudice and self-interest. We rightly condemn the attacks on foreigners in Germany but we must also be on guard against issues such as Maastricht, or the GATT (General Agreement on Tariffs and Trade) talks being exploited to fuel a hatred of others. This is a particular danger at times of economic political difficulty.

We discussed some of these issues at a recent conference in Birmingham. The theme of the conference was the relevance of religion to today's society. To me, it's clear that religion will remain of little relevance so long as religious people continue to stand in moral smugness on the sidelines of life. But if religions are prepared to soil their hands in actual involvement, their role will become both real and vital to making tolerance, compassion and concern for others, integral aspects of our daily living.

2 December 1992

Ethnic Cleansing in Former Yugoslavia

For the past few days, my family and I have enjoyed the company of a young Sikh doctor staying with us on his way back to the USA. He had been working in Bosnia with the French medical charity, Medecin Sans Frontiere. Baljit's first-hand account of torture, rape and mass killing brought home to us the real horror behind the sanitised euphemism, 'ethnic cleansing'.

Dr. Bontros Gali, Secretary-General of the United Nations, also referred to the suffering in former Yugoslavia in a speech made earlier this week. This, unfortunately, got pushed out of the headlines by our concerns over the pound and the escalating media pressure against the Heritage Secretary – culminating in yesterday's resignation.

In his statement at the opening of the forty-seventh Session of the General Assembly, Dr. Gali likened the ending of the cold war to the opening of a Pandora's Box of causes and conflicts long dormant under the pressure of power block politics. Dr. Gali warned that conflicts such as those in former Yugoslavia could easily lead to a doubling of nation states within a decade – leading to a heightening of tensions and further disputes. The only way to prevent this scenario becoming a reality, Dr. Gali concluded, was to strengthen international mechanisms for protecting the legitimate right of minorities.

Most of us would agree with Dr. Gali's sentiments. But how far can we really go in this direction? Yesterday the UN issued a report on sanctions against Serbia. This gloomily concluded that the main impact to date had been on infants in hospital denied essential drugs and medicines.

Ethnic conflict is not new. It existed at the time of the Gurus who also taught the need to protect minority rights – by force if necessary. But this respect for the rights of others, the Gurus taught, should be set in the context of a recognition of a common humanity. As Guru Gobind Singh, the tenth Guru, put it:

Some call themselves Hindus
Others call themselves Muslims
Amongst these there are the Shiahs
There are the Sunnis also
And yet man is of one race in all the world

Yes, we do have different cultures, beliefs and aspirations, and yet these are transcended by a common humanity that underlines the importance of that which we hold dear.

The universal recognition of this simple truth is our best safeguard against the growing evil of ethnic cleansing and the further fragmentation of society.

3 December 1992

Yes, Minister and the Need for 'Failure Standards'

An industrial tribunal recently criticized a large employer for dismissing two ethnic minority employees for alleged fraud. The tribunal said 'they had done this' without a scintilla of evidence. The company protested its innocence. 'We have an equal opportunities policy'. They were reminded by the tribunal that simple statements of intent were, in themselves, no guarantees of good behaviour.

To me, much the same danger lies with the Citizen's Charter, now a year old. There is also the Patient's Charter, and many other charters from public bodies, falling on us like autumn leaves. I make it twenty-nine at the last count! Soon, no self-respecting employer or provider of services will be without a charter!

Such charters seem, at best, crude indicators of aims or targets, and are no substitute for genuine dedication or concern. At worst, they give rise to complacency. A framed 'Passenger Charter' at the entrance to a London Underground does little to ease the suffering of an elderly lady, hobbling painfully down a broken escalator.

There are also glaring inconsistencies. Last week's Court's Charter, for example, set targets for reducing waiting times for civil and criminal cases. Maps are to be provided to help users get to court. But it's difficult to square these measures with parallel cuts on legal aid, and this week's increase in court fees. On reflection, perhaps there is logic: fewer people using courts will certainly cut down waiting time!

In many ways, all these Charters are like religious creeds. There was a bewildering number of these in the India of Guru Nanak's day some 500 years ago. Guru Nanak didn't quarrel with the beliefs of these creeds but was concerned that people seemed more interested in reciting their articles of belief than in living by them. He gently reminded:

Truth is high, but higher still is truthful living

And in another verse:

He alone is a man of God Who practices right conduct.

Our charters are at least a step towards 'right conduct'. But I've always felt something was missing – until I remembered an episode from the TV comedy, 'Yes, Minister'. In it, a young efficiency expert wants all civil servants to state in writing what would constitute failure in their job! Sensing danger to responsible civil servants, Sir Humphrey skillfully talks the Minister out of it. But the idea of 'failure standards' is a powerful one that could be used in the real world to concentrate the minds of those behind the charters ... if the real Sir Humphries allow it!

16 September 1993

Economic Well-Being

For the last few days I've been working in the garage. Not on the car, but in clearing a space out for the car to get in. I've got rid of lots of junk, but now I've hit a problem. What do I do with the things that are 'not quite junk'?

The biggest offender is a large fridge; slightly the worse for wear, but otherwise in perfect working order. It was relegated to the garage when we decided to get a 'built-in fridge'. That is, one with a door to its door. With food inside the fridge in plastic containers its now a Russian doll-like exercise to get a quick snack.

The new fridge isn't as nice as the old one. But it is new. Its purchase is the Singh family's contribution to reviving the economy. When the green shoots of economic recovery finally show... this year, next year – or whenever, you'll know where they had their origin!

We are constantly reminded by the economists that spending money we don't necessarily have, on things we don't really need, is a GOOD THING. It stimulates production which creates more jobs and in turn greater purchasing power. It's a cycle of growth fueled by need and greed.

This idea of a market economy isn't new. It certainly existed in the India of Guru Nanak's day. The Guru's father was a typical businessman who would have fitted well into today's times. He gave the young Nanak some money and told him to invest it in merchandise for sale at a profit. He said to his son 'put the money to good use'.

The young Nanak went off towards town and, on the way, saw some poor people, hungry and shivering in the winter cold. He bought them some food and blankets. Soon, all his money was gone, but the young Guru felt he had put it to good use.

His irate father clearly thought otherwise, and it took all the diplomatic skills of Nanak's sister to restore peace. It's not recorded, but the Guru was probably penalized by a reduction in his money supply.

The Guru wasn't against commerce or the possession of material goods but warned against this becoming a compulsion that blinds us to our social responsibilities and the very real needs of others. To underline this, he gave Sikhs the injunction: earn by your own effort and share your good fortune with others.

My fridge, and other discarded items in our homes are not the only casualties in our sometimes crazy quest for more and better. Today, the cold and hungry that Guru Nanak saw by the wayside, are seen at our railway stations, bus shelters, or huddled and shivering in the doorways of our cities; in the unemployed and other victims of recession. Their needs should be paramount; even at the cost of upsetting the economists!

23 September 1993

Knot the Gun

Just outside the United Nations building in New York, there is an impressive statue of a man holding a gun. The barrel is twisted in a knot. It's a poor pun but a powerful message; 'not the gun'. It's a message that we all hope will be foremost in the minds of all at the United Nations as it starts its forty-eighth assembly this week.

The dramatic turn of events in Russia reminds us, if we still need reminding, that we live in a very dangerous and unstable world, where conflicts in areas once considered remote, can instantly affect us all. It's a world in which we should work to reduce armed conflict for selfish as well as for moral reasons.

And yet we continue with an arms trade that we know will increase instability and involve the killing and maiming of innocents. The world shrugs helplessly at the suffering in Bosnia and other areas of conflict experiencing appalling shortages of food and medicine. Yet the supply of guns and bullets continues unabated.

It seems a sad commentary on the mixed morality of our times that the sale of a weapon to an individual is recognized as a crime; yet the export of large quantities of arms is seen as an act of merit, even when sold to a country like Iraq. We saw this in David Mellor's frank admission to the Scott Inquiry this week that he would have stopped a sale of arms to Iraq but for the effect on our exports.

The sale of arms to 'friendly' powers is still seen as a good thing despite the dubious nature of such friendships. The Sikh Guru, Guru Ram Dass warned us about such alliances when he wrote;

All human powers men make pacts with
Are subject to death and decay
They are dishonest and will not endure

The Guru continued, that the only worthwhile pact was one that recognized our common humanity.

The nature of world trade is such that arms sold to one country do not always remain in that country. 'Leakages' from arms sales, have, for example, resulted in Libya acquiring arms from Britain, Germany, Poland and Japan.

New entrants to the arms trade make existing instability even more hazardous. Chinese arms are increasingly seen in areas of conflict. Even India, the land of Mahatma Gandhi, now boasts that it is a major exporter of arms.

This merchandising of death, will in years to come, almost certainly give rise to the sense of revulsion that we now reserve for the slave trade of the last century. Meanwhile, the UN needs to act urgently, to give practical effect to its message of 'not the gun', to give us a real chance of peace.

2 February 1994

Marketing Religion

The Templeman Commission Report recommending closure of up to twenty-four out of thirty-six historic City of London churches on grounds of cost effectiveness, shows that not even the Church is safe from the accountant.

The move has caused dismay, not only to Christians, but also to many people of other faiths. We all live in the same social and economic environment and what affects one community, affects us all. Churches, like industry, are prey to the same market forces that govern ever-increasing aspects of our daily lives. Whether we like it or not, organized religion has become something of commercial activity, looking to sales or number of customers, or as one newspaper put it, number of people in pews. And in this it has steadily lost ground to sporting activities, television and the pub and more recently, to Sunday shopping.

Not surprisingly, many look to solutions in purely marketing terms. Better promotion, more attractive packaging. Trendy clerics in trendy clothes and trendy music have all been used, but to no real effect. Others, still thinking in marketing terms, look to increasing market share – with claims that their religion or particular denomination, washes sins whiter and more effectively than other brands. Nonetheless, as we've seen, the drift away from religion, continues.

I think there is much in the view put forward by Guru Nanak, that religion fails to make its true impact, not because of poor packaging, but because of an excess of it. He taught that the real power of religion lay in its simple but clear guidance. He wrote:

Religion does not consist of visiting places of pilgrimage Or going into meditative trances. He who looks on all alike and lives to serve others, is truly religious.

Guru Nanak did not seek to create an exclusive market share for his own beliefs. Instead, while criticizing the ritual and superstition that commonly passed for religion, he reminded the Hindus and Muslims around him, of the high ideals of their own teachings. Ideals like honest living and compassion for the less fortunate – in a word 'basic values' – where have I heard that phrase before? Values that should underpin and give a much sense of direction to our daily lives.

Today we need that sense of direction more than ever before. Now here's a problem! While commercial activities look to people's tastes and trends and then move to meet these, religion needs to move people towards its values. A much harder task, but clearly one worthwhile!

9 February 1994

Bosnian Suffering

The tough new NATO response to last weekend's shelling of a local market in which sixty-eight people lost their lives, underlines growing concern at the plight of the Bosnian people.

For me, one television picture said it all. A young girl, perhaps in her early teens, was shown lying wounded and in obvious pain. As the picture moved to a close-up, the girl turned full-face to the camera, physical pain clearly visible. But more than the pain, the face showed bewilderment, a sense of disbelief, of betrayal. It asked the voiceless question—why?

It's a question that has echoed through human history. It's a question that Guru Nanak faced as an eyewitness to the Mughal Barbar's conquest of India, some 500 years ago. In describing the detail of what he saw: the mindless brutality and the suffering of the innocent, he could easily have been talking of Bosnia today.

Surprisingly, the Guru's greatest condemnation, was not of the perpetrators, but of the Delhi rulers, who had neglected their duty to protect their subjects. In a famous passage, Guru Nanak wrote:

When a tiger falls on a tiger
There is no great grief.
But when a tiger falls on a defenceless herd,
The herdsman must show his responsibility.

Today, the world sees the UN as the herdsman. The marketplace slaughter in Sarajevo has finally goaded member states into promises of action, and one can only wish and pray for the success of the promised NATO action. My hope however, is that today's NATO meeting will also look to the lessons of Bosnia for a better approach to international peacekeeping.

The UN clearly needs to move from its present crisis containment role, to one of crisis or tragedy prevention. Festering ethnic unrest in the former Soviet Union and other parts of the world could all too easily erupt into new Bosnias, or worse. Unthinking kneejerk reaction to conflicts, are themselves cause for concern. Yes, the UN herdsman must show its responsibility. But it can only do so if we give it unstinted moral and concrete support to meet the awesome challenges of the new world order.

23 February 1994

Religion: a Holistic Approach to Social Ills

The Church Commission for Racial Justice, has this week, called on the government for a one-off amnesty for families that have fallen foul of the immigration laws. They say that this would be an appropriate gesture to mark 1994 the International Year of the Family.

While the move to keep families together is certainly welcome, I must confess that I'm a little worried by this annual highlighting of different areas of concern. The year of the child, the year of women; this year, the year of the family; next year the International Year of Tolerance.

Of course, we should be concerned about the position of women in society; about our responsibilities to our family and to future generations. But what bothers me is that this selective focusing on individual issues, one at a time, can lead us to forget the real and important links between them.

The Sikh Gurus were alert to the need for a more holistic approach to a better social order. They saw family life as central to this end and put it on a higher plane than a monastic life of renunciation, which they saw as an opting out of responsibilities.

The Guru's teachings are encapsulated in the Sikh Marriage Service, which stresses the full equality of the marriage partnership, and the synergy that results from two people acting as one for the betterment of society. 'One light in two bodies', as the Guru put it. In the service itself, the couple, with the man leading, walk four times around the holy scriptures, each holding one end of a silken scarf. This symbolizes the soft but strong bond between them.

The equality between men and women taught by the Gurus, is not always mirrored in society, and Sikhs too, have constant discussion on respective roles. When my daughter Mona got married, she was asked, referring to the ends of the scarf held by the couple in the marriage ceremony, why did you allow your husband to lead? She replied, she saw the scarf as a rein. The male leads, but the hand at the other end of the rein, is no less important!

The Sikh Gurus saw the family as a microcosm of our wider human family. If the smaller unit functions well the larger one is bound to do so. For most of us, there is an added advantage to family life. If we can put up with the often-impossible behaviour, of husband, wife, child, parent or sibling, we can put up with anything! Perfect training to face the outside world. It all calls for a lot of tolerance. But we don't have to worry about that just now. 1995 is the International Year of Tolerance.

29 September 1994

Obsession with Self

The number thirteen is considered lucky by Sikhs. This is because the Punjabi word for thirteen, 'thera' also means 'thine' or God's. There is a Sikh story that Guru Nanak once had a job weighing measures of wheat grain and would count aloud as he weighed 1,2,3,4… When he got to thirteen, absorbed in God, he continued repeating the Punjabi thera or thirteen, with its alternative meaning central to Sikhism, that nothing is ours; everything belongs to the Creator.

I was reminded of this story when our grandson, Simran, celebrated his second birthday over the weekend, by adding the word 'mine' to his rapidly expanding vocabulary. It's a tough lesson at two, but I'm sure that this obsession with 'self' and 'mine' is a passing phase in the process of growing up and learning to share and interact with others.

The importance of children, especially older children, learning to work and play together, was emphasized earlier this week by one of the Prince of Wales' charities. The Report drew attention to rising youth crime: nearly 50% of all recorded crime, costing a staggering seven billion pounds a year. The Trust argued that it would be more cost-effective to spend more money on better youth facilities in an effort to reduce juvenile crime.

The Trust's findings were immediately challenged by Michael Howard, the Home Secretary, who said there was no hard evidence that better facilities for young people would reduce crime, and that further research was under way, although it would be at least March 1996 before findings would be available.

I must confess that it bothers me that we have to have lengthy and expensive research to prove what has been known for donkey's years. That the devil makes work for idle hands. Nevertheless, I do have some sympathy with Mr. Howard's sense of caution. After all, there have been many disappointments. Short sharp shocks, safari holidays, fines, community penalties. We seem to have tried everything!

Perhaps we're starting at the wrong end, as Guru Nanak reminded us, if you want to do something about the evil around you, start by looking at yourself. But this could be uncomfortable. It might show that our emphasis on 'mine', on our individual and collective greed, and our obsession with self might be giving the wrong signals to the young in developing their sense of right and wrong. Children learn by imitation. We need to look urgently at the confused and dangerous moral environment we have created for them.

6 October 1994

Words Words Words

Words seem to be very much in the news these days. Yesterday, the French listed 2,500 English words they want to ban from the French language. Earlier in the week, Sir Thomas Bingham, the Master of the Rolls, said lawyers use far too many. Nor is there any shortage of words at Party Conference, where we have to rely on political commentators to distil meaning and substance from rousing speeches to the party faithful.

Sir Thomas, in his address to the Bar Conference, referred to this at a training seminar that he and other senior judges attended recently. They had come with five-to-ten-minute presentations and found that reducing these to ten seconds had made their arguments more cogent. Shortened presentation, would certainly be welcome to those pursuing justice in the law courts. But I'm not sure that television-type sound bites are the answer for the rest of us, facing the ever-growing barrage of words. Words often used with dangerous or mischievous intent.

Yesterday's gruesome discovery of forty-eight bodies of a religious cult in Switzerland, graphically illustrates how a charismatic cult figure, can, by the power of words, condition rational people into irrational behaviour. Religion in the past, particularly in India relied heavily on conditioning and unquestioning acceptance of rituals and practices that defied common sense. Guru Nanak preached against emphasis on rituals and the blind acceptance of questionable religious practices. He gave us the sound advice that if a practice didn't stand the test of common sense, it must be questioned.

Conditioning in the Britain of today is far subtler; but nonetheless still a threat to independent thinking, with those in authority or positions of responsibility, using words to fog issues and do our thinking for us. Nor is the media without blame in its use of coded signals to appeal to prejudices – words like terrorist, extremist or freedom fighter to tell us who are the good guys and who are the bad. Today, by force of unthinking repetition, words like 'extremist' or 'fundamentalist,' sit comfortably alongside 'Sikh' or 'Muslim', or names of other faiths.

Language is a God-given gift, that we should use to inform and illuminate, rather than add to existing prejudice and stereotyping that harms us all.

13 October 1994

Questioning sacred Dogmas

Guru Nanak constantly warned the people of his day against rituals and superstitions that can easily become surrogates for true religion. He told us to be wary of questionable dogmas that defied common sense and cluttered our thinking. Religion, he taught was respect for God's creation and active concern for our fellow human beings. Nothing more and nothing less.

Last week, we saw Tony Blair trying to discard what he felt was unnecessary clutter and dogma held sacred by many in the Labour Party. He shocked some of the Party faithful at Blackpool by questioning the relevance of Clause 4, which holds that nationalizing the means of production and distribution necessarily leads to greater efficiency and fairness.

I think it would be helpful if John Major at Bournemouth this week, were to do a Tony Blair by questioning the other extreme of political dogma held sacred by many in his Party – the belief that salvation lies in the free play of market forces. It's a belief, incidentally, that seems to have created large new bureaucracies, some of which are as insensitive as those of the former nationalized industries.

Of course, market forces are real. They are a fact of life and no bad thing in themselves. But as Guru Nanak reminds us, the unrestrained pursuit of material wealth, can carry with it a culture of selfishness and greed. The Guru was not over impressed by material wealth.

He once chose to stay at the house of a poor carpenter rather than accept the hospitality of a rich businessman. The powerful merchant was extremely angry. He summoned the Guru to his house and demanded an explanation. The story goes that the Guru took a piece of bread from the poor carpenter's house and squeezed it and milk flowed from it. He then took a piece of bread from the rich man's table and, as he squeezed it, blood came out. The Guru explained "the carpenter has earned by honest effort, while you have acquired your wealth by oppressing the poor."

It's a story that makes a point. We can't ignore market forces any more than a sailor can ignore the wind. But, as the Guru taught us, market forces are not gods to be obeyed whatever the consequences.

Just as a yachtsman uses the wind to move in the direction he wants to go, we too should be able to use, constrain and harness opportunity and talent, not only for wealth creation, but also to move us towards greater respect for our environment and far greater concern for our fellow human beings.

27 October 1994

Tenth Anniversary of Operation Bluestar

Next week holds sad and bitter memories for Sikhs. It marks the tenth anniversary of the massacre of thousands of Sikhs throughout India in November 1984, in what Justice Sikri, a former Chief Justice of India described as the "worst carnage since the partition of the subcontinent".

The then Indian government, somewhat glibly, blamed the killings on a 'spontaneous outburst of grief', at the assassination of the Indian Prime Minister, Indira Gandhi by two of her Sikh bodyguards. No one questioned the absence of spontaneous grief at the assassination of Mahatma Gandhi by a Hindu extremist. In Britain, newspapers put it all down to 'communal violence'—something to be expected in India. Clearly religion was to blame.

Some Sikhs, still embittered by the June '84 Indian army attack on the Golden Temple and the huge loss of life, felt that the atrocities against their community were politically inspired. And these concerns were supported by some independent observers. A BBC 'File on 4' report at the time, noted that the army was conspicuously absent, and the police acted either as silent spectators or active participants in the destruction of Sikh life and property. According to official figures, more than 2000 Sikhs were killed in Delhi alone, and many thousands more throughout the country.

The immediate reaction of most Sikhs however, was to blame Hindus, which was precisely what those who organized the violence wanted! And nothing could have been further from the truth! It soon became clear that thousands of Hindus had risked life and limb to protect their Sikh neighbours. My own brother, visiting India at the time, would not be alive today, but for the shelter given him by Hindus he scarcely knew. Hindu civil rights workers bravely led unity marches in the disturbed areas. To their amazement, they saw known politicians leading and inciting the mobs.

Centuries earlier, Guru Nanak warned us against such people; 'butchers of the world,' as he called them, 'who use the garb of religion to hide a murderous knife!'

Next week, Sikhs throughout Britain will attend special services dedicated to the memory of victims of the November 1984 massacre. They will also pay tribute to thousands of brave Hindus who, in risking their own lives, demonstrated the powerful unifying force of true religion.

20 October 1994

'Violence in the name of God is Doubly Evil' -Chief Rabbi, Dr. Jonathan Sacks

Yesterday's bus explosion in the centre of Tel Aviv, killing twenty-two people and injuring some forty others, underlines the fragile nature of the Middle East peace process. Coming hard on the heels of last week's kidnapping and killing of a young Israeli soldier, grief and anger at yesterday's outrage, has, as we saw on last night's TV pictures, raised new tensions and calls for retaliatory action, jeopardizing the very future of the peace process. This of course, is the very objective of those who claim responsibility for the carnage.

Fortunately, the response from both Israeli and Arab leaders, has been swift and positive. The Israeli Prime Minister, Yitzak Rabin, has expressed his determination to continue the move to peace, and the Arab leader Yasser Arafat, in condemning the massacre, stressed that the best response was to strengthen the drive for peace.

Yesterday's bomb explosion brings to mind an earlier incident, in February of this year, in which a Jewish settler entered a crowded mosque in Hebron and shot dead fifty men and boys as they knelt in prayer; a powerful reminder that religious bigotry and opposition to peace exists on both sides of the religious and political divide.

Some 500 years ago, Guru Nanak, in stressing the need for tolerance between different faiths, taught 'no one faith has a monopoly of truth'. Today, it's sadly necessary to add that no one religion has a monopoly of fanatics, whose actions are an affront to the faith they claim to defend. As Dr. Jonathon Sachs, the Chief Rabbi observed at the time of the Hebron massacre, 'violence is evil and violence committed in the name of God is doubly evil'.

Unfortunately, bad news has the capacity to overshadow the good. It's easy to forget that this week also saw a peace agreement between Jordon and Israel and encouraging conciliatory moves from Syria.

Looked at in this way, the desire and momentum for peace in the Middle East, is strong enough for it to continue and succeed, despite the attempts of extremist groups to sabotage it.

My hope, and I'm sure that of people of all faiths, is that calm nerves prevail in the Middle East, and that yesterday's outrage becomes a new and compelling catalyst for peace.

10 January 1995

Collective Worship

Most of us enjoy a little praise, now and then. It helps us feel important and appreciated, and we all welcome a little boost to our ego. After all, we're only human.

I must confess that I've often wondered why our different religions place so much emphasis on the praise of God. Why in the universe should the Creator of all that exists, and of space and time itself, need or want the praise of us puny humans? If God needs to feel appreciated and has problems of insecurity, we're all in deep trouble.

The paradox of worshipping a God that clearly doesn't need our worship, emerged again last week with the comments by the Archbishop of York, Dr. Habgood on the problems of collective worship in schools. The debate seems to be: should there be more of it, or less of it, with little discussion on why we should worship God.

A line from the Sikh holy Granth reminds us: -

If all were to gather and sing His praises
It would not make God any greater or less great

And yet Sikh scriptures are full of page after page on God's greatness and the wonder of His Creation. Guru Gobind Singh, the tenth and last of the Sikh Gurus, whose birthday we've been celebrating this last week wrote: -

God has no name; no dwelling place
No shape, or colour or outer limit
Unborn, ever perfect and Eternal
To the east or to the west
Look where you may
He pervades and prevails as Love and Affection
The Scriptures continue:
From the Divine Light all creation sprang
Why then should we divide human creatures into the high and low?

Worship or reflection of this sort, contained in all our holy scriptures, benefits not God, but ourselves. It reminds us of the vastness and wonder of Creation, of our human frailty and the absurdity of our pretentions of God-like knowledge and wisdom. It reminds us of our inhumanity to our fellow beings, and how in our greed, we continue to destroy the environment that sustains us.

It would be a real pity, if the opportunity made available to our children for such daily reflection, was curtailed to accommodate fears of compromise of belief expressed by some. The best worship of God, according to all our major faiths, is fuller concern and active appreciation of God's creation. A daily act of worship that reflects on this, and provides a sense of perspective and direction, must be worth preserving.

17 January 1995

What's the Harm?

It's always a bit dangerous to question cherished national institutions. The Anglican House of Bishops were almost asking for it last week, when they voiced concerns over the National Lottery. They were accused of bleating and were branded hypocrites and killjoys – and that was by papers like the Times. Tabloids were far less restrained!

The gist of criticism against the bishops, and similar views expressed earlier by the Archbishop of Canterbury, was – what's wrong with an occasional flutter? To me as a Sikh, the answer must be, 'not a lot'. The Sikh Gurus reminded us that life itself was often like a game of chance, and it was our responsibility to make the best of whatever hand had been dealt us. Chance and risk is all around us. We make conscious calculations of odds and risk, whenever we take out insurance, invest in a bank or building society, or consider a service agreement on a washing machine.

The trouble with what is more generally understood as gambling, as the bishops remind us, is that little flutters can, all too easily, become big flutters with drastic effects on individual and family. What bothers me more, is the way publicity and hype are used to bolster a weak, 'what's the harm in?', type argument, and turn a mundane event into a national obsession.

There's that ridiculous huge hand in the sky that dominates our TV screens, billboards and shops. What's it meant to represent? The hand of fate, or God pointing to the chosen one? It's a sure sign that we've got things badly out of proportion when even the government of the day regards the creation of the National Lottery as one of its main achievements in office.

Any suggestion of misplaced emphasis in these things, is sure to be met by the 'what's the harm argument', that seems to govern our thinking. 'What's the harm in an occasional flutter?' 'What's the harm in sex and violence on TV?'... and it's easy to go on.

The trouble is that the harm is not always immediately apparent, and that such attitudes combine to dull our senses to real concerns and responsibilities.

Guru Nanak constantly reminded the people of his day of the need for a more positive attitude to life. He asked us to address ourselves to the question, 'what good will it do'. It would be easier to live with the hype over the lottery and similar obsessions that seem to dominate the public mind, if, in addition to asking 'what's the harm in?', we add balance by asking, 'what good will it do?' But I'm not laying odds on this happening in the near future.

24 January 1995

Brutal Suppression of the Chechen Uprising

It's hard to imagine a more unfortunate start to 1995, the International Year of Tolerance, than the broadcast statement of Andrei Kozyrev, Russia's Foreign Minister. Defending the use of Russia's armed might against the Chechen people, he said: – '*We are not the first or only ones to have spilt blood to keep our State together'*. The saddest part of his frank admission, is that it is undoubtedly true. But questionable behaviour in the past cannot be used to justify the killing of innocents today.

If history teaches us anything, it is that many of today's nation states are themselves the product of war and aggression. Their boundaries, as we see in the Middle East, the former Yugoslavia and in Russia itself, often contain communities historically divided by religion and culture.

Yet again and again, we look benignly at those who spill the blood of their fellow humans in the cause of national sovereignty. This is particularly so if the country involved happens to be a 'friendly' power. This is underlined by the West's reaction to the bombing, shelling and destruction of Grozny. The objection has, for the most part been confined, not to the subjugation of a brave and proud community, but to the moral embarrassment caused to us as potential friends of the new Russian government by the President Yeltsin's poor estimation of the strength of Chechen resistance, leading to prolonged and messy conflict. The protection of religion, culture and basic human rights, it seems, is of secondary importance if the offending country is, however fleetingly, a friendly power.

Andrei Sakharov, the former Soviet human rights campaigner stressed that for real peace we must be even-handed in our pursuit of justice. And concern for human rights, must transcend national boundaries.

Earlier, the fourth Sikh Guru, Guru Ram Dass also reminded us of the need to put moral considerations above personal or political loyalty. He wrote:

All these human powers men make pacts with
Are subject to death and decay
I am of the Lord's faction; unequalled is His power.

What the Guru was saying was that we should be true, not to fleeting human alliances, but to enduring moral principles. And the most important of these is tolerance; a far better alternative to mindless violence in the pursuit of conformity.

24 March 1995

'Communitarianism' – the New Religion

'Responsibility and concern for others, has been in the news a lot recently'. In the USA – why have short words when long ones will do – they call it 'communitarianism'. I call it religion.

For years now, whenever I've spoken to children at gurdwaras, I've said that 'in school you learn the three Rs. But for Sikhs there are six Rs. You come to the gurdwara to learn about right, wrong and responsibility.

Whatever our background or perspective, most of us are painfully aware of cracks and fissures in our social order that seem to be widening at an alarming rate. We see rising crime, not always for greed or gain, but sometimes, simply for a so-called 'buzz' or thrill. We see family breakdown, a culture of self before others and survival of the fittest. Equally evident is a growing coarseness of speech and aggressive behaviour to others.

The scale of the problem is seen in the 'communitarian' movement across the Atlantic. Here, parents who try to move their children away from the drug culture of the streets into more worthwhile pursuits, call themselves 'mad dads'. And it does take a sort of madness of dedication to fight children's peer pressure, and a massive sense of alienation.

Sometimes, when talking to teachers, social and health care workers and others, I feel that we are making real progress. But it is politicians, however well-meaning, that give me cause for concern, by their vague and seemingly fragmented approach to clearly linked issues.

In a recent Spectator lecture, attention was drawn to the problems of truancy from schools and it was said that parents of persistent offenders should be prosecuted. Yes, but most such parents, are already on income support, and others are often single parents, struggling to bring up a family in near impossible circumstances.

Similar vagueness characterised the earlier 'back to basics' campaign. We live in a largely secular society in which it is difficult to discern what basics are we talking about? But at least, all parties claim to be looking in the same direction towards a more just and caring society, underpinned by emphasis on right, wrong and responsibility. Values at the heart of all our major faiths. Call it communitarianism if you like; I call it religion.

31 March 1995

What's in a Name?

A short time after Rhodesia became Zimbabwe, I accidently referred to the new country by its former name at a meeting of our local Council for Racial Equality. There was stunned silence in the moment before I could correct myself. 'Rhodesia?' someone echoed, and I felt I needed to wash my mouth out.

I must confess that I do find it difficult to keep up with today's frequently changing place names, with towns and countries, and chunks of continents like Eastern Europe, disappearing in political black holes, to re-emerge in new and fragmented form.

In India, it was announced last week that, following the triumph of the extremist Shiv Sena Party in the state elections, Bombay, will now be known as 'Mumbai', after a local Hindu goddess.

Well, what's in a name? On the face of it, not a lot. But, as we've seen in former Yugoslavia, a change in name is frequently used to emphasize particular ethnic or religious identity. And here's the danger, as 'Indarjit's' law of human behaviour states:-

When a group of people find sufficient in common, to call themselves 'us', they strengthen their sense of identity by finding a 'them' to hate.

We see this in appalling conflicts around the globe, with ethnic cleansing in Europe, the calculated genocide of more than half a million in Rwanda and now, similar conflict in Burundi.

In Bombay, sorry Mumbai, it is difficult to see Shiv Sena, a militant Hindu organization which campaigned for the expulsion of Muslims and expressed delight at the destruction of an historic mosque, being satisfied with a simple change of name.

This is not to say that the assertion of ethnic and religious identity is necessarily evil, but, as Sikh teachings remind us, it becomes so when it ignores our wider common humanity. Guru Gobind Singh taught: -

Some call themselves Hindus; Others call themselves Muslims
Among these there are the Shias; There are the Sunnis also
And yet man is of one race in all the world.

It's a fine balance between ethnic and religious diversity that can enrich us all, and bigoted xenophobia that ignores our common humanity. But it's one that the people of Mumbai and its sister regions around the world, must get right.

7 April 1995

The Final Vision of Justice

The twenty-four hour stay of execution, granted to Nicholas Ingram illustrates the mental torture of his twelve years on America's death row. This in a country where the constitution forbids 'cruel & unusual punishment'.

The rising crime rate in the USA, Britain and in many other parts of the world, has brought the whole question of crime and punishment into increasing focus, with vocal calls, for exemplary punishment.

In America, some States have reintroduced the death penalty, years after its abolition, and in this country, many are also calling for its restoration. In support of their argument, proponents go back to religious texts – to an eye for an eye, and a tooth for a tooth.

Sikh teachings state that, while the use of force to oppose evil might occasionally be necessary, but the evildoer falls into a different category once apprehended and must be treated humanely.

These Sikh principles dictated state policy in the Punjab, in the kingdom of Maharaja Ranjit Singh where in the thirty-eight years of his rule, not a single person was put to death by the State.

As a Sikh I am firmly opposed to the death penalty. But I do accept that it might have a deterrent effect, as indeed would the recent life imprisonment of a man in California for theft of a pizza. Public beheading, the severing of limbs, and public stoning as practiced in some countries in the Middle East might well act as a further deterrence but these acts also brutalise society. And is this really where we want to go as we move towards the Millennium?

I find it really difficult to believe that any religion condones state vengeance, or the taking of life merely to set an example.

There is also the question of human or judicial fallibility, dramatically underlined by yesterday's Appeal Court acquittal of Kevin Callan after he had completed more than three years of a murder sentence. He and at least half a dozen other innocents in the last few years, would now be dead, if the death penalty had been in force. Unlike God, we are not all knowing. Guru Nanak reminded us of this when he taught:

The final vision of justice
Lies not with man; nor with any creature of the universe
But with God alone.
As humans, we clearly lack the wisdom to play God.

1 July 1995

Fiftieth Anniversary of the Signing of the UN Charter

One of my favourite English hymns has the lines:

We see dimly in the present
What is small and what is great
Small of faith how weak an arm
May turn the iron helm of fate

I thought of these lines earlier this week, on the fiftieth anniversary of the signing of the UN Charter on June 26, 1945.

The birth of the United Nations took place when much of Europe and many other parts of the world, lay devastated in the fight against political and racial bigotry. It was against this background that the UN was formed, to quote from the preamble of its Charter,

'*To save successive generations from the scourge of war, and to reaffirm faith in human rights and the equality of men and women in nations both great and small*'.

In the fifty years since the signing of the Charter, we have seen these worthy ideals, often flouted or ignored. But there have been very real successes in the formation of UNICEF, numerous other agencies and in peacekeeping operations that have saved thousands of lives.

In a week in which countless acres of newsprint have been devoted to the details of the lives and aspirations of John Major and John Redwood and the more gossipy features of the Conservative leadership contest, a little discussion on ways of preserving peace for our children's generation, would not have gone amiss. Today the UN finds its resolve being continually tested by new challenges to its authority, and clearly needs new policies to meet the needs of the future.

This theme of looking to the world of the future, will be picked up at the Wembley Conference Centre tomorrow, when Sikhs celebrate the 400th anniversary of the birth of Guru Hargobind, sixth Guru of the Sikhs. It was he who taught Sikhs to be tolerant ... up to a point! The Guru put forward the idea of boundaries of bad behaviour, beyond which Sikhs were duty bound to respond to aggression.

It is this clarity of resolve that is needed by member States of the UN, to put would be aggressors on notice that certain types of behaviour will bring a certainty of response. Today, in the aftermath of the cold war, we need to give the UN our support, not our apathy.

7 August 1995

Searching for Intelligent Life

Scientists, these last few days, have been getting really excited over the remains of a 3.5-million-year-old foot found in South Africa – the missing link between ape and man. It identifies a point in our history, when some apes, bored with climbing trees for food and shelter, turned to other ways to test and expand their intelligence and ability.

And so it came to pass that some apes became men who abandoned crude animal ways, and the occasional mugging of other animals, and turned to more systematic ways of killing and maiming, not only other animals, but also those of their own species. Who says nature never puts a foot wrong!

I'm reminded about the doubtful nature of our supposed civilization, by a common theme in a number of alien space stories brought out for the holiday season. Such stories generally end with the question – if there is intelligent life out there, why hasn't anyone attempted to contact us? The answer surely lies in the question. Any intelligent being observing life on Earth from the safety of space-time remoteness, would certainly conclude with Dr Spock type logic, 'if they can do that to one another, what would they do to us?'

And he, she or it would be partly right, but not wholly so. For in addition to our often brutal and uncaring behaviour to others, there is a spark of divinity, admittedly often difficult to notice, in all human beings.

As Guru Nanak taught:

'There is an inner light in us all
And that inner light is God Himself.'

Today, amid all the atrocities and mass killings in former Yugoslavia, Rwanda, Chechnya and seventy-five other countries at the last UN count, there are also thousands of men and women, parted from loved ones in far off countries, risking life and limb to serve and support those less fortunate than themselves.

But looking again at the world about us, we clearly have a long, long way to go before any intelligent life from outer space sees us as anything more than homicidal jumped-up up apes!

9 August 1995

Fiftieth Anniversary of the Defeat of Japan

As the fiftieth anniversary of VJ Day draws near, some people have already begun to question the wisdom of raising issues and reviving memories, perhaps best forgotten. Former allied prisoners-of-war have been recalling brutal and degrading treatment at the hands of the Japanese and are seeking an apology for their beatings, starvation and use as forced labour.

Yesterday's commemoration of the fiftieth anniversary of the dropping of the world's first atomic bomb on the Japanese city of Hiroshima, has also aroused painful memories in Japan and controversy abroad. 70,000 men, women and children suffered instant incineration, and thousands more, mutilation and lingering death. Others were later born with missing limbs, suffering the cancerous effects of radiation-induced illness.

It's been argued that the Hiroshima and Nagasaki bombs hastened the end of the war. Possibly so. But the terrible moral conundrum remains. Can the deliberate mass killing of innocent men women and children, ever be justified?

The teaching of Sikh scriptures is an unqualified 'No', The Gurus taught that the innocent should be protected, and never made to suffer for the actions of others. And it's a view that finds echoes in the teachings of many other faiths.

Looking back to the world of 1945, while still painful to many, can help us to understand the imperatives of today. Whilst, as a Sikh, I can sympathize with those seeking apology and redress for the suffering of half a century ago, the best commemoration of VJ Day must be to look to a world free from the obscenity of modern war.

Today, as Croatian forces over-run large areas of Krajina causing as we've just heard, a vast new exodus of terrified refugees, and despite this morning's welcome news of a possible ceasefire, it all seems a distant dream. Nonetheless, we owe it to a generation that gave so much, to continue their quest for real and lasting peace.

14 August 1995

Researching the Glaringly Obvious

I often feel that religion and science start from opposite directions in helping us cope with the complex business of life.

Religion reminds us of responsibilities and gives us a code of behaviour to guide us. We are told that if we follow this, all will be well with us and the world around. Devotees of science, on the other hand, say '"hold it" before we can do anything about a problem, we must know its size and extent'. The first commandment of the statistician is 'measure and quantify'. Today, the business of measuring this, is one of the world's largest growth industries, accounting for as much as 6% of the gross domestic product of the USA.

It would be fine if all this research could tell us what we are doing wrong and how we could make this world a happier and safer place. But all too often, the academic goes to tortuous lengths to tell us the glaringly obvious.

Two studies reported in the current issue of the British Medical Journal, on sex education in schools, illustrate the point. These, complete with details of control groups and statistical tests come to the not very startling conclusion that some carefully structured sex education in schools, probably does more good than harm.

Well now we know! But few people have ever objected to the teaching of the facts of life to children in a responsible manner. The concern, particularly of Sikhs and other minority faiths in this country, is about the scope this gives to some adults to transfer their own hang ups and obsessions onto vulnerable children.

We've seen this recently in calls for condom machines in schools, and gender education for three-year-olds. And we see it in pressure on minority communities to put aside old-fashioned notions of restraint and responsibility and be like the rest of us.

Academic studies that ignore practical concerns are of little real use. Guru Nanak reminded us of this when he wrote:

One may read cart loads of books, with many more to follow,
But it's all of no avail, unless knowledge is used for the common good.

For me, I think I would rather follow the simple teachings of religion, than get excited over academic studies that tell us what we already know.

At least the guidance of religion is clear. But simple recitation of religious texts is not enough. Following religious teaching is far more useful.

21 August 1995

'For your tomorrow, we gave our today.'

On Saturday, I attended the Service of Remembrance outside Buckingham Palace. We came to the reading of the Kohima Epitaph:

'When you go home, tell them of us and say:
For your tomorrow, we gave our today.'

Sad, haunting words that force reflection – for your tomorrow, we gave our today. It's as if we we're presented with a baton of challenge and responsibility, to nurture freedom and justice, and extend it to those in other lands.

And yet today, looking at the world about us, I can't help reflecting how little real progress we've made in the intervening half century in the realization of their hopes and dreams.

In the last week, in between reflections on the brutalities of 1945, we saw something of the world of 1995. TV pictures of children in Rwanda who personally witnessed the rape and machete killing of close relatives; aerial photographic evidence of the mass graves of hundreds murdered in so-called UN 'safe areas' in Bosnia, and the beheading of an innocent Norwegian tourist in Kashmir by separatists trying to make a point.

Atrocities in war are not new. Guru Nanak was himself an eyewitness to the suffering caused by the Mughal advance into India. And his writings poignantly reflect his compassion, and his concern for what we now term, human rights.

We too are eyewitnesses to suffering through TV coverage of conflict in other lands, but I fear that this distant 'eyewitness' exposure to violence, seems to desensitise us – to accept the utterly evil, as a regrettable norm.

The argument that sustains much of the violence around the world today is 'they did it to us, so we'll do it to them'. It's the eye for an eye and tooth for a tooth argument taken out of context, and as a Rabbi friend once observed, it can only lead to ever increasing numbers of blind and toothless people.

To me, the only real and lasting way to honour the memory of those that gave so much in World War Two, is to work for wider renunciation of armed conflict as a means of settling territorial disputes. Paradoxically, this renunciation is now contained in the Japanese Constitution. In a sense, it forms the second and perhaps most important part of any real apology; 'We will never do it again'.

18 November 1995

Meeting the Needs of the Younger Generation

For the last week or so, Britain's half million Sikhs have been celebrating the birthday of Guru Nanak. For Sikhs it's a bit like Christmas, but without the shopping and the routine exchange of presents. It's a time when our gurdwaras echo to stories of Guru Nanak's kindness, wisdom and courage, and his strong emphasis on tolerance and respect for all faiths.

Tomorrow, festivities will end with a large celebration in West Bromwich where the presence of guests from other faiths will be a visible reminder of the Guru's teaching that God is not interested in religious labels, but in the way in which we conduct ourselves.

The meeting at West Bromwich will attempt to focus on how religion can help us meet the common problems of the day. The paradox for Sikhs is that while it is the young that face the brunt of these challenges, it is they who show the greatest reluctance to be involved in this religious dialogue.

The same problem is mirrored in the experience of other faiths. Yesterday, I attended a meeting of the Interfaith Network, a body dedicated to the improvement of religious understanding. The theme was 'Young People and Interfaith Dialogue.' It was young people who were most noticeable by their absence in the audience!

The generation gap is frequently blamed. But I feel it is more a communication gap. A failure to translate the teachings of religion into guidance for everyday life. After all most of our Holy Books are books of guidance; teachings on moral and ethical values to help us shape action and response to events around us. Yet, so often in our places of worship, we sing or chant this guidance, or recite it in a ritual way as if this is in itself, sufficient.

Our young clearly deserve more as they face a breakdown of family life, dwindling employment opportunities; the blurring of moral values, and the false promise of instant happiness through drink and the use of drugs.

While as we've just heard police continue to search nightclubs for those that supply drugs to teenagers like the tragic Leah Betts, some blame must also lie with those in religious authority who are failing to give the young clear spiritual and moral guidance in language that is easy to understand and guidance that gives hope, perspective and wider horizons.

25 November 1995

Peace in Bosnia

The best news of this week, pushed a little into the shade by headline grabbing events at home, was undoubtedly the signing of the Bosnian peace accord, which despite the difficulties we've just heard about, still seems to be holding.

While all parties seem to agree there are no winners, there was right from the start of the conflict a clear loser, tolerance; a vital ingredient that cements human relationships; that enabled Serb, Croat and Muslim in former Yugoslavia to respect their neighbour's faith and way of life.

The break-up of Yugoslavia and the conflict in Bosnia have been sombre reminders of how easily such tolerance can be swept aside by the easy manipulation of ethnic and religious difference leading to genocide bringing the phrase 'ethnic cleansing' into our growing vocabulary of human shame.

I was brought up in a generation taught to believe that the German atrocities against the Jews were an aberration that could not have happened elsewhere. We could not have been more wrong. Yugoslavia and the genocide of hundreds of thousands in Rwanda, vividly remind us, in this the UN's international year of Tolerance, of the fragile nature of that precious commodity.

It was because the Sikh Gurus realized that tolerance was the key to true and lasting peace, that they continually stressed its importance in all walks of life. More than this, they lived this teaching in the example of their own lives.

Tomorrow, Sikhs will be commemorating one of the saddest events in the Sikh calendar; the martyrdom of our nineth Guru, Guru Tegh Bahadur.

The Guru lived at a time of intense religious persecution of the Hindu majority by the Mughal rulers. A delegation of Hindu priests decided to ask Guru Tegh Bahadur, to intercede on their behalf.

They said to the Guru, 'we know you don't agree with many of our beliefs, but if a person of your standing speaks up for us, the Mughals might just relent'.

The Guru knew that such a mission would almost certainly cost him his life, but he agreed to go to the capital Delhi to try to help the Hindus. The Mughals refused to listen, and the Guru was cruelly tortured. And then on a cold November day in 1675, publicly beheaded for his brave stand on behalf of the Hindu community.

This higher vision of tolerance, the willingness to die for another's beliefs, may be too much to expect in the world of today, but it is a powerful ideal that can inspire us against all too easy exploitation of superficial ethnic and religious difference.

2 December 1995

'Religion – the sigh of the oppressed, the heart of a heartless world' – Karl Marx

It was Karl Marx who famously described religion as 'the opium of the people'; something that deadens the reality of pain and suffering that is a part of life. This week's news that more than 10% of City employees are taking drugs, reminds us that religion as a possible opiate, is being pushed aside by the real stuff, drugs in varying forms, and by a growing use of alcohol.

The study carried out by the Institute of Personnel and Development, shows that 10-15% of job applicants, many already holding positions of great responsibility, tested positive for drugs. I found it even more disconcerting that a Times report on the study, went on to give a sort of yuppie 'best buy'.

'LSD is easy to get hold of at the moment and appears to give good value for money, because it is cheap and has a long-lasting effect'.

Before this Report, we were led to believe that the use of drugs was mostly confined to teenagers, and was a passing reaction to family breakdown, the growing spectre of unemployment and massive peer pressure. This report on the large-scale use of drugs among the business community gives the lie to this view. It shows that even the outward glamour of life in the city, hides real anxieties tensions and insecurity.

The advice given to drug users by various agencies, leaves me even more concerned. It seems to concentrate on making the act of drug taking a little safer without any clear message that the use of drugs leads to drug dependency – a soul destroying and life-threatening condition. Instead, the advice is couched in terms that might be given to lemmings. 'Take care as you go', without mentioning that it's a journey that leads to the cliff edge.

When Guru Nanak taught – *'Where self exists, there is no God: where God exists there is no self'* – he was reminding us that obsession with personal happiness, through drink, drugs or whatever, leads to misery, while looking to the needs of others, leads us to true contentment.

Curiously, Karl Marx accepted this wider view of religion, when he wrote, 'Religion is the sigh of the oppressed creature; the heart of a heartless world.'

That's no bad agenda for religion, and I don't mind it being called the opium of the people, if it can move us away from a culture that seeks happiness through buzzes, kicks or trips, by helping vulnerable teenagers, young city workers and others, cope with very real tensions and anxieties in an increasingly heartless world.

9 December 1995

Spotlight on Human Rights Abuse

I've recently been trying my hand at DIY security lighting. I was given a couple of infra-red detector lights as a sort of early Xmas present, and decided to fit one at the front of the house, and the other at the back, but with mixed success. The one at the back refuses to work, other than as a floodlight. The one at the front does work, but with a will all of its own.

It generally goes on as expected, but also lights up at unexplained random intervals. And it absolutely refuses to come on when I put the rubbish out at night, unless I wave to it with outstretched arm. Our neighbours probably put my waving of arms at an inanimate object, down to some strange Singh custom to appease the forces of light! But however imperfect my system, we all know that better lighting does help reduce crime. Fear of identification is a powerful deterrent to the would-be criminal.

Amnesty International and other human rights organizations have long held that the same principle applies to those responsible for human rights violations. These human rights groups believe that the focusing of media attention and international concern on those who torture maim or kill innocent people in distant lands, can in itself act as a powerful deterrent.

Tomorrow is International Human Rights Day, and the day will see a renewal of concern for hundreds of thousands of innocent human beings, including the elderly and infirm, and the very young, suffering for their beliefs, or the beliefs of those close to them. In our different places of worship, we will reflect on how such abuse can take place in half the nations of the world.

There are many who argue that the focusing of attention on international wrongdoing, is itself flawed and biased, with a common tendency to keep the spotlight away from trading partners and 'friendly nations', and that instead of subjective blacklists and whitelists, we should be looking at and quantifying various shades of grey. But these things, like my own security lighting, can be improved.

What is important is that we do not let doubt and cynicism stand in the way of our continuing support to organizations, groups and individuals, who by their relentless focusing on human rights violations give light to those in darkness and serve as the voice of the voiceless.

6 March 1996

Violence in our Genes

There is the story of the little boy who brought home a school report. His father looked at it and declared 'It's terrible! How do you explain such poor results?' The sharp-witted boy replied, 'I'm not sure, it's either something to do with my genetic make-up or my environment.'

Daily examples of growing coarseness in language and rising violence, also read like a bad school report, but unlike the small boy we can hardly blame our genes, and instead have to look to falling standards in public and private life, and particularly to the role of the media.

And here there is evidence of mounting concern. Jaci Stephen, television critic with national newspapers for the past ten years announced that a major reason for her decision to quit was that she was no longer able or willing to watch the violence that has increasingly come to dominate the TV screen.

In a report in yesterday's Times, the BBC agrees that standards have to be updated and that it is to tighten its code of practice on bad language, sex, violence and blasphemy in response to growing public concern. But why do we always have to wait until there is evidence of outrage or concern before we do anything to clean a moral environment in which, as Jaci Stephen put it, '"Every aspect of life is reduced to a metaphorical soundbite: a punch in the face?' And many of those that punch or kick the hardest, or swear the loudest are the good guys to be copied in street culture, as indeed they are.

The news of the BBC's guidelines to curb mindless violence and offensive language is nonetheless welcome. But why not also look a little in the opposite direction? Guru Nanak reminded us that 'sweetness and humility are the essence of all virtues.' Sweetness and humility on TV? Such a quantum leap might prove too much of a shock to the system, but there is no evidence to suggest that the occasional portrayal of husbands and wives being faithful to each other or having programmes without bad language or violence can seriously damage our social health.

We Talk of 'V' chips and watersheds to protect our children from exposure to the unacceptable, but what about some protection for vulnerable adults? Of course, there is always the 'off' button and my children frequently use it… when my wife or I come into the room as they watch a programme unfit for our tender eyes and ears. But then our children aren't always around!

11 July 1996

Machete Rampage in a Wolverhampton School

Just four months after the horror killing in a school in Dunblane, a man armed with a machete runs amok in a Wolverhampton infants school, and several children and adults are seriously maimed. There are calls for greater security, but even if schools are turned into mini-fortresses, they still won't be wholly safe. And what message would this give to our children about the world in which they live? What is to prevent a similar outrage in a crowded shopping precinct, a busy railway station or any other place where people congregate?

While increased safety measures are right and proper in Dunblane, and now Wolverhampton, are reminders of increasing violence in society; violence which manifests itself in adults attacking children, teenagers attacking the elderly, so-called road rage and much else. It is society that needs to change, rather than, as suggested, the physical structure of our buildings and institutions. Dr. Carey's recent call for much greater emphasis on moral teaching, must, I believe, be seen as the way forward.

There is a clear need for urgency. We cannot afford the sterile debate over whether this teaching is the responsibility of schools or parents. It is the responsibility of all of us, to set and live by standards that to me, are not exclusive to practicing Christians.

Sikhs, and others, share the same concerns about material greed, the need to care for the weak and vulnerable and our responsibilities to those around us. Many of the parables of Jesus Christ have remarkable echoes in Sikhism. There is Jesus Christ's reference to the eye of a needle and the story in Sikhism of Guru Nanak giving a needle to a rich miser and asking him to take it into the next world.

When Guru Nanak taught 'there is neither Hindu nor Muslim' and by implication, neither Christian, Sikh nor Jew, he reminded us that God is not concerned with our various religious or non-religious labels but with the way we behave.

At the time of the Dunblane tragedy, I wrote to the school offering the sympathy and support of the Sikh community. A reply was not expected. But a few days ago, received a lovely letter which contained the sentence:

'Your letter highlights the similarities between us all, and how irrelevant differences of any kind are.'

These words of warmth, showing tolerance and respect, are perhaps the most important of our many shared values and priorities.

18 July 1996

Mind Your Language

A fat and jolly little monk at the top of my calendar, gives words of wisdom for each month of the year. Last month it was, 'start each day with a smile, it makes people wonder what you are up to.' For July, we're told: -
'speak in words that are soft and sweet, for tomorrow you may have to eat them.' Useful advice, not only for the politician of the 'watch my lips, no new taxes' variety, but for all of us. And not only in this country.

Over the weekend, the Speaker of the Indian Parliament, appalled at the threatening abusive and decidedly un-parliamentary language used by newly elected members of India's Lok Sabha, called them to his residence to see videos of proceedings in the House of Commons as examples of proper standards of debate. I know we all get a little concerned at times over questions to the Prime Minister and the rowdiness of some of the debates in the Commons, but at least the use of obscenities in the Commons, is still considered unparliamentary. But for how long, one wonders?

It's now many years since I started my working life as a mining engineer. There in the heat, dust and underground danger, I heard language so colourful, that the same miners would have blushed to repeat it in the streets above. Today it is common currency on buses and trains as children, boys and girls, come home from school.

My concern has been heightened by a recent report in the Times, captioned, 'Swearing is good for you'. It was about a seminar organized by —you'll find it difficult to believe this, The Better English Campaign. At the seminar, a speaker told children that, 'Despite what your teachers say, you can use mucky word and sexual expressions in your writing.' She added, 'If you don't use swear words, kids won't think the work is relevant.' So now we know.

The Better English Campaign, launched in Easter this year, by Gillian Shepherd, the Education and Employment Secretary, was, we were told, 'designed to raise standards and end communication by grunt'. It's a poor choice, but I must confess I prefer grunts to mindless obscenities.

Of course, we should call a spade a spade, but to add an expletive before the word 'spade' does nothing to enhance understanding. And, as Sikh scriptures constantly remind us, uncouth speech has its effect on both attitude and behaviour. Even if we don't have to eat our words, we all have to live with deteriorating standards in the way we behave to each other.

1 August 1996

Boundaries of acceptable Behaviour

Sikh scriptures teach that everything we do has either a godly dimension, or a baser human dimension, or more generally, a bit of both: As humans, there is a bit of the saint and sinner in each one of us.

The aim of religion is to move us gently towards more godly or responsible living, and away from what Sikhs call 'the five predators': lust, greed, anger, undue attachment and pride, which pander to our baser instincts.

In this way, religious teaching is quite different from the law of the land. Laws do not try to move us in any direction. They simply set the boundaries of bad or socially unacceptable behaviour. Race relations legislation and the Public Order Act do nothing to promote good behaviour, they merely tell us what is unacceptable.

But, as a well-known hymn reminds us, *'New occasions teach new duties; time makes ancient good uncouth'*.

Laws that are socially acceptable in one age, are often seen later as unjust, or even barbaric. In this country, we no longer have a death penalty, or flogging, or other forms of cruel and degrading punishment, and the boundaries of law are frequently moved inwards as society develops greater social responsibility, or as Sikhs would say, moves in a more godly direction.

What worries me about this week's call for the legalisation of brothels is that the proposal seeks to move us to less responsible behaviour. Of course, legalisation of brothels would move many prostitutes off the streets, but in the process, it would seem to me, to be giving a mark of social approval to an activity that demeans women, panders to baser male passions and encourages infidelity as an acceptable way of life.

Perhaps the most usual, and therefore the most dangerous, argument for legalizing activities that diminish us as human beings, is that the activity: prostitution, use of soft drugs or whatever, is so common that we can't do much about it so we might as well move the boundaries of the law to accommodate it and give it respectability.

It's a weak and negative argument that gives a cloak of normality to otherwise unacceptable social behaviour. It's an argument that panders to the very passions that our scriptures warn us against, and one that pushes norms of behaviour in a decidedly ungodly direction.

6 September 1996

Disentangling Culture from Religion

This week, we learnt that a survey of young Asian Hindus, Muslims Sikhs and Christians found that 10% felt that so-called honour killings, that mostly target women, could be justified in certain circumstances. It's a highly disturbing statistic. But is it right to link religion with dated and perverse social attitudes to justice and honour? Any examination of Hindu, Muslim, Sikh and Christian teachings will show that they, in no way support or condone such murder.

In today's sensitive times, I believe it's important to differentiate between dubious cultural attitudes, and religion, that frequently condemns such practices. The Sikh Gurus, for example, were strident in their criticism of rituals and social practices that demeaned or gave a less than equal role to women. They condemned infanticide, which generally meant the killing of infant girls, and forbade Sikhs from associating with the then common practices of sati, that is widows, under pressure of society, throwing themselves on a deceased husband's funeral pyre. In a further move, the Gurus gave Sikh women the name or title 'Kaur', literally princess to emphasize their elevated status.

Background culture reflects the norms of a community, while the purpose of religion is to lift us to higher planes of responsibility and behaviour. The reality however is frequently different. Questionable cultural practices often attach themselves to religion, distorting or blurring true religious teachings.

I think it's particularly important that we differentiate between religion and culture in the current debate over how to make ours a more cohesive society. We can have all the commissions of inquiry we want, producing impressive reports, but we will never make real progress until we disentangle culture from religion, ditching the nastier bits, like so-called honour killings. I feel that a useful first step would be to get rid of the ugly word 'multiculturalism' which unhelpfully lumps religion and culture together as something we should be for, or against; difficult when you don't know what it means.

When we remove the distorting overlay of culture from religion, we see our different religions as they are, overlapping circles of belief with much in common.

Taking culture out of the equation will also help us see areas of religious difference in a fuller perspective and develop strategies to promote integration, based on genuine understanding and respect.

13 September 1996

The war on Terror

An opinion poll this week suggests that most people in this country feel that we are losing the war on terror. I don't know about that, but I do feel that since 9/11 we've been losing the fight for clarity of language. Soundbites, well, sound fine, but they don't do much for discussion and action.

If doctors wish to contain a new and virulent illness, they first try to identify and isolate its exact cause, and then go on to look for cures. We would feel less than re-assured if doctors and scientists went on and on, year after year vaguely talking about their determination to fight 'nasty germs'.

Five years after 9/11, I suspect many of us feel the same way when we hear talk of 'fighting global terror', as if suicide bombers in Iraq, Tamil tigers in Sri Lanka, Chechnyans, and countless others all have the same aims and objectives.

To me, the real struggle against the evil of 9/11, is between what some see, as the West's brash smugness about the superiority of its way of life, and a long dormant, resurgent Islam, itself deeply divided by religious and factional differences, trying to come to terms with itself and the realities of the twenty-first century.

It's a struggle for hearts and minds, and as a Sikh, I believe that it's not one that can be won either by terrorism, or with bombs and bullets.

Of course, it's necessary to respond to and be vigilant against terrorist attack, but detention of suspects for years without trial in Guantanamo Bay, torture at Abu Graib, 'extraordinary rendition', and talk about an axis of evil, are not the best way to win friends, and simply add fuel to the spiral of hatred and violence. By the same token those that believe that killing innocent people in the name of religion will take them to paradise, insult their own religion, and worse, God himself.

Despite the gloomy findings of the opinion polls, I feel that we can move forward to peace by showing a little more humility about our own way of life and focussing on values like democracy and freedom of speech and belief; values that resonate with hearts and minds. I'm sure that many in moderate Islam, deeply unhappy about bigots twisting their beliefs to justify hatred and killing, would welcome any move in this direction.

23 October 1996

One World Week

This week is 'One World Week'. Every October at this time, we are asked to put aside our general view of 'abroad' being a dodgy place full of foreigners for just seven days and try to take a more charitable view of other members of our human family.

We are asked to remember the vulnerable and disadvantaged, not only 'abroad' but also those far closer to home. We hold multicultural events and interfaith services and celebrate the richness and variety of different cultures and recognize, however faintly, what Guru Gobind Singh called, 'the oneness of the human race'.

In a famous passage the Guru elaborates on this teaching:

Some call themselves Hindus; others call themselves Muslims
Yet all men have the same form: all men have the same soul.

It's a sentiment with which most of us, whatever our faith, would agree. And yet when we take even a fleeting glimpse at the world about us, we see widespread inequalities, unbelievable torture and cruelty inflicted by petty tyrants on their own people, and the suffering of innocent children around the world. We see TV pictures of continuing famine and learn of the plight of hundreds of thousands of refugees such as those now fleeing the camps in Zaire.

But all this seems too much for us. We feel helpless, and instinctively turn away, and focus our attention on issues that are easier to understand, like the plight of tigers in India.

So is there really nothing that we can do to make the sentiment of 'one human family', a bit more of a reality? Well yes there is. For a start, we could stop making things worse.

We can, along with other more affluent nations, end the obscenity in which poorer countries pay more to the rich than they receive in aid, and thus become ever poorer. We can ensure that terms of trade are not fixed to favor the rich at the expense of the poor. We can stop selling sophisticated weaponry to petty despots to use against impoverished neighbours.

We can do all these things and much more at little real cost to ourselves if we have the will. Excuses are easy: compassion fatigue, and problems of our own. But there is also an urgency. In a shrinking and interdependent world, the concerns of 'abroad' are in every sense, the problems of us all.

30 October 1996

Celebrating the Millennium

The proposed giant Ferris wheel, to be sited opposite the House of Commons to celebrate the millennium, has had my head in a bit of a spin ever since I first heard the idea.

My first reaction was what on earth has a Ferris wheel got to do with the celebration. of the millennium? But the more I think of it, the more convinced I become that nothing could better encapsulate the values and spirit of our times. Forget the fact that it will be an architectural eyesore. At 500ft, it will be the biggest such structure in the world; it will provide instant thrills and above all, in the words of the chairman of Lambeth's Planning Committee, it will get tourists and business into the area. What more could we ask!

And why stop there, why not turn the House of Commons into a gigantic funfair and make the Lords a plush gambling casino? The money should come rolling in!

But what has all this to do with the Millennium, the 2000th anniversary of the birth of Jesus Christ, who, in common with Guru Nanak and other leaders of religion, taught many of the values that we have so arrogantly ditched and are now scrambling to rediscover through conferences, seminars and party-political rhetoric.

As a Sikh, I'd be happy if the main focus of Millennium celebrations was on the life and teachings of Jesus Christ; teachings that have powerful echoes in all our different faiths. The Sikh Gurus constantly emphasized this essential unity of religion and the commonalty of core values essential for sane, balanced and responsible living in any age.

The end of the twentieth century is also an opportunity: like the end of a year, only more so, for us to do a little stocktaking, and to reflect on achievements, failings and our hope for the future. It's been a century of unbelievable scientific advance. But it has also been a century of shame and blurred moral compromise in which our obsession with 'self and rights', has led us to forget others and common responsibility.

The Millennium celebrations will be an ideal opportunity to try to get the balance right. To take a hard look at ourselves and the world we wish to leave our children. It would be a pity to blow it through over emphasis on shallow celebrations and cheap fairground thrills.

6 November 1996

Effigies of Hate

John Harington, who lived at the time of the Gunpowder Plot, wrote:
Treason never prospers: And what's the reason
For if it prospers, none dare call it treason
Guy Fawkes's treason certainly didn't prosper and last night, despite the stormy weather, effigies of the poor chap were burnt on bonfires. accompanied by ever bigger, noisier and more spectacular fireworks.

It's also at this time every year that Hindus celebrate the victory of Lord Ram over Ravan the demon king of Sri Lanka who had kidnapped Sita, the wife of Ram. Huge effigies of Ravan are burnt, and celebrations finally conclude with the all-important festival of Diwali, the festival of lights. This marks the triumphant return to India of Ram with his wife Sita; an occasion for more celebrations, and more firecrackers.

Sikhs also celebrate Diwali, but for quite a different reason. It was on Diwali day, nearly 400 years ago that Guru Hargobind, in his concern for freedom of belief, secured the release of fifty-two Hindu princes imprisoned by an intolerant Mughal emperor. And yes, Sikhs too celebrate with fireworks and lights.

The fact that all these bonfires and displays of pyrotechnics in different cultures and in different parts of the Northern Hemisphere, take place at about the same time, is too much of a coincidence. It seems we all feel the need to show a last blaze of defiance against the inevitable onset of winter. All harmless fun, but for the practice of making and burning effigies of those who disagree with our way of thinking or our belief.

Poor Guy Fawkes was a member of a persecuted minority which frequently endured torture and death for simply being Catholic. There was no democratic means of protest. And discovery of 'a plot' was itself used as an excuse for further repressive legislation; a formula since used across the world to keep minorities in their proper place.

The burning of effigies of those of different belief, is all too easily seen as harmless, particularly with the passage of time. But even religious minorities have feelings. Let's have the bonfires and the fireworks, and if we must have effigies, let's have a giant effigy of intolerance; a demon still with us today.

6 March 1997

It's not fair

It's measure of our morally muddled times that we've come to use words like 'do-gooder' and 'liberal' as a form of abuse or contempt. The same trend is found in sport. When our team does badly we criticize them as being a 'hopeless bunch of amateurs', literally, those who play for fun rather than for monetary gain. But fun is rapidly going out of sport.

A recent flood of court cases reminds us that sport is no longer a game. It's a serious business that affects the livelihood of players, the profits of shareholders and even the emotional well-being of spectators. We read that fans of Leicester City are planning to sue the FA over last week's much disputed penalty in the match with Chelsea. A distraught fan claims he was off work for two days because of 'emotional upset' and is seeking compensation. And we've been reading about the rugby player who went to court over his suspension. This week, a hugely expensive High Court case, over alleged match fixing in football ended in a draw, with the prospect of a costly replay still on the cards. What is sport coming to?

As someone who used to play cricket – an amateur – in every sense of the word – I agree that the immediate aim of any sport or game is to try to win. But surely there's much more to sport than simply winning or losing. The way we play is or was considered equally important. Guru Nanak himself often compared life to a game. A game in which we should be prepared to risk our life for our principles; a game that should be played in such a way as to meet the approval of God – the ultimate referee.

In playing the game of life, the Guru reminds us:

"Not to be cast down in sorrow, or over elated in joy"

Here, the Guru gives us one of the most important lessons we can teach our young. That life is not always fair, and that in the game of life, we should have the equanimity to accept the seemingly unfair along with the better fortune that comes our way without being over-affected by either.

It's a vital lesson for today's times as nursery cries of 'it's not fair' carry into adult life. Winning is of course important. But perhaps even more importantly, sport can and should teach us to accept the rough with the smooth, both on and off the playing field.

13 March 1997

Gun Rampage in Dunblane

Seldom can a single event have united a nation in collective grief and deep introspection as the tragic shooting in Dunblane twelve months ago today. As news of the carnage filled the airways, there was initial disbelief, and then a sense of common loss that cut across all divisions of class, ethnicity or religion.

At the time of the massacre, I wrote to the school offering the sympathy and support of the Sikh community. I never expected a reply and was moved by a letter of thanks highlighting similarities between our faiths.

Sikhism takes a very philosophical view of life and death. We believe that life in this world is part of a longer journey and that we should not grieve for those that leave us. At the same time the Gurus recognized the very real emotional gap that is created in our lives when someone near and dear dies.

This sense of hurt or betrayal, is natural and felt by us all, particularly if the loss of someone close takes place in tragic circumstances. But the passage of time does eventually, help to heal. Guru Nanak recognized this and taught that we could assist this healing process by looking beyond our loss to an active concern for others. Not easy. Yet it is a measure of the courage and spiritual strength of the people of Dunblane that they have done just this.

The highly successful 'Snowdrop Campaign' against the ownership of handguns has been a humbling lesson to us all in looking beyond personal grief to ways of preventing such tragedies in the future. The success of a small and bereaved community, in forcing us to look afresh at the evil in such weapons reminds me of the line of a Christian hymn of how, *with faith, a weak arm can turn the iron helm of Fate.*

In a moving interview with James Naughtie on this programme yesterday, Eileen Harrid and Mary Blake, two of the teachers injured in the shooting, reflected on the continuing physical and emotional hurt still being suffered by children, parents and teachers and the need for continuing support. And how the sense of hurt might be lessened if they felt something good might come out of it.

To my mind, we can best show this continuing sympathy and support for the people of Dunblane by following the lead they have so courageously given by working to make the word Dunblane, synonymous not with tragedy, but with a single-minded determination to curb the violence that has become so endemic in our society.

20 March 1997

Is an Apple a day Good for Us?

An apple a day keeps the doctor away? Perhaps not anymore. Last Sunday, travelling on the train to Birmingham, I'd just settled down with a newspaper and a nice red apple, and was into my second or third bite when I came across a report headed 'Parents told to peel pesticide fruit'. I wasn't unduly alarmed. Newspapers are always trying to scare us.

Taking another bite from my unpeeled apple, I read on. The report, based on a Ministry of Agriculture briefing, warned that excessive levels of organophosphates, which attack the body's nervous system, were found on some fruit. The Report warned that in extreme cases, eating even a couple of sprayed apples without peeling, could lead to stomach pains, particularly in children. I eyed my half-eaten apple more suspiciously.

The Report concluded with the usual, cheery 'Don't panic' advice that always leaves me a little concerned. To me, the one certainty of the food industry is that we don't really know much about even the short-term effects of various fertilizers, pesticides, preservatives, colour enhancers and other chemicals added to our diet, let alone their long-term effect in possible combination.

Every so often, as with the apples, we get scare stories of possible carcinogenic or other health damaging effects of things put in our food, but these are easily forgotten, particularly when the same products continue to be sold in different forms. Of course, we have E numbers and other information on the back of packets, but it needs a degree in food processing to understand their true significance.

Sikhs do not have dietary laws. We are told all food is the gift of God and therefore holy and pure in a religious sense. We are advised to eat in moderation. At the same time, it is recognized that not all foods agree with all of us, and we should refrain from that which causes us harm. This used to be easy, but not anymore in a world of preserved and processed food where even an unpeeled apple might benefit from a government health warning.

And it's here that we look to the world of science; to those now celebrating their achievements in science week, for clearer guidance. My plea to scientists is to be less detached, more responsible and more open about the possible downside of their research and their products, in a way that informs both the food industry and the confused consumer.

27 March 1997

Fiftieth Anniversary of the Partition of India

Earlier this week, I attended one of the many events that are being held this year to mark the fiftieth anniversary of the transfer of power in the sub- continent of India.

The ending of the Raj was remembered with predictable nostalgia, and generous praise for those involved on all sides in the peaceful hand over of power, and there was much reminiscing and mutual congratulation. But to me, the function also showed how nostalgia can add its own spin or slant to historical fact, blurring important lessons we cannot afford to forget.

The reality of life on the sub-continent of India fifty years ago was one of appalling conflict between the predominantly Hindu and Muslim communities. When Partition became a fact, whole train loads of dead and mutilated bodies hurtled across the newly created borders of India and Pakistan in macabre gestures of mutual hate. Minority communities also suffered, and Sikhs were driven from the land of Guru Nanak's birth. It is estimated that some ten million men women and children perished in this communal carnage, and millions more fled their homes.

The West, with the colonial smugness of the day, put it all down to religious madness to be expected in Eastern cultures. But in these last few years we have grown used to seeing religion exploited and used as a blunt instrument in Bosnia, the Middle East and as we saw with yesterday's bomb blasts in Cheshire, other places far closer to home.

The lesson of the Partition of India is one of the ease with which religion can be manipulated and used as a badge of superior identity, leading to bigotry and all-consuming hate. Sadly, as we've heard this morning, the same sense of superiority and certainty can also lead to self-inflicted San Diego (mass suicide) type tragedies.

The Sikh Gurus were keenly aware of these dangers and reminded us that religious labels, and false notions of caste or race had no place in God's Court. They taught that no one religion had a monopoly of truth and underlined this by including some writings of Hindus and Muslims, alongside their own in our Holy Book. It was for the same reason that the Guru asked a Muslim saint to lay the foundation stone of the Golden Temple.

The Gurus taught that religion will continue to be a cause of conflict if we simply look to its false, man-made, outer shell of bigotry and supposed superiority. But, if we look to the reality of religion beneath, we will see a common concern for tolerance, responsibility and respect for the rights of others, vital to a common quest for peace and justice.

18 June 1997

Subtle and Unthinking Racism

In this programme yesterday, we were given a timely reminder in this the European year against Racism., of the horrors perpetrated on Jews and other minorities in the '30s and '40s and reminded of the visible xenophobia still around us today.

Racism however is not something new, nor something confined exclusively to the West, as some would have us believe.

A verse from the Sikh holy Granth reminds us:

From the one Divine Light the whole of creation sprang
Why then should we divide human creatures
Into the high and the low?

Fortunately, the law of the land, and a real sense of natural justice, makes open discrimination difficult in the Britain of today. But, aided and abetted by complacency and bureaucratic inertia, it still exists in subtler forms. A recent Church of England report drew attention to the difficulties faced by members of minority faiths in prisons, where funding is provided for a Christian chaplaincy, with no comparable provision for other religions.

The Church has also drawn attention to similar anomalies in other areas of local and national government only to be met by the response that existing data gives no information on the size or distribution of religious communities. Christian groups and representatives of other faiths have therefore been pressing for a question on religion in the next Census.

After some initial hesitation, the Office for National Statistics finally agreed to consider including a question on religion in the Census that would help to provide this basic information.

At the same time it was made clear that the proposal, in common with other new requests for data, had to be first accepted by representatives of users, mainly government and local government departments. Then there would be more consultations with the same users, with further opportunities for rejection. And then, even more hurdles. A business plan would have to be prepared evaluated and prioritised against other calls for census data, and likely sales would have to be considered. But we were not asking for academic information on religious affiliation; our concern was with the very real social and cultural needs of vulnerable minorities.

It was then that we realized that a simple proposal to introduce greater fairness in society, might well be lost in the workings of a cumbersome bureaucracy geared only to the needs of the majority.

25 June 1997

Looking beyond our Genetic Make-Up

Almost every day, we are told something new about our genetic or inherited characteristics. Sometimes it's simply the obvious, expressed in ponderous scientific language; like girls being nicer than boys. This week we are told that scientists at Cambridge, have discovered the gene responsible for obesity, so that some people in years to come may be able to eat a little more and still keep their figure. Perhaps, more seriously and worrying, we're told of the possibility of genetic fortune telling, where genetic profiles can predict nasty disorders, for which there is no cure, that can affect us in the years ahead. As Guru Nanak warned about astrology, such predictions simply create sorrow and suspense in one's heart.

Nonetheless, we do need to come to terms with the huge explosion in knowledge and understanding of our genetic structure. Scientists playing with the very building blocks of life are increasingly able to identify the effect of individual genes with possibilities for combating or eliminating, a whole range of serious and not so serious disorders. The same research also opens the possibility for future generations to influence the physical characteristics of their children. There are then, clearly difficult ethical dilemmas in such research. But the real question is how far we want to go on this road in the quest for perfection.

This pursuit took quite a different form in Guru Nanak's day. Then, people would sometimes spend their whole life subjecting themselves to various austerities or disciplines in the hope of gaining mastery over mind and body as a means to an understanding of God. The Guru taught time spent on such devices was simply a waste of the precious gift of life.

In our evening prayer, Guru Nanak gently nudges us back to reality. The prayer reminds us that our life span is finite, decreasing by the day. it's what we make of the opportunities of life in serving our fellow human beings, and thus God, that is important, rather than the false pursuit of power, health or worldly acclaim.

Of course, we do need to set limits to research that may in some way demean or trivialise human life. But the more effective safeguard against misuse of any such research, lies, as the Guru reminds us, in curbing our own vanity and false aspirations to near immortality. In the end, it's not our genes, but what we make of life that really counts.

20 September 1997

Lessons of History

There is the story of a history professor who was asked by a little girl at a party, what he did. He replied that he was a student of Roman history. The little girl, clearly not impressed, answered, 'Oh, we finished the Romans last year!'

My reaction was a bit like the little girl's when I first heard of the current BBC documentary on the rise of Nazi Germany. We could be excused for thinking we'd finished with Hitler and racism a couple of years ago when we celebrated the fiftieth anniversary of the end of World War Two. But, watching the series, I realized how we still continue to ignore major lessons of history.

At a time of ethnic conflict in India, the Sikh Gurus reminded us that man is of one race in all the world, and that nothing but sorrow, misery and suffering results from attempts to divide people into the high and the low, the superior and the inferior.

What this latest documentary does is to show how easy it is to manipulate people to forget such ideals and the lessons of the past, by appeals to baser, but ever powerful human instincts. There was the harshness of the Versailles Treaty and the resulting suffering. All it needed was a Hitler to articulate and capitalize on the sense of national desolation and identify a convenient scapegoat: the Jews. Importantly, the documentary also reminds us how those that see the evil in such irrational emotion are all too easily cowed into silence and tacit support. More recent events in many parts of the world remind us that there are ever more Hitlers waiting in the wings and no dearth of potential scapegoats.

Could it ever happen here? Frankly, I think any would-be dictator would have a tough and miserable time. What bothers me far more, is the growing ability of an ever more powerful media, concentrated in fewer and fewer hands to tell us, what constitutes *normal* behaviour. When to be happy, when where and how to grieve, and more worryingly, what people want and supposedly think.

My concern is that this can lead to narrowness in thinking and an intolerance towards those that don't share our views which in its extreme form can lead a nation astray. The safeguard, as Guru Nanak taught is that we base both private and public life, not on expediency or fickle public opinion but on the more abiding values of tolerance compassion and concern for the rights of others: values common to all our major faiths.

27 September 1997

The Story behind the Koh-I-Noor Diamond

The news this week that a Red Indian chief who died in this country in the 1800s is to have his remains flown back to his family in the USA, has a poignant echo in the story of Maharaja Duleep Singh who also died in England more than 100 years ago.

Duleep Singh was the son of the legendary Maharaja Ranjit Singh, a Sikh who ruled over the whole of north India, including much of present-day Pakistan, Kashmir and parts of Afghanistan in the 1830s. True to Guru Nanak's teachings, Ranjit Singh's empire was a model of religious tolerance. He gave generously towards the building and upkeep of Hindu, Muslim and Sikh places of worship. Though a Sikh, Ranjit Singh appointed ministers to his government on merit alone, and Hindus and Muslims occupied prominent positions. The Sikh Maharaja would also travel incognito to distant parts of his kingdom to ensure officials did not usurp their authority.

Then, in 1839 the Maharaja died, and in the space of ten short years, through a combination of palace intrigue and two closely fought wars with the English, nothing but memories remained of one of the world's first truly secular states.

Maharaja Duleep Singh, a boy of eleven at the time of the collapse of his father's empire, was converted to Christianity, forbidden to have any contact with his mother and brought to England as a ward of Queen Victoria, giving her, as instructed, the famous Koh-i-noor diamond as a gift.

As Duleep Singh grew older, he learnt how he had been separated from his mother, his religion and the land of his birth and eventually died, a bitter and broken man and was buried in a Norfolk cemetery.

It's a sad story. And to me, the sadder part is that all that is remembered, even by most Sikhs, is the incident of the Koh-i-noor diamond, with occasional half-hearted demands for its return. To me the real poignancy of the story lies in the contrast in the respect that the all-powerful Ranjit Singh accorded to his subjects of different faiths with the treatment of his son Duleep Singh.

And, in this fiftieth year of the partition of the subcontinent on communal lines, there is the tantalising thought of what might have been if, what the historian George Bruce described as India's first experiment with secular democracy had taken firmer hold and given the lie to the belief that people of different faiths cannot live together in peace and harmony.

2 March 1998

Artefacts in Religions

I'm frequently asked to talk to RE teachers and advisers on the teaching of Sikhism in schools. I enjoy talking about the religion but not the inevitable request for information on useful artifacts. Teachers, like the rest of us, know that young children are always happier with things they can pick up, examine or draw, than with boring teachings. The problem is that Sikhs have so few of these things, that we probably come bottom in the artefacts stakes.

The Sikh Gurus refused to have any paintings made of themselves and argued that the veneration of any man-made object detracts from true worship of the one God of all creation. Despite such teachings, artists impressions of what the Gurus might have looked like, are freely available and worse, clay idols of the Gurus are sometimes found among the aids to religious teaching used in some schools.

1 was reminded of this Sikh attitude to religious artefacts when I attended a preview, of an exhibition to be held at the Victoria and Albert Museum next year to mark a very important year for Sikhs, the 300th anniversary of the creation of the Khalsa, the visible community of Sikhs and the 500th anniversary of Guru Nanak's first sermon in which he preached the importance of tolerance and respect for all faiths. Sikhs regard 1999 as a sort of mini millennium, and it will be celebrated with much enthusiasm.

It's right, particularly on such occasions that we admire beautiful and historic works of art, and through these works, the sacrifice and contribution made by men and women in Sikh history. But it's also important to remember that however beautiful they may be, works of art are not a substitute for the guidance of religion so relevant to today's times. Teachings such as the Guru's emphasis on the need for positive living rooted in service to others; a powerful antidote to the 'me' culture of today. Then there is the Sikh stand against religious bigotry, sadly, still very much with us, and how the nineth Sikh Guru gave his own life to protect those of a different religion, and much else in the lives and positive and uplifting teachings of our Gurus. Anything that reminds us of such teachings, must be welcome, which brings me back to religious artefacts which in becoming objects of veneration, paradoxically simply divert us from the religious message.

Sikhs are no different from anyone else. Our celebrations in 1999 will inevitably produce their crop of gaudy trinkets and souvenirs. The hope is that we'll also find time to reflect on the guidance for today, contained in the actual teachings.

20 May 1998

Walking the Talk

My long-suffering wife and daughters have constantly had to listen to me saying that they make too much fuss of packing to go on holiday. 'Simply make a list of the things you want to take and throw them into a suitcase, it's easy', I'd boast. I recently got my comeuppance.

We'd decided to go on a short break to Cheddar Gorge. As usual, I'd left my packing to the last minute. But I had my list, and soon I had put my things in a case and off we went.

When we got to the hotel, we started unloading the car, and then embarrassment! I'd left my suitcase at home—to the intense amusement of the family. And I've never been allowed to forget it since.

I remembered this incident as I packed my case last weekend for a two-day conference on 'Values for the twenty-first century' I double checked, and this time did remember to take my case with me. But the idea of lists followed me with a vengeance. For two days representatives of all walks of life, worked together to produce list upon list of core values considered desirable for life in the twenty-first century. Eventually these were narrowed down to a summary list. Looking at it, a colleague from industry said with some frustration, that our core values were beginning to look more and more like those common to religious teachings! And they did. Values that we've arrogantly discarded in our obsession with self, personal rights and synthetic supermarket shelf type happiness.

It's important in our quest for more responsible living, that we learn from the failings of organized religion, where those in religious authority rarely lived the values of truth, humility and concern for others taught by religion. For many, religion became a list of good intentions wrapped in dogma, to be recited or chanted to make us certain candidates for paradise.

Guru Nanak, concerned by this subversion of religious teaching, constantly stressed in parables and a memorable verse:

Words do not a saint or sinner make
It is deeds alone that are recorded in the book of fate.

My list of things to take on holiday was defective in that, it should have had an additional item: take suitcase and contents with you! In much the same way, a list of core values is of little use unless we carry these with us into our daily lives.

During our conference, I came across an American expression new to me. 'Walking the talk', turning words into action. Core values to underpin life in our rapidly changing times are clearly desirable, but they need a commitment to 'walk the talk'.

3 June 1998

Creation of an International Criminal Court

Today's news of rising violence in Kosovo reminds us of the ease with which old religious conflicts can be rekindled into new violence. The same concern was highlighted in a recent TV documentary about religious tensions in the region. Christians and Muslims spoke of the other community with uniform fear and distrust. And then there were the leaders, robot-like figures programmed on hate, with the clear ability to turn fear and distrust into an orgy of murder.

The documentary was about Kosovo, but it could easily have been about Bosnia, Rwanda, the Sudan, or a dozen other places around the world. Weak or compromised national governments and, until now, the absence of any international machinery to touch them, have allowed perpetrators of communal violence to act with impunity.

Fortunately, there are now signs, that at long last, the international community is waking up to its responsibility. A few days ago, I attended a small meeting that gave me real hope. It was a preparatory meeting for a United Nations conference in Rome in a few weeks' time, to create the world's first International Criminal Court to examine crimes against humanity in any part of the world.

As far back as 1945, the United Nations indicated its determination to deal with such offences, but little happened in the politics and moral compromises of the Cold War. Now, with experience from ad-hoc tribunals dealing with genocide in Rwanda and former Yugoslavia, much of the groundwork has already been covered. The Court would have the right to examine evidence from any source in seeking and punishing the guilty, establishing truth and providing redress.

Many hurdles still remain. The Court would need to be totally independent of political pressures of any sort, and yet work with and complement existing national and international organizations. Not easy.

A few years ago, the very idea of an International Criminal Court would have been dismissed as unrealistic. Now a growing revulsion against gross human rights abuse, coupled with an increased emphasis on ethically based foreign policies, can lead to real progress.

Guru Gobind Singh reminded us that an emotional and indiscriminate response to injustice was wrong. It was the perpetrators alone, who should be singled out and punished. It is this singling it of individual offenders and bringing them to justice that could make the work of the new Court, the most effective venture of its kind in our strife-torn century.

25 June 1998

Inner peace is not Enough

Sikhs are constantly reminded to look beyond obsession with self to a wider concern for those around us. Trying to be true to such teachings, I readily accepted an invitation to an interfaith conference last weekend on the theme of world peace.

In the event the conference was the very opposite of what I had expected. 'World peace can only come through inner peace', we were told again and again. There was much chanting of peace prayers and similar mantras. I felt a little irreligious in wondering how any of this could help the suffering in Kosovo, or other scenes of conflict. Then there was the planting of a multinational flag, with a hollow flagpole filled with peace messages. It was announced with the pride of real achievement that dozens of such poles had been placed in different parts of the country. The irreverent thoughts continued. Could such rituals really help those suffering the physical wounds and mental trauma of ethnic cleansing? Could peace mantras really help the skeletal starving in Africa that we see on our TV screens?

I felt like someone who had turned up to the wrong party. It was my turn to speak. Hesitantly I affirmed the importance of self-improvement. It's given considerable emphasis in Sikhism, but the teachings also say there is more, much more to balanced or godly living. I inquired what was the point of charging spiritual batteries unless these were then used to help the needy and move society towards greater equity and justice.

Despite my early fears of verbal lynching by peace activists, my words were listened to with kindness and courtesy as an interesting thought by people genuinely committed to the pursuit of peace. But I fear that my plea for more active involvement will probably soon be forgotten.

I can readily understand religion being pushed to the margins of life by those obsessed with the pursuit of material happiness, but I feel saddened by the unthinking marginalization of these teachings by those clearly aware of the suffering and hurt in society.

Guru Nanak criticised as selfish those who left their families and went to the wilderness in search of God. Today there's not much wilderness left but it's all too easy to escape our responsibilities in narrow and blinkered lifestyles that see the pursuit of personal happiness or personal inner peace as ends in themselves.

The great parliamentarian, Edmund Burke reminded us that for the triumph of evil, it's only necessary for good men to do nothing. Wise words that are perhaps, even more relevant to the world of today.

2 July 1998

Football. Not a Matter of Life and Death; It's Much More Important

I'm delighted the England squad came back home in style on Concorde to a warm welcome at the airport. They have every reason to hold their heads high.

Anyone who watched England's inspired performance on Tuesday evening will share their sense of emptiness and dejection at being knocked out of the World Cup by the narrowest of possible margins. The team had been improving with every match and there were real hopes of going on to the final. A missed chance in a penalty shoot-out, and suddenly it was all over, not only for the team but for millions of others for whom football had temporally become central to life.

Looking to the future, England played well and are poised to go from strength to strength, particularly with the discovery of new talents such as that of the 18-year-old Michael Owen. As for the rest of us, well there was life before the World Cup.

As the Sikh Gurus remind us, it is important to keep a sense of proportion or balance in such things. I suppose we'll have to get back to some of the jobs or chores we've been putting off.

The last few weeks have reminded us of the tremendous passions and prejudices that football excites. It was Bill Shankly who said, 'football isn't a matter of life and death—it's much more important'. I wouldn't go quite that far, but it is almost a religion to devoted followers of the game. There are real parallels with religion, some good and some bad. Focusing on a *common* event; a *common* interest has led to an, albeit short term sense of community in pubs and clubs throughout the land, and in many homes, a rare gathering of family around the TV set.

For me, one of the negative sides of sport creeps in at the very start of a match, when both teams raise their eyes to the heavens as their national anthem is played, in the unsaid belief or hope that God, knowing the superiority of *our* nation or culture, will quietly intervene to ensure *our* success. In much the same way religions frequently talk of exclusive or special relationships with God. From there, in both football and religion, it's a short step to xenophobia and active hatred, sometimes seen on the terraces, and more dangerously, in the wider world.

The Sikh Gurus encouraged sport as a way to physical fitness and spiritual equanimity.

We are told that life itself is like a game that requires strength, conviction and compassion. It should be played in such a way, that we are neither elated by success nor despondent at failure. Sane advice for those experiencing the momentary extremes of either success or failure in sport, or in wider life.

19 September 1998

When All Else Fails, Look to the Instructions

One of the proposals for a prayer area in Millennium Dome complex shows it placed between a first-aid room and a room for lost people. The unintended symbolism is a light-hearted reminder of the way we often turn to religion when something goes wrong: a vehicle of last resort.

Religion can of course be helpful in easing inner-hurt and guiding those that have lost their direction in life. But religion as taught by Guru Nanak and all major faiths, has a far more important role: that of giving us a fuller and less self-centred perspective on life. The teachings of religion provide much more than short term spiritual comfort, by helping us avoid many of the pitfalls of life to which our more selfish urges often lead us, made more so by the news of Monday's planned release of video-taped evidence, we can applaud Bill Clinton for his prayer meetings and his belated appointment of religious guides to keep him on the straight and narrow, but it would have been more helpful to him, if he had looked to, and lived the guidance of religious teaching in the first place. Unfortunately. there's a bit of the Bill Clinton in all of us. I'm not referring to sordid liaisons, but to this turning to religion when all else fails. It's a bit like me and self-assembly: when despite my best efforts, things look all skewed, or fall apart, I reluctantly turn to the instructions.

The instructions; the teachings of religion help us get a balanced view of right and wrong. All religions have clear guidance on personal behaviour and social responsibility. Christians warn us of the seven deadly sins, while we Sikh, who believe in moderation in all things, have only five. But both lists include lust, which today has become a bit of a laugh until something goes wrong. Then the same tabloids who would have us believe there is little more to life than sex, bring out banner headlines of 'Sex Monster'.

It's the same in other areas of life. Like obsession with wealth and what we call the good things of life. A verse from Sikh scriptures reminds us:

Blessed and beautiful is the hut where the Lord's praise is sung
Worthless the palace where the Lord is forgotten
To live by grinding corn wearing only a blanket
Is better than ruling a kingdom without inner peace.

Such teachings seem to be out of touch with the way we are building society, but we could unwittingly be assisting social disintegration. We'd do well to look at the instructions before our skewed social values collapse around us. The consequences could be disastrous and require much more than spiritual first aid.

15 January 1999

Religious Bigotry

I've just come back from a visit to Punjab in India. It was there on the spring festival of Baisakhi, 300 years ago come spring this year, that Guru Gobind Singh, gave Sikhs the distinct identity or uniform that we have today, to encourage us to stand out from the safety of the crowd in pursuit of Sikh ideals of social justice and religious freedom.

It was my first visit to the sub-continent for more than eighteen years. I must confess that I've been in a bit of a sulk with India ever since the attack on the Golden Temple in 1984 on one of the holiest days in the Sikh calendar, and the subsequent mass killing of Sikhs later the same year. How could people behave in such a way against a tiny minority?

But one can't sulk forever. Nor sadly can human nature be changed that easily. On our arrival in Delhi on Christmas eve, newspaper headlines screamed 'Christians attacked in Gujerat; nuns raped, churches and a missionary school burnt by Hindu extremists.' It was deja-vu with a vengeance. This week, only hours after the Indian Prime Minister Atal Bihari Vajpaee visited the affected area to appeal for calm, another church was set alight.

The instant or knee-jerk reaction to these attacks on Christians in India, would be to blame Hindus or Indians in general for the actions of a lunatic fringe, but this simply fuels hate and fear between communities. From there, it's only a short step to saying that the beliefs of others, or other ways of life are necessarily inferior to our own.

The reality is that it is all too easy to appeal to our baser passions through the false trappings of religion, in common hatred of the stranger. Jesus Christ was certainly alive to such dangers when, against a background of popular prejudice, he applauded the action of the good Samaritan. Similarly, the Sikh Gurus attacked all notions of race or caste. As Guru Gobind Singh taught 'people may have differences in religious belief or the customs of different environments, but more importantly, we are all members of the same human family.'

The Guru also taught that these religious teachings common to our different faiths, will continue to be subverted by cynical politicians and fanatics in religious garb unless we have the courage to voice our beliefs, and stand up and be counted, not only against the actions and prejudices of others, but more importantly, the bigotry of those in our own community.

22 January 1999

Striving for Peace in Former Yugoslavia

Yesterday's plea by the six nation Contact Group, for Serbians and ethnic Albanians to get together in talks, seems a strangely muted response to the recent massacre of ethnic Albanians in Kosovo. In his refusal to allow independent observers to investigate the massacre and by his attempts to pressurise western ground monitors, the Serbian President Slobadan Milosevic, like Saddam Hussein in Iraq, has in effect, thumbed his nose at the United Nations and NATO. And to tell the truth, short of some brilliant commando-type action, there seems to be little we can do about it.

Aerial bombardment, our modern equivalent of the nineteenth-century gunboat, may make us feel better, but it is inevitably the innocent that suffer while the despot remains safely ensconced in the safety of a bombproof bunker. And much the same could be said about sanctions, which, while preventing food and medicines reaching a prohibited area, seem to have little effect on the supply of arms.

Strident denunciation of Serb action, as witnessed in the Commons this week, accurately reflect a nation's sense of outrage, but words like 'insufferable' or 'unacceptable', have no real meaning unless followed by action. The harsh reality is, that in a world awash with arms, and numerous unresolved ethnic and religious conflicts, Saddams, Slobodans and more of their ilk, could pop up anywhere.

I believe the only hope of moving away from this gloomy scenario is to look to disparity and injustice, and the potential for regional conflict before would-be dictators have a chance to exploit it. But to do so, we have to move away from blinkered, old fashioned notions of 'friendly nations', and 'national sovereignty', to an even-handed approach to human rights for all people, particularly religious and cultural minorities Preventative maintenance must surely be better than later cries of 'unacceptable'. As Guru Gobind Singh, the tenth Guru of the Sikhs taught: '*All humans though different in habit and environment, deserve the same respect and the same protection*'. And this applies to those in far off Tibet, as it does to those in Kosovo.

Some will say that this is being unduly idealistic, but our different religions teach that for progress we need to aim at an ideal. And, as we approach the start of a new millennium, it is right that we look closely at the wisdom of the short-term pacts and moral compromises that have made the twentieth century, the bloodiest in human history.

29 January 1999

Stress Can Be Good for Us

A report in the Times this week of an American study on rats by the National Institute of Mental Health, suggests that much maligned stress may in some ways be beneficial. Research showed that jumpy rats, called 'New Yorkers', produced large levels of stress hormones which reduced the body's immune system, leaving the rats liable to a greater risk of colds or flu. But for the calm, laid-back type rats, called 'Californians' in the study, it was worse. Un-used overcapacity in the immune system caused a greater incidence of rheumatoid arthritis, allergic skin diseases, asthma and much else.

So it seems that some stress is actually good for us, and we can, if we dare, say 'that's nice' to the next person who complains to us of being a bit stressed.

Stress is a normal part of life, as Guru Nanak reminded us that true contentment can never be gained from withdrawing from the challenges of daily life in search of God, but by putting minor irritations in their true proportions and addressing real challenges in our personal life, and those arising from our responsibility to create a fairer society.

Despite such teachings, escape from the 'heartache and the thousand natural shocks that flesh is heir to' has its own allure. A few years ago, I was invited, along with a visitor from India, to record some short television epilogues. After dinner in the hotel, the man from India talked about his life at his ashram near Delhi. It seemed a haven of peace and tranquility. As I went to bed I thought of my own hectic lifestyle. I could do with less stress and a larger than average dose of tranquility.

It all changed next morning. The man from the Ashram was late coming down to breakfast. He'd slept badly. Gone was the air of calm detachment. He blamed the hotel, and repeatedly criticised a terrified disciple who was accompanying him. Although there was plenty of time to get to the studio, he was convinced that we would be late, and everything would be a disaster. The man, who I had looked to as the epitome of calmness, had gone to pieces when faced with the minor pinpricks of daily living.

I immediately realized the wisdom of the Guru's word to recluses from daily life in the wilderness. In the language of the American study on rats, I'd rather be a jumpy New Yorker living life to the full, than a laid-back Californian opting out of the adventure of life.

7 April 1999

Merchandises Grief and Suffering

Every now and then, we come across an item of news that reminds us of the depths of depravity to which humans can sink. I'm not referring to the systematic genocide of ethnic Albanians in Kosovo, horrendous and heart rending though it is, but to the activities of those who literally trade on human suffering.

It was a report on last weekend's Sunday Programme, on the commercialisation of the holocaust with site-seeing tours of Auschwitz and other scenes of mass murder that caught my attention. The report described and detailed, souvenir sales of camp style pyjamas and even an application for a license, mercifully turned down, for the manufacture of Anne Frank jeans.

I wonder about human nature. We pride ourselves that the tearing down of the Berlin wall in the autumn of 1989 marked the triumph of democracy over communism. But, as we've seen since, it was more the defeat of state-controlled capitalism by virtually unfettered free market forces. Forces that are truly global and recognize no national boundaries and as we've seen, have few constraints.

Financial statistics speak for themselves. The income of the poorest fifth of the world's population has virtually halved in the last ten years, while that of the richest fifth has increased by some 15%.

Let's face it. The appeal to human greed seems to be a more powerful motivator than the democratic right to freedom of speech. I suppose the good news is, that this does at least show our common if flawed humanity. Human greed seems to transcend all notions of caste, colour, creed or nationality.

The Sikh Gurus never criticised wealth in itself. But they were extremely critical of the ways in which it is sometimes accumulated and the pride that goes with it. Guru Nanak once pointedly chose to stay at the house of a poor carpenter, ignoring the lavish hospitality of a rich merchant who had made his money by exploiting the poor.

Another of the Sikh Gurus wrote:

Blessed and beautiful is the hut where the Lord's praise is sung.
Worthless the palace where the Lord is forgotten.

The Gurus taught that we should earn by honest effort and share our earnings with the less fortunate. Sound advice then. Vital in a world that merchandises grief and suffering; a world of growing inequality.

14 April 1999

300th Anniversary of the Creation of the Khalsa

Today is a very special day for Sikhs. A sort of mini millennium. It is the 300th anniversary of the formation of the Khalsa, a community of equals ready to stand up and be counted for their beliefs.

Two centuries earlier, Guru Nanak, the founder of Sikhism who lived at a time of often violent rivalry between Hindus and Muslims, made the startling observation that in God's eyes there was neither Hindu nor Muslim. He taught that God is not interested in our different religious labels, but in the product beneath. In the first move to inter-faith understanding, Guru Nanak taught that our different religions are different paths to the same one God, and that all should be respected.

Guru Tegh Bahadur, the nineth Guru of the Sikhs, gave 'tolerance' a new and more powerful meaning – 'the willingness to give one's life for the freedom of belief of others.' A delegation of Hindu Brahmins from Kashmir had visited the Guru and said, 'We know you don't agree with many aspects of our teachings, but you and earlier Gurus have always spoken up for freedom of belief. Will you intercede on our behalf against the Mughal rulers who are daily forcibly converting thousands of Hindus?'

Guru Tegh Bahadur readily agreed. It cost him his life. He was publicly beheaded by the Mughals for his defence of the rights of another faith. At that time Sikhs had no distinguishing appearance, and they hesitated to come forward and claim their master's body.

It was to guard against such momentary lapses of courage that, 300 years ago today, Guru Gobind Singh the tenth and last of the Sikh Gurus, gave us a visible identity, long hair covered with a turban and other symbols to remind us to always stand up and be counted for our beliefs. In themselves, the symbols make us no better or worse than anyone else. They are symbols of our beliefs and ideals. Reminders of the Sikh path, and the values embedded in it. It was a higher view of tolerance, a belief in the oneness of our human family, gender equality, an obligation to put others before self and a readiness to stand up for the weak and oppressed.

Today, we are all overwhelmed by the suffering in Kosovo. Such horrors start with the silence of those who see injustice inflicted on friend, neighbour or workplace colleague. It is this silence that gives strength to those who exploit superficial difference. The real message of the creation of the Khalsa 300 years ago is the need for us all not to look the other way but to stand up for the rights of others whatever the cost.

22 April 1999

Not Barriers, but Gateways

While Sikhs were both surprised and delighted over last week's media coverage of the 300th anniversary of Sikhism in its modern form, there was some understandable concern from others; 'Britain is a Christian country. Why should viewing and listening time be used to focus on other faiths?'

It's a question I can understand and similar to one I asked years ago as I hurried home from my new school with an exciting discovery. Catholics didn't have to go to assembly or attend R.E. classes. I didn't know much about Sikhism, but I knew that I wasn't C of E! All I had to do was to get a note from my parents and I'd have lots of free time.

My usually reasonable parents wouldn't have any of it. My mother said 'Good try. But your religion teaches respect for other faiths. And you can't respect what you don't understand.' I thought at the time that my mother was being utterly unreasonable, but over the years I've grown to understand that those simple words that 'you can't respect what you don't understand' give us both the cause and the cure to much of the conflict and bigotry in the world today.

People of different faiths and cultures often live in close proximity for generations, without any real understanding of the belief of their neighbour. It's a fragile and superficial sort of tolerance rooted in assumed superiority of our way of life against that of our neighbour.

What we see in the world today, as in Kosovo, Rwanda and places nearer home is the ease with which latent prejudice can be exploited by the power hungry and turned to active hatred and brutal killing.

We all know, how in a fog or mist, familiar objects like a bush or a tree can assume frightening proportions. To me, ignorance and prejudice acts in much the same way, and in such a mist it's all too easy to believe those of different beliefs and cultures as threats to our way of life. When the mist clears, we see things as they really are and recognize shared values and aspirations.

In today's much smaller world, knowledge of other ways of life is no longer an academic luxury. It's essential for peace and harmony that we learn to respect differences and rejoice in the many things we have in common.

More positively we learn that different ways of life are not barriers between people, but gateways to a greater understanding and enrichment of life.

28 April 1999

Simple Language

This week, British courts have suffered their biggest culture shock for years. They've been told to use plain English in civil litigation. Out go words like 'plaintiff', to be replaced by the ordinary sounding 'claimant'. 'Chancery Motions' become 'Interim Applications' and stern sounding writs, will now be simply, 'claim forms'.

You'd think everyone would welcome this move to plain English, and to making the working of the court more intelligible to lay people. But no. Some lawyers have criticised the changes as a pandering to political correctness. Others see the removal of Latin and the demystifying of the legal process eroding the dignity of the law.

Similar arguments have always been used against those attempting to make religion more intelligible to lay people. Plain words are said to diminish the dignity and sense of awe contained in religious texts. Guru Nanak met this argument when he started preaching in the language of the day, instead of Sanskrit, the then language of religion, understood only by a small priestly class who interpreted the sacred scriptures in return for food and money.

But even simple everyday language becomes dated with the passage of time. For example, the teachings of the Gurus contained in our holy book the Guru Granth Sahib, are in a language current on the sub-continent several centuries ago. Easy to understand then, not so easy to understand today, particularly by children here whose first language is English.

The logic of Guru Nanak's teaching is that in this country, Sikhs should make greater use of English and, despite cultural resistance, this is increasingly being done. But it's not only language that changes with time. Social concerns and priorities also change. We all joke about judges whose comments show them to be way out of touch with real life, yet religious teaching which needs to address issues and concerns of today, all too often finds itself rooted in the past. Just as the law needs to adapt to social change, religions need to look at the ethical needs of today's times.

As the words of an English hymn remind us *'New occasions teach new duties, time makes ancient good uncouth; they must upwards still and onwards, who would keep abreast with truth'*. Our different religions have a lot to offer a world that at times seems to be drifting in a sort of a moral vacuum. But to do this, they must address *today's* concerns in a language that we can all understand.

6 August 1999

What's in a Name?

The Indian city of Calcutta is changing its name to Kolkata. It's not so long since Bombay became Mumbai and Madras Chennai in a rejection of Raj names.

This renaming of towns and countries has quickened in recent years particularly in the former Soviet Union and in the continent of Africa. While it's a bit of a nightmare for travel agents and tourists and those like me who are chronically bad at geography, it's not really a big deal. As Shakespeare observed, 'a rose by any other name would smell as sweet'. An observation that, with some imagination, also holds for the streets of Kolkata.

A recent article in the Times however took Kolkata to task for creating 'international confusion'. Winston Churchill was similarly concerned about name changes.

Two weeks before VE Day, he wrote:

'I do not consider that names that have been familiar for generations of Englishmen should be altered to suit the whims of foreigners living in those parts If we do not make a stand, the BBC will be pronouncing Paris Paree. Foreign names were made for Englishmen, not Englishmen for foreign names'. I wonder where that leaves the Scots, the Welsh and the Irish?

I feel that the increasing assertion of local identity, culture, language and religion, are, in many ways, a reaction to increasing globalization with its narrowing uniformity of thought and its market-place ethics. This year, the 300th year of Sikhism in its modern form, Sikhs have been asserting their own distinct identity and recharging spiritual batteries from the high ideals and values taught by the Gurus. Christians, no doubt, will be doing much the same in celebrating the millennium. The world is richer for its different cultures and their different view of life.

There is however, a very real danger in asserting pride in difference. It's the all too human temptation to show the superiority of our way of life by belittling that of our neighbour.

Guru Gobind Singh the tenth Guru of the Sikhs, reminded us of the importance of identity, but he also stressed that we are all of the same one race responsible to the same one God of all humanity.

The challenge for the good citizens of Kolkata, and for the rest of us as we approach a new millennium, is to ensure that legitimate cultural pride also recognizes our over-riding *common* humanity.

20 August 1999

Perverse Unifying Effect of Manufactured Hatred.

It seems ages ago, but it was only early this summer that India and Pakistan were poised to meet in the cricket world cup at Old Trafford. It was at a time of heightened conflict between the two countries over the disputed area of Kashmir, and violence was feared between rival supporters. But the match passed off peacefully, showing that in this country, the things that unify people from the sub-continent: commerce, language, common concerns over the erosion of religious values, and of course, and importantly, a shared passion for cricket, are stronger than real or supposed differences.

It should be the same on the sub-continent, but clearly, it's not. There tensions, hype and threats of nuclear action are clearly on the increase in the run-up to India's general election next month. The problems of the sub-continent are however, simply an illustration of a more general concern. How can communities that live in peace and harmony in one country, be at each other's throats in another?

To my mind, the reason lies in the ease, the frightening ease with which whole communities can be manipulated to fear and hatred of their neighbour. The formula is simple, and it has been tried, tested and used throughout the world. All it takes as a trigger is an exaggeration of supposed difference, a smear of suspicion, and an appeal to envy or greed. Then, in an all too familiar sequence, suspicion turns to active hatred, violence and as we've seen in Kosovo, atrocities and counter-atrocities.

It's a scene all too familiar in our conflict scarred twentieth century. But it has been with us all through human history and it was certainly present in the India of Guru Nanak five centuries ago. His formula for preventing this downward spiral of human depravity lay in a single word, 'dialogue'. It started with his very first sermon. In it he taught that God isn't interested in our different ethnic or religious labels, but in our piety, tolerance and concern for others. The Guru followed this up by entering into dialogue with the different faiths of his day, respecting them as different paths to the same one God.

Despite all our clever means of communication, there is still little dialogue between different ways of life today, and it is dialogue alone that can dispel the ignorance and latent prejudices that so easily gives rise to conflicts that still plague the world today.

27 August 1999

Preventative Maintenance

'If it isn't broken, don't fix it', sounds like good common sense, particularly if we are talking of a domestic appliance or changing an already sound way of doing things. But it has its limitations. Industry has long recognized, in preventative maintenance, that it's often better to prevent things breaking down in the first place.

It's much the same with social problems. We are all aware of questionable behaviour, and attitudes and practices around us that give us cause for concern. But we ignore the warning signs and look the other way, until something goes wrong! Then there is ritual beating of breasts, and cries of how can such things happen in our society, as in the aftermath of the Macpherson inquiry into the death of Stephen Lawrence.

The Sikh Gurus, faced with problems of rigid social divisions and conflict between different faiths, stressed the need for a sort of 'preventative maintenance' to guard against social ills. Their aim was to develop and strengthen, tolerant and positive attitudes to others. Looking at the friction between different religions, each claiming superiority and exclusive access to God, Guru Gobind Singh taught:

God is in the temple, as He is in the mosque
He is in the Hindu worship as He is in the Muslim prayer
The Hindus and the Muslims are all one
Have each the habits of different environments
The one Lord has made them both

Earlier, his father had given his own life in the defence of those of a faith different to his own, to worship in the manner of their choice.

The merit of the Gurus' approach is its constant and unremitting attack on the ignorance on which prejudice thrives. The Guru's aim was to replace ignorance and prejudice with tolerance and understanding.

It's an approach that John Stephens, the new Metropolitan Police Commissioner might bear in mind when he takes up his post and begins to tackle the problems of institutional racism identified in the Macpherson inquiry.

The planned recruitment of more police from ethnic minorities, though welcome, won't in itself be enough. The new commissioner will have to dig deep to get to causes of institutional racism and tackle the ignorance and prejudice that gives rise to a canteen culture that pokes fun at difference. To change this culture to one in which difference is respected is a mammoth task. But it's one that must be tackled to restore shattered public confidence.

18 October 1999

'Medecin Sans Frontiere' Awarded Nobel Peace Prize

Throughout this year, Sikhs have been celebrating the 300th anniversary of what in effect was an early declaration of human rights when Guru Gobind Singh emphasised in stirring terms, the Sikh teaching:

Manas ki jaath saab ek he pachanbo
–Recognize the oneness of the human family.

He reminded Sikhs of the need to stand up for such ideals however testing the circumstances.

This week, we turn to those same thoughts of a single 'human family', with the same rights and opportunities, with different faiths joining together in the annual celebration of One World Week, and the founding of the United Nations. But we are all too aware that the celebration is an aspiration rather than reality. We live in a world of gross inequality in which the poverty line in one country, would be the height of luxury in another; a world in which half the members of the United Nations practice torture and the gross abuse of human rights against their own people.

But despite all our failures there are genuine grounds for hope. We have in recent years been moving slowly and, sometimes painfully, to international action against both countries and individuals who abuse human rights. Campaigning by movements such as Jubilee 2000, has clearly influenced powerful nations to move to a more compassionate attitude to Third World debt.

And there are others working to alleviate poverty and suffering, like this year's recipient of the Nobel Peace Prize, 'Medecin Sans Frontiere' whose very name encompasses the one world ideal.

Sikhs believe that the ethical teachings of religion can help us move faster in such positive directions, if we can move away from the arrogance that says my religion is better than yours, highlighting apparent differences in a way that itself provokes conflict.

Sikhism teaches that our different religions are, in effect, overlapping circles of belief. If we look at religion in this way, we'll see that the degree of overlap is far greater than smaller areas of difference. We'll see common ethical standards of tolerance, justice, compassion, and responsible living, for both individuals and nations that have the power to make today's vision of a truly one world society, a practical reality.

27 October 1999

Recreational Drugs for Instant Contentment

We humans pride ourselves as being the cleverest creatures on the planet, but watching a programme on drug abuse the other night, I'm not so sure. We never seem to learn!

500 years ago in India, Guru Nanak taught that, life had both material and spiritual dimensions, and that both were necessary for true contentment. Centuries earlier, Jesus Christ had preached much the same thing when he said that man shall not live by bread alone.

But despite such clear teachings on the need for balanced living, we still look to money and the things it can buy in our search for instant gratification and quick fix, synthetic happiness.

Monday's BBC documentary on drug abuse in South Wales showed us at what cost. The statistics are frightening, surpassed only by our complacency. Half the 16-year-olds in British schools now experiment with drugs. One child a week dies of solvent abuse. 90% of those who go to clubs, use so-called 'recreational drugs'. One third of all property crime is drug related. And so on.

In the programme, a group of concerned women, and some former drug addicts showed how much can be done in fighting the drugs menace. One former user described in graphic terms that cannot be repeated on a breakfast programme, the pain and suffering he endured while on drugs, and he made an impassioned plea to schoolchildren to stay clear.

Perhaps even more depressing than the use of drugs by the young is the realization that it is we that have led them down this road, with our false values and false priorities, and the false mantra of give the people what they want.

The use of liquor and drugs to give a sense of wellbeing was also common at the time of Guru Nanak. He gave this advice:

Avoid false intoxicants that blur the mind,
And mar the distinction between right and wrong
Look instead to the more enduring contentment
Found in the service of God and fellow man.

It's a message that can easily be tested. I'm sure those former drug addicts now giving their time warning children of the danger of this false road to happiness, are, in doing this, themselves experiencing a contentment far greater and more lasting than that of the needle and the syringe.

3 November 1999

Diwali and the False Imprisonment of Guru Hargobind

This weekend, British Hindus will be celebrating Diwali, 'the festival of lights'. It's a celebration that marks the triumphant return to India of the Hindu god Ram after an epic struggle in Sri Lanka. Diwali is also important to Sikhs, though for a different reason connected with a dramatic stand for religious freedom by the sixth Guru of the Sikhs in the early years of the seventeenth century.

Guru Hargobind had been incarcerated in the notorious Gwalior fort by India's Mughal rulers for his insistence on freedom of worship. The imprisonment of the widely popular Guru created a groundswell of resentment against the Mughal authorities. The Emperor Jahngir realized that he had blundered and, in an effort to gain popular support, he announced that the Guru would be set free on the festival of Diwali. The news was conveyed to the Guru who bravely responded that he wasn't the only one falsely imprisoned in the fort, and that he would refuse to leave unless fifty-two Hindu princes held there, were also released.

Now, the Mughal Emperor knew that the only way out of the fort was through a narrow passage, through which only one person could pass at a time. Not wanting to lose face, and in a false show of generosity, he declared that anyone holding onto the Guru's cloak would also be free to leave. He was confident that at most, only one other person would be able to leave with the Guru.

When the Diwali festival came around, the Guru put on his cloak. But it was a *cloak with a difference*. A cloak with *fifty-two tassels of differing lengths* allowing each of the Rajas to keep hold of an end as they walked together in single file through the narrow passage to the anger and annoyance of their Mughal captors.

I thought of the Guru's brave stand, while at an international conference at Australia House last weekend on the theme of religious and cultural diversity. Speaker after speaker stressed the importance of recognizing and respecting the beliefs and practices of others. But consensus among like-minded people is not enough. It needs the sort of courage and commitment shown by Guru Hargobind who risked his own freedom for the rights of others to make a real difference. A valuable lesson for today's times, when we so often put expediency before principle.

The story also reminds us of the importance and value of difference. The tassels on the Guru's cloak would not have been of much use if they'd all been the same length. Difference has its own strengths.

10 November 1999

Wiping the Slate Clean

As the turn of the century draws near, more and more people seem to be looking to smaller projects, that recognize the importance of the individual in effecting change as a way of celebrating the new millennium. One of the best that I've come across is a project called the Clean Slate Campaign. The idea is simple. Think of someone or some group that you've wronged and offer reconciliation. Wipe the slate clean on a bruised relationship. It's the brainchild of Edward Peters from Oxford. The idea came to him after he fell out with a valued friend over a foolish and cutting remark that he'd made. Eventually, years later, he apologized and a valued friendship was restored. It's a simple idea that we can easily carry into our daily lives. My problem would be where to start. I'd be spoilt for choice.

The idea of forgiveness and the seeking of forgiveness is central to many of our religious traditions. The Christian Lord's Prayer reminds us to forgive those that trespass against us. Our Sikh Ardas, or daily prayer, applauds those who forgive the faults of others. And, in another verse in our holy scriptures, Guru Nanak reminds us to *'never let the night fall on our anger', or* in the metaphor of the Clean Slate Campaign, to wipe the slate clean every night.

The question of apologies and forgiveness comes up regularly in international relationships. A couple of years ago, while the Queen was on a state visit to India, some vocal groups were asking for a public apology for the Jallianwala Bagh massacre of several hundred people in Amritsar in 1919.

Last weekend, during the Pope's visit to India, there were demands for an apology for the treatment of people in Goa by Portuguese Christians 400 years ago. And the same sort of apologies are routinely demanded for undoubted wrongs in other parts of the world.

As we enter a new millennium, perhaps it's time to wipe the slate clean on the wrongs done by generations long gone and look instead to the wrongs that we as individuals and wider groups are currently inflicting on both those close to us and those further afield. The Sikh Gurus constantly reminded us of the need to seek the forgiveness of those we wrong, while at the same time, working for a kinder and fairer society A tall enough task from which we can easily be deflected if we look only at wrongs of the past.

18 January 2000

Religious Communities Living in Harmony

This year marks the 200th anniversary of the Punjab being united under a single ruler, Maharaja Ranjit Singh, lion of Punjab. He was a ruler with a difference. The Mughal rulers he helped overthrow placed a price on the head of every Sikh caught, dead or alive. Yet Ranjit Singh's first act on conquering the capital, Lahore, was to pay homage and respect at the city's two major mosques. True to Sikh teachings he defended the right of Muslims to call their followers to prayer against Hindu and Sikh complaints and gave generously to all places of worship. He refused to have coins minted in his name, and lived simply, refusing the pomp and ceremony of power. As a result, Hindus, Muslims and Sikhs lived in peace and harmony in the near half-century of his rule.

This little example gives the lie to one of the most dangerous fallacies of our time, in common currency in Northern Ireland, Israel, the sub-continent of India, the Balkans and many other parts of the world that different religious communities cannot live together. Ranjit Singh's rule showed that despite superficial differences, people of different faiths can live together in harmony if given a positive lead by those in authority. The danger of the lie of irreconcilable difference is that it can be self-fulfilling, a means of separating people of different beliefs into areas of exclusivity and difference as happened on the Indian subcontinent and Cyprus. What particularly concerns me is that the lie is the proposed basis for solving the dispute between Israel and the Palestinians.

I visited some of the holy sites in Israel in the run up to Xmas, sites that are intertwined and holy not only to Jews and Palestinians but of course to Christians. It's a sad commentary on the times that Bethlehem was truly silent, devoid of pilgrims.

It was my first visit to Israel, and I marvelled at the rugged beauty of a country steeped in history. A country that in more peaceful times could comfortably exist on the tourist trade alone.

Of course, with existing passions of suspicion and hatred it would be foolish to expect Jews and Palestinians to easily embrace commonalities and focus on shared interest, but it is dangerously short-sighted to suggest solutions on the basis of permanent difference. Guru Gobind Singh's famous verse on the fallacy of irreconcilable differences come to mind:

Some call themselves Hindus, others, Muslims. Among these there are Shias and Sunnis; yet man is of one race in all the world.

Looking to commonalities rather than superficial difference is the only way to true and lasting peace.

24 January 2000

Religious Affiliation in the Census

This week, the House of Lords will be debating a private member's Bill for a question on religious identity to be included in the 2001 census. It recalls the ticking off I got on the same subject some ten years ago.

It was at a meeting of a government Religious Advisory Council. We were discussing census topics and I had suggested that self-identity by religion, might be more meaningful than identity by so-called race. A steely eyed official from the then Office of Population, Census and Statistics, cut me short with, 'We consider religion to be a private matter.'

Yes. Religion has over the years become a private matter; something we don't talk about in polite conversation. But this was never the intention of the founders of our great faiths. Guru Nanak saw religion as a guide to both self-improvement and the creation of a compassionate tolerant, and just society.

When Guru Tegh Bahadur, the nineth Guru of the Sikhs was beheaded in the centre of Delhi for defending the right of Hindus to freedom of worship against Mughal oppression, he made religion a very public matter. as did Jesus Christ, who centuries earlier, gave his life for values and ideals that seek to curb the nastier side of human behaviour.

I see the proposed question on religious identity as, not so much related to the teachings of religion, but more to a recognition of the importance of self-esteem and valuing others for what they are. Most of those whose parent or grandparents came from the sub-continent were born in this country. They see themselves as British Muslims or British Sikhs, able and willing to make a full contribution to industry, commerce, the professions and sport at all levels—including England's fight to regain the status of a top cricketing nation!

More accurate statistics on the size and distribution of religious communities, would end the guessing game and help target local and national government resources in a more effective and equitable manner, particularly in such areas as education, and prison and hospital chaplaincy. But for me, the real gain would be in moving us towards a recognition and understanding of what is important to our neighbour. Today we talk of institutional racism, but to me the real villain of the piece is institutional and personal ignorance of the way of life of others. Any information that helps combat this ignorance must be welcome.

25 January 2000

Damilola Taylor

Yesterday's moving interview on this programme with the father of the murdered schoolboy Damilola Taylor must have touched a chord in many of us. One can feel for him in his search for meaning and solace after the fatal stabbing of his son. His feelings must be similar to those of the parents of the murdered toddler James Bulger and those of the parents of another teenager, whose murder only streets away from the area of the Damilola stabbing, went virtually unreported.

Mr. Taylor was quite right. There is something wrong with a society in which violence is so endemic. No person, particularly children should feel the need, or desire, to carry a knife or other weapon, or feel compelled to carry or push drugs. But that's the reality of life in many deprived urban areas.

The question is where do we begin in our search for a better way? Of course, we must improve the quality of life and opportunities in such areas. But Sikhism reminds us that the real effort must be within us. Tackling the inner evils of lust greed, anger and pride.

Not easy. Greed, a compulsive desire for more and better, is, almost, built into our market driven society. Lust is widely seen as a bit of a laugh, while cheating on your partner has become a common ingredient of comedy, soap and serious drama.

I'm not sure that simply emphasising good social and family values, as Mr. Taylor seemed to suggest, will do much good. Only a few years ago, papers on values appeared like autumn leaves from the different branches of government. And of course, we have the sane and responsible guidance of our different religions. Following such guidance is far more challenging. It needs the rare courage shown by those like Guru Nanak or Jesus Christ, who frequently went against the norms of the day in showing a way to more enlightened attitudes.

I feel that our main concern today, should be with the powerful 'what's wrong with it' brigade, who seem to set many of our false values. What's wrong with mindless violence, foul language and sexual depravity on our TV screens, after all, as they say, 'we're all adults'. The trouble is we're not. Children are quick to copy our norms, our attitude to violence, our lack of social responsibility and our ways to quick fix happiness. If we can challenge these false norms, Damilola Taylor's death will not have been in vain. If we don't, we can lie back and wait for the next inevitable tragedy.

1 February 2000

Retention of Organs of Deceased Children at Alder Hey Hospital

As hospital switchboards continue to be inundated by anxious relatives, it's easy to understand the anger over the retention of organs of deceased children at Alder Hey and other hospitals. The ghoulish actions of those, like pathologist Dick Van Velzen, can in no way be justified by the need for research. Speaking in the context of his own times, Guru Nanak argued 'that disregard for human life is akin to butchery'. Strong words, but I'm sure that many will agree that some of the incidents detailed in this week's report on Alder Hey, fall into this category.

But media focussing on the behaviour of one individual can easily blur the wider issues. Today, doctors do not command the uniform awe and respect that once existed. 'Trust me, I'm a doctor', is not enough. Modern society requires fuller information on all aspects of health care. Doctors, like the rest of us are fallible human beings; prone, by ambition or arrogance to err from the higher ideals associated with the medical profession.

Hospitals do themselves no credit when, like high-pressure salesmen, they ask distressed relatives to tick boxes to secure permission for the removal of what they term 'tissue', for research. My concern is that our revulsion over such practices, might lead to the withholding of consent for genuine and badly needed research that in the end, could benefit the lives of many. And of course, there is the real and added danger, of this adverse publicity, extending to those who carry, or are thinking of carrying, donor cards.

The Sikh Gurus set up many hospitals, and by personal example showed the importance of tending to the sick and dying with love and respect for life. At the same time, they taught us the importance of letting go at bereavement; in trusting to God's will, but for many today, who have moved away from organised religion, it's harder and more painful to accept the finality of parting.

For all of us, whatever our belief, or lack of belief, the common reality of bereavement, is the gap that is left in our lives. It's a gap that can only be filled with the passage of time, and the love and sensitivity of those around us.

The clear in need for some in the medical profession is to come down from their false heights and keep this need for sensitivity in the forefront of all they do.

2 February 2000

Dangers of Democracy

Sikhs often look with envy at religions that have a hierarchy of central authority. The problem is that we're a bit too democratic. All our gurdwaras are run by managing committees generally elected in annual general elections, and gurdwaras remain independent entities. Not surprisingly, Sikhs in both India and Britain have suffered through this excess of democracy.

A more serious reminder of potential flaws in the democratic process is this morning's news that Jorg Haider's democratically elected Freedom party is set to share power in Austria. A declared dislike of foreigners has been central to Herr Haider's success. His personal popularity was clearly demonstrated in numerous lavish political rallies last weekend in celebration of his fiftieth birthday.

It all amounted to a personality cult reminiscent of Europe in the '30s, when Hitler also gained legitimacy through the ballot box, on a popular mandate of xenophobic hate, which saw its ultimate expression in the evil of the holocaust.

While the new Far Right in Austria were flexing their political muscles, a parallel demonstration by hundreds of neo-Nazis at Berlin's Brandenburg Gate, voiced anger over the proposed erection of a holocaust memorial. Nothing wrong in an expression of opinion, but, the protest couched in clearly racist language served to underline both the vulnerability and fragility of the democratic process. The sad reality is that it is all too easy to gain mass support by pandering to majority prejudice. Even easier, if vulnerable minorities are made the focus of popular discontent.

When Guru Gobind Singh, the last in the line of Sikh Gurus, told Sikhs that in future they should choose their leaders by democratic consensus, he added that both those chosen and the process itself must be true to Sikh teachings, particularly a recognition of the equal worth of every human being.

Unfortunately, Sikhs, and I suspect others sometimes take democracy and equality, a little too literally, with an equal right to opinion often leading to interminable discussion; a minor weakness of democracy. But the main thrust of the Guru's teaching, that those who aspire to lead through the democratic process must recognise the equal worth of all involved, is an important one for all democracies. Without it, as we are seeing in Austria today, the democratic process itself, can all too often spawn populist bigotry.

9 February 2000

'His Mum has Taken My Dad Away'

Last Saturday, my wife and I attended the wedding of the daughter of a Sikh friend of ours. In the ceremony the couple were reminded of Guru Nanak's teaching on the complete equality of men and women. And the following verse by the Guru was then sung, explaining the Sikh stress on total commitment in marriage:

Don't consider those who merely live together
As husband and wife
Only they are truly wedded
When two bodies have one soul

I thought of these teachings on marriage, while reading a Times interview last weekend, with the chairman of Relate. It's a measure of today's changing times, that Relate is the new name for the former Marriage Guidance Council. The interview was conducted to coincide with this week's celebration of National Marriage Week. In the article, the chairman of Relate asks the questions 'who needs marriage?' He then goes on to say that it's relationships, rather than formal marriage that is all-important.

I think though, that the real answer to the question, 'who needs marriage', lies in a recent playground fight between two small boys. A teacher finally managed to part the two and asked what it was all about. Amid tears and sobs, one of the boys said, 'his mum has taken my dad away'. Words of anguish that underline the misery of children caught in today's frequent transient relationships, something we often ignore in promoting the equal validity of all lifestyles.

To my mind, responsible national bodies should highlight these dangers and stress the importance of commitment and responsibility that are the essence of our different marriage vows. Others see things differently and argue that if you teach marriage, you turn off half the class that come from unmarried homes. Possibly, but isn't there a danger that if we don't, that half might soon grow to three quarters or more.

In National Marriage Week, it's important that we look at marriage from the principle of not destroying something that works until we find something better to replace it. Of course, marriages are rarely perfect, and domestic violence and ill-treatment of children often occur reminding us of the danger of complacency. But, for all its flaws, marriage still has a lot going for it. While respect for other lifestyles is important. Guru Nanak reminds us that it's the challenges of marriage and family life that best equip us to serve wider society.

23 February 2000

Commitment: a Question of Priorities

All eyes will be on David Beckham, the twenty-four-year-old midfielder, in tonight's match against Argentina. He's reported to be in fine form after last week's trauma of being dropped from the Manchester United side. Even now, the complaint of his manager, Sir Alex Ferguson and some United fans, over a lack of commitment, must still be ringing in his ears. But, was it a lack of commitment to football, or perhaps a higher commitment to his sick child that made him miss that training session?

Of course, football is big business and success important to clubs. But it's the worship of success and the demand of total allegiance that worries me. To my mind, it's this narrow focus on success, with its compulsions to win by fair means or foul, with huge financial rewards for clubs and individuals, that has led to an alarming increase in physical violence on the football pitch. A violence that's mimicked by schoolchildren hoping to become the stars of the future.

Guru Nanak taught us to keep a sense of proportion on our attitude to success and fame. He wrote:

Were a man to live through the four ages,
Or even ten times longer
And his reputation to spread over the nine shores
With universal acclaim,
Yet, if false to God, he would be like a worm amongst vermin

This need for balance between domestic and work priorities affects us all, and is particularly difficult for those in high profile positions. In a few months' time the Prime Minister will be faced with a similar dilemma with the arrival of the new baby. I'm sure that no one will really mind if he skips the occasional boring cabinet meeting. But then he's lucky. Politics in Britain has yet to match the passions of sport in the nation's consciousness.

8 June 2000

Addressing Inequality

Yesterday's speech by the Prime Minister to the Women's Institute, with his reference to respect, responsibility, and traditional values, reminds us that the wider debate on equality, is far from over.

We still have some way to go, to be a society that is grounded in equality of opportunity and social justice and is seen to be so. Such a society is regarded as a common goal by both politicians and religion. In the Sikh view, our different religions are overlapping circles of belief in which lie common values of tolerance and active concern for others. Values that should underpin all aspects of our national life and make for a more responsible society.

Talking about responsibility is easy. Living responsibly is a lot harder. Even understanding responsibility in the complex, part science, part greed-driven world of today is hard enough. We see this in the current debate over GM foods, where three members of the Royal family give us three different opinions. The reality over this, and similar scientific advances, is that we don't know, and cannot know, the full long-term consequences. We are groping in the dark, trying to balance short-term benefit, against long-term uncertainty.

The other problem is that values or principles sometimes get in the way of each other. For example, everyone agrees on the idea of equality of opportunity. But, for such equality we need information on the nature, scale and distribution of disadvantage. And yet tomorrow, a government-supported private member's Bill, to get such information, will almost certainly be killed off, by short-term insistence, on wider debate, for which there is no Parliamentary time.

This week, Sikhs commemorate the martyrdom of Guru Arjan, the fifth Guru, who preached tolerance and freedom of worship, at the cost of his own life. He taught that, whatever the personal cost, we should always look to the long-term consequences of what we do, or neglect to do. It is difficult to come to terms with the competing moral complexities of today's times. But if, in line with the Guru's teachings, we constantly ask ourselves the simple question, 'is what is being proposed likely to be good, or harmful to future generations?', we won't go far wrong.

15 June 2000

Nearly Expelled on My First Day at School.

I nearly got expelled on my first day at school. The building was on a hill, and there were a series of steps leading to the classrooms. To me, the steps looked boring, and the moment my mother's head was turned, I began to climb a small mountain of builder's sand to reach the same goal. Knee deep and sometimes waist and almost neck deep in sand, I eventually made it to the top, only to receive a furious telling off from worried watching teachers, and later, from my parents. 'Other children use the steps, why did I have to be different?'

My motive was simply a misplaced sense of adventure. But there are often good reasons for not following the crowd. Guru Nanak once travelled to the banks of the Ganges where people would throw water from the river in the direction of the sun in, what the Guru considered, a superstitious belief that this would somehow, reach their ancestors in heaven. The Guru got in the river and began throwing water in the opposite direction. When asked why, he replied that he was throwing water to his fields in Punjab. 'How can water thrown from here reach your fields hundreds of miles away', they argued.

To which the Guru replied, 'in the same way as it reaches your ancestors in heaven'.

The Guru's message was that of the need to distinguish between ritual and superstition, and true religion that gives meaning and direction to life. He taught that we should try to avoid supposedly religious practices that fail to meet the tests of reason and common sense.

I thought of this as I watched the extraordinary crowd scenes on television of half a million uniformly smiling people, in the North Korean capital Pyongyang. Thousands carried identical plastic flowers, as they lined up to welcome, until then a figure of hate, President Kirn Dae Jung of South Korea. While fervently hoping that the meeting between the two presidents would lead to an end of a half century of conflict, in what President Clinton has described as the scariest place on earth, I find it strangely disturbing that a whole population, can be made to alternate between hate and welcome, as if at a turn of a switch.

To me it's a reminder of, how easily we can all be manipulated to behave in ways that are either devoid of reason or call us to love or hate on demand. Our best defence is to keep common sense to the fore and have the courage not to blindly follow the crowd.

29 June 2000

The New Human Rights Act

I've been doing some hard training at Wimbledon recently; not on the hallowed tennis courts, but, at the magistrate's court, on the new Human Rights Act, which comes into force on October 2nd. The Act introduces the concept of 'proportionality', or the need for a sense of proportion in balancing the human rights of an individual, against those of wider society.

The importance of a sense of proportion or balance in life is central to many religious teachings. When Jesus Christ taught that man shall not live by bread alone, he was reminding us that there is a spiritual side to life, as well as the material. The Sikh symbol, the Khanda – our equivalent to the cross in Christianity – carries two swords, signifying spirituality and social responsibility. Both are considered important for balanced living.

The need for balance between conflicting ideals is highlighted by a proposed new European Directive, giving equality of employment opportunity to all applicants for a post in a religious school. On the one hand it's clearly desirable. But, what if the successful applicant to a Muslim school, were a born-again Christian proud to declare his faith, or a gay or a lesbian equally proud and open about a way of life. Their employment could affect the very ethos of the school and its long-term viability. Well-meaning legislation in such areas, can, sometimes, do more harm than good.

A visit to Britain's only voluntary-aided Sikh school, at Hayes in Middlesex, suggested a different approach to the needs of equity and balance. As I entered the school, I went through a lobby decorated with colourful pictures and posters of a forthcoming religious festival. It was the Jewish festival of Purim. In the school hall a drama teacher was honing the acting skills of children rehearsing a play about the Sikh festival of Vaisakhi. She happened to be of the Muslim faith and had been employed for her expertise.

Here, free from the pressure of compelling legislation, the governors and the Head had shown an enlightened attitude to both employment and religious education, and had got a difficult balance, just about right. To me, it was a reminder that, essentially religious teachings on the need for sensitivity and respect for others, can reach parts of life that narrowly focussed legislation cannot reach to produce a more cohesive and fairer society.

14 September 2000

Problems at the Millennium Dome

Yesterday's announcement of a £90 million grant to help keep the Millennium Dome open to the end of the year, underlines the extent of the Dome's misfortunes. And I can't help feeling that it's probably all my fault.

It's a known fact in the Singh family that anything I touch generally falls to bits. In what seems like a previous incarnation, I joined the mining industry. The newly formed National Coal Board had invested millions in what was heralded as the industry of the future. A few years later, I was planning the closure of coalmines. It was much the same story with civil engineering, and then I moved to management consultancy in local government. And we <u>all</u> know what is happening to local government.

About two years ago, I was invited, along with people of other faiths, to help plan the layout and contents of the Faith Zone at Greenwich. My family say that this was the beginning of the end for the Dome. We weren't paid a penny for many hours of hard work. But, had the New Millennium Experience Company known something about my dubious credentials, they would probably have paid me a small fortune to keep away. Perhaps I'm being a little a bit hard on myself. Ours was at least an effort to include *something* of religion at Greenwich.

In many ways, the story of the Dome is a parable of our times. The celebration of the Millennium now seems a long way in the past. The focus should have been, on the life and teachings of Jesus Christ; teachings that are viewed with great respect by Sikhs and others. Instead, a historic opportunity was hijacked in a jamboree of populism to show how clever we are as a nation. The object of veneration was <u>us</u> and our cleverness in the things we can build and do. In many ways, the very opposite of the teachings of Jesus Christ.

Naturally, my sympathies go to the people at the Dome, many of whom I know personally. But the story of the Dome is a sharp reminder of the impermanence of man-made structures. Sikh scriptures remind us that these are like 'walls of sand', or, in words uncannily descriptive of the Dome, 'momentary bubbles', they will not endure. The same teachings remind us that 'seva', or service to help others, the essence of many lesser-known millennium projects, has a more lasting effect, with ripples that carry through space and time.

21 September 2000

Reverse Evolution in Burma

A report on Burma on this Programme a couple of days ago, described the plight of the Karen people, who have suffered brutal persecution for over half a century. Many thousands have sought refuge in neighbouring Thailand; others are used as slave labour. Some, men and women, have fled to the depths of the jungle. One of these women described her plight in particularly moving terms, *'It's like reverse evolution. Humans are said to have evolved from apes. But we're being forced to live like monkeys in the jungle, feeding on leaves and plants for our very existence'*.

Her poignant account of the suffering of her people puts our grumbling over the recent petrol shortage in its true perspective. It also reminds us that there are two sides to human evolution. The cleverness to invent things, at which we have made unbelievable progress, and our moral responsibility to others, and to our environment, which lags far behind our cleverness, and, as we see in Burma, often seems to go in reverse.

Today the spotlight is on the Burmese government's abuse of power, but we are all too aware that similar behaviour common in many parts of the world in the past, is still widespread today. Our different religious traditions have all recognised the extent of our moral fallibility. The Sikh Gurus were careful not to prescribe precise moral solutions that become frozen in time and custom. Instead, they emphasised lasting principles; such as the need to protect the weak, work for social justice, to be wary of the arrogance of power and, in our personal lives, not to allow obsession with personal well-being, blind us to concern for others. Guidance, which clearly has resonant echoes in other faiths. Guidance, which can give us moral vision to match our undoubted cleverness.

The trouble today is that we've largely ditched this guidance, without recognising its worth. Organised religions must share the blame, with their emphasis on uniqueness of doctrine blurring the reality of a common moral thrust.

But it's not all doom and gloom. Despite occasional hiccups, there are, in Britain, at least, real signs of active co-operation between different faiths. There is also the recognition of a common responsibility to ensure justice and compassion extends to those parts of society that cannot be reached by politics alone.

28 September 2000

Looking to the Needs of the Poor: Hoerst Kohler Managing Director IMF

Behind much of the anger surrounding the IMF and the World Bank meetings in Prague this week, there is a deep and growing sense of unease, that globalisation of trade and commerce, is making rich countries richer and the poor poorer. The statistics are compelling. Jubilee 2000, a broad-based religious coalition, estimates that debt repayments sought by the industrialised West from the world's poorest countries, cost the lives of 19,000 children every day.

Today's protesters range from concerned individuals and religious groups campaigning for the cancellation of all third world debt, to anarchists and neo luddites who by burning, smashing and looting, sadly move the focus away from genuine concerns. But there are signs that the message is getting through. A couple of weeks ago, I attended a small seminar on third world debt. The guest speaker was Hoerst Kohler Managing Director of the IMF.

His words surprised me.

'We need to look at the world. What happens in poorer countries must be the concern of richer nations.'

This hard-headed economist wasn't speaking emotionally; he was speaking about the reality of the world we live in. A world in which a change in oil production in the Middle East, can within days, cause social unrest in Europe and the threat of world recession; a world in which trade, commerce and their social repercussions, defy national boundaries.

Globalisation of trade and commerce is a fact of life that can't be reversed, any more than we can turn back the tide. It can be a force for good as well as a means of perpetuating unacceptable extremes of poverty and wealth.

Such extremes have always been with us. They certainly bothered Guru Nanak. He once upset a powerful local ruler by refusing to eat with him claiming he was accumulating wealth while those in his employment grew ever poorer. The Guru taught that there was nothing wrong in improving our material life by 'kirt', or earnest effort providing this is balanced by 'wand chakna', the sharing our good fortune with the needy.

It's the huge and growing disparities of wealth that concern many in and well beyond Prague. In the interests of the poor, and in the long-term interest of all of us, both economic and moral imperatives require simultaneous action.

18 January 2001

Keeping Fit

As a start to the New Year, the Singh family moved into the keep fit business in a big way. We bought a treadmill. After my first go on the machine, a jog of about twenty minutes, one of the dials revealed in a depressing way, that the calories lost were less than those contained in half a packet of crisps. The clear message on the dial, was that clever exercise gadgets are no substitute for a healthy lifestyle.

A number of articles on stress, in the papers this week, remind me that it's not only physical health, that we need to watch in our rushed times. A generation or so ago, few people talked of stress, and stress-related illness. Today, despite growing affluence, it's a common subject of conversation and a problem that in its more acute form, affects some 10% of the population, with a linked effect of reducing ability to fight illness.

The pace of life wasn't a problem in Guru Nanak's time, but skewed priorities were as much in evidence then, as today. One of the Guru's most consistent teachings was the need for balanced living. Earn to live comfortably and decently, but don't let an obsession with material wealth dominate your life. Be spiritual, but don't let spirituality blind you to social responsibility. Love and care for those around you, but don't get over attached.

It's a lack of balanced living on the ever-speeding treadmill of life that to my mind, is responsible for much of the stress and tensions of modern living. We see this in false, widely accepted priorities that are increasingly centered on self, personal fulfillment, and a wholly material view of life that leaves little room for concern about others.

Sikhism, emphasizes the importance of seva, looking to the needs of others in achieving both personal contentment, and a healthier and fairer society. To this end, Chancellor Gordon Brown's recently announced scheme to encourage over fifties with spare time, to do voluntary work is a welcome first step, but why only the over fifties? A culture of finding time for others needs to be embedded in society if we really want to reduce the stress and narrow selfishness of modern life.

Of course, there are other ways of tackling stress: therapy, popping pills, alcohol and so called 'recreational' drugs. But, as a way to a truly stress-free life, they are about as useless as my 'half packet of crisps worth' of exercise was, in achieving, physical fitness.

8 February 2001

Searching for Peace in the Middle East

It now seems like an age, since my visit to Israel last December. Ehud Barak had just resigned as Prime Minister as a ploy to getting more support for the stalled peace process; a miscalculation that has now given the premiership to his hard-line rival, Ariel Sharon.

My visit to Israel was on the invitation of the Chief Rabbi, Dr. Jonathon Sacks, who'd asked me to join him on a fact-finding trip to explore ways to assist the search for peace. We spoke to politicians, academics and religious leaders, as well as to mothers of teenage conscripts, and saw the common yearning for peace. We also saw the reality of the fear and prejudice, with which each side views the other.

The hope, of course, is that that the peace process that came so tantalisingly close to success a couple of months ago, will resume in an atmosphere of hard-headed realism. But, judging from the belligerent noises from both sides, it's not going to be easy. The clear need is, for enlightened self-interest to replace prejudice and distrust in a beautiful part of the world, rich in history.

During our visit, a university professor spoke of the management and control of Temple Mount and other religious sites and structures in Jerusalem that are holy to both Jews and Muslims. She expressed the fear that neither side would trust the other, and third-party management of disputed areas would be necessary until confidence was restored. Then, to my surprise, she turned to me and said that perhaps Sikhs, with their strong teachings on religious tolerance, could be that third party.

It was a kind and generous comment, but a complete non-starter. With our proven ability to argue at length over trivialities, Sikhs have enough difficulty in managing their own shrines! But on the wider issue of tolerance, she had a point. To my mind, the key to peace in any religious conflict lies in Guru Nanak's teaching, that God is neither bothered, nor impressed, by our different religious labels, and that our various faiths are simply, a common quest for God, rooted in responsible living.

I believe that if Palestinians and Israelis accept this basic reality, the road to peace will be clear, and a dispute between two sides transformed into a shared problem. How to bring peace, education and opportunity to existing and future generations of both Jews and Palestinians.

20 September 2001

Aftermath of 9/11

Yesterday's deployment of American ships and planes is a predictable response to last week's terrorist carnage. At the same time, it is becoming increasingly clear that the exercise of military might alone, has severe tactical and human rights limitations. The vulnerability of open societies to lethal terrorist attack remains a new danger that demands new thinking.

Sadly, much of the evidence of the past few days suggests that we are still treading in the grooves of a violent past and exemplary revenge. Inflamed public reaction is seen in news reports from the United States, of brutal attacks on Muslims for being Muslims. Two Sikhs have been murdered and Sikh places of worship firebombed because of our passing resemblance to Muslims. These attacks on the innocent, now spilling over into this country, remind us yet again, of the ease with which normal rational human beings can be whipped into a frenzy of hate against those of other ways of life.

I think it's important that we now stand back a little and look at last week's events from a wider perspective and consider the lessons we must learn if we are to move to a better world. For example, almost hidden in today's newspapers is the report on a Christian pastor charged with aiding and abetting in the murder of 800,000 people in Rwanda in 1994. A figure almost beyond comprehension.

This mindless murder of innocents in the name of religion has gone on throughout history. Guru Nanak, a witness to the Moghul invasion of India, wrote of 'butchers of humanity', clad in religious garb. Surprisingly Guru Nanak reserved his strongest criticism, not for the perpetrators, but for those in authority who neglected their responsibility to those they governed.

Today, the United States is clearly the most powerful nation on Earth. Its power also gives it unique responsibility. The hope of all of us is that this sleeping giant, rudely woken by terrorist outrage, looks beyond the immediate, in its response.

The war against terrorism needs a totally new thinking which, while seeking action against the perpetrators of evil, also challenges perverted religious beliefs and a real or perceived sense of injustice in which terrorism thrives. It calls for a new sort of war that also recognises the needs of the dispossessed, and the evil of gross inequalities of opportunity and wealth, in a world of plenty.

20 September 2001

9/11 Responsibility of Religious Leaders to Condemn Perverted Ideology

There are times in life, like the bereavement of a close relative, when the routine concerns of normal life pales into insignificance. Tuesday's terrorist carnage in the USA falls into such a category. It is still difficult for those of us thousands of miles away to comprehend the scale of horror, suffering, and a probable death toll of thousands.

Inevitably, because we are all human, grief and a sense of disbelief, will turn to anger and calls for revenge against the perpetrators. The argument that anyone who deliberately plans the mass murder of innocent human beings, deserves to be punished in the sternest way, is supported by Sikh teachings of 'single out and punish' those responsible for atrocities against their fellow human beings.

The dilemma faced by President Bush and the free world lies in the words 'single out and punish'. Terrorists are by nature shadowy figures with perverted skills of hiding behind the innocent. A justifiable sense of outrage and the frustration of pinpointing those responsible, can all too easily lead to broad brush action against those possibly responsible, and the further killing of innocents. It's a temptation that must be resisted if we are to make real progress in combating terrorism.

While every effort must be made to find those responsible, we can all do much more than we have done in the past to fight the bigotry on which terrorism thrives. A bigotry of belief that perverts and grotesquely inverts all that the founders of our great religions taught. It is for the leaders of religion to respond to Tuesday's horror in the USA, by emphasizing that God is a God of all humanity; that to thank God for the deaths of innocents, as Osama Bin Laden has, is blasphemy of the worst kind. It's absurd to preach that anyone of any faith is looked on with Godly approval for planning or executing the mass murder of his fellow human beings. Those who fail to condemn such absurdities will be condemned by their silence.

27 September 2001

Carrying Identity Cards

The proposal that we all carry identity cards will require an unusual degree of honesty to succeed in reducing crime and terrorist activity. As a Sikh, I've got nothing against being identified for who or what we are. I've often thought it would be an excellent idea if we went a bit further and everyone wore name badges, to save me the embarrassment of forgetting names, particularly when I meet someone away from their normal location.

Seriously, identity cards would mildly inconvenience the majority, but I doubt if they would deter criminals or terrorists, whose way of life depends on falsification. Identity cards, would however, place additional pressure on would-be asylum seekers, and I fear that this may be their main purpose. The question is, is it worth it? Is this what we really want?

Just as a person's health is measured by the movement of mercury in a thermometer, the prevalence of persecution and starvation, are measured by the number of refugees forced to flee their homes. Record numbers of people enduring appalling conditions and near starvation in refugee camps or seeking entry to more affluent parts of the world, should act as a spur for urgent international effort to reduce their suffering.

Guru Nanak saw such misery when he once went to a nearby town to invest some money on behalf of his father. He saw some poor and starving people at the roadside shivering in the winter cold. It was clear that they hadn't eaten for days. The Guru decided to spend his money on food and blankets and, in reply to his father's wrath, declared that there was no better investment.

It's this generosity of spirit that should influence our attitude to refugees. Sadly, the opposite is happening. In the more affluent parts of the world there is a perverse, battening down of hatches and ever tightening controls that contrast with the generosity of poorer lands.

While Australia, a vast and affluent country, defies maritime law in denying entry to a few score impoverished souls, Pakistan, a country beset with political and economic problems doesn't go around asking its two million Afghan refugees if they are economic or political migrants. It simply invites them to share in its poverty. Instead of identity cards, we should be looking to a similar generosity of spirit.

22 November 2001

Demolishing Barriers of Belief

Next week, Sikhs will be celebrating the birthday of Guru Nanak, the founder of the Sikh faith. The celebrations come at a difficult time for all religions.

Following the events of September 11th and its aftermath, religion now finds itself in the dock, as the cause rather than the cure for conflict. The evidence for the prosecution is impressive. Even the most cursory glance at current, international disputes will show that most have a strong religious dimension.

Sadly, conflict between and within religions is nothing new. It's always been with us. It's as if we choose to use our different religious books as offensive weapons to batter those of other faiths, rather than to look at the guidance within their covers.

This was very much the state of affairs in Guru Nanak's time. Commenting on the absurdity of conflict between Hindus and Muslims, with each proclaiming superiority of belief. Guru Nanak declared, in his very first sermon, Na koi Hindu, Na koi Mussalman. That is, in God's eyes, there is neither Hindu, nor Muslim, and by today's extension, neither Christian, Sikh nor Jew. That God is not interested in our different religious labels, but in how we conduct ourselves.

In this simple, but powerful sermon, Guru Nanak gets at the root of much of the so-called religious conflict in the world today. Let me explain what I mean. We all know that when two boys (it's always boys), start arguing that 'my dad is taller, stronger, bigger or in some other way, better than your dad', the almost inevitable result is physical conflict! In the same way, much of the conflict between religions has resulted from child-like claims that my religion is better than yours. Today, in our smaller, inter-dependent world, the consequences of such claims carry the potential for wider and more serious conflict.

We all know that when a large building is demolished to make way for a new development, we see the surrounding area in a newer and fuller perspective. In the same way, if we knock down the barriers of bigotry of belief between our different faiths, we find that our different religions are not all that different. Our different faiths provide a common and powerful emphasis on social justice, putting others before self, and the need for balanced and responsible living. Values that remain the key to lasting peace and justice, in today's troubled world.

2 January 2002

Institutionalizing False Difference

It has been more than a year now, since I saw the end of day flag lowering ceremony at Wagah, on the Punjab border with Pakistan. The impressive and colourful experience is vividly etched in my memory, for all the wrong reasons.

The Indian border guards, impeccably dressed in ceremonial uniform with starched plumed turbans, marched and saluted impressively A few feet away, Pakistani soldiers, in their ceremonial dress, performed with equally faultless precision. It was an impressive sight. Yet I found the whole spectacle profoundly depressing.

Here were two of the poorest countries in the world, with much in common, blindly emphasising the near religious sanctity of an arbitrary, man-made frontier the defence of which, hugely impoverishes both India and Pakistan. To me, the far more encouraging sight at that border crossing was the huge crowd of sightseers on one side of the border waving and cheering good-naturedly to those on the other side. People, with whom they shared a common language and culture. Recent TV pictures of weeping relatives stranded at now closed border crossings, underlines the same close relationship.

Guru Gobind Singh, the tenth Guru of the Sikhs, whose birthday we celebrate later this month, reminded us of the importance of looking beyond our obsession with seeming difference, to the reality of a common human destiny. He wrote:

All men have the same form,
All men have the same soul

To me it's this failure to recognise our common human identity and shared aspirations that has led the subcontinent to the brink of nuclear conflict. Recognition of common interest and a common destiny, must, by the same token be the way forward. It is clearly in the interest of both subcontinent neighbours to reduce military expenditure and ensure that the people in the disputed region of Kashmir enjoy basic human rights.

The tensions between India and Pakistan are not very different from those in other parts of the world and again, there is a clear choice. Following the path of exploiting seeming difference for short term political gain, can lead to horrendous conflict, whilst recognition of a common entwined human destiny can bring true peace to our twenty-first century

9 January 2002

Dr. Carey Archbishop of Canterbury Steps Down

I must say that despite all the media speculation, Dr. Carey's decision to step down from his post as Archbishop of Canterbury, still comes as a bit of a surprise to me. I've had the good fortune to have known Dr. Carey since he first became Archbishop some eleven years ago, and have always admired his honesty, plain speaking, and quiet sense of humour, in coping with those who saw him as too liberal, or not liberal enough; too conservative in his approach to the ordination of women priests, or, in the view of some, not conservative enough.

The start of Dr. Carey's tenure of office, coincided with a time when different religions in this country actually started to talk to each other, voicing common concerns and aspirations. It is to his credit that he has always supported this move to inter-faith dialogue. It was Dr. Carey who, working with other faiths, helped establish the 'Lambeth Group' of different faith representatives, to plan the faith zone at Greenwich and the highly successful celebration of the Millennium in the House of Lords.

In the early days of his appointment as Archbishop, Dr Carey invited some of us from different faiths, to discuss ways to greater cooperation, and he began by expressing frustration at the difficulty he found in identifying leaders of other faiths. I remember re-assuring him that that wasn't a problem in the Sikh community, as all Sikhs are called 'sirdar', literally 'chief and all consider themselves leaders. I didn't explain the democratic anarchy that this creates! It's not quite so bad in the Church of England.

The new leader of the Church of England will face many other challenges, some shared with sister faiths. Perhaps most importantly, how to show that much maligned religion, far from being the cause of conflict, carries in its underlying message of sane and balanced living, the cure to overlying perversions of belief. Not easy. Then there is the need to show how concern for others is a better and healthier alternative to our present selfish, preoccupation with 'me' and 'my happiness', with its attendant hurt to family and society.

Some words of advice on the qualities of a true leader to Dr. Carey's successor, from Sikh scriptures may well be relevant:

Not cast down in sorrow, nor over elated in joy.
Aloof from the power of pride, greed, or coveting.
Who frightens none, nor fears any,
Indifferent to the world's praise or blame,

Or, as Kipling later put it, 'keep your head when all about you are losing theirs'.

16 January 2002

Torture and Humiliation of Al Qaeda Suspects at Guantanamo Bay

News reports of Al Qaeda prisoners being hooded, manacled, sedated and otherwise humiliated, are profoundly disturbing, and, if only half true, are to my mind a severe setback in the fight against terrorism.

The September atrocities in New York and Washington, described by President Bush, as an assault on civilised society, resulted in worldwide revulsion against those who had shown such callous disregard for human life. In the Sikh view, it is regard for human life, and recognition of the worth of others, that is the hallmark of civilised society. The Sikh Gurus, who were forced to fight many battles in defence of religious freedom, taught that compassion and concern for others, must extend even to foes on the battlefield.

In a particularly fierce battle at the time of Guru Gobind Singh, a Sikh water carrier by the name of Khaniya was seen to be serving water to the enemy wounded, as well as to Sikhs. Some Sikh soldiers, incensed at Khaniya's behaviour, dragged the water carrier before the Guru, demanding suitable punishment. The Guru asked Khaniya to explain himself. Khaniya looked at the Guru and replied, 'you have always taught us to treat others, even our enemies with compassion and respect. In giving water to the enemy wounded, I was simply doing what you taught us to do'. The Guru was delighted by the reply. He embraced Khaniya, calling him 'Bhai', or 'brother'. He then gave him ointment and bandages and told him to look to the needs of the suffering on both sides of the battle line.

Words like 'civilised', are often used far too glibly. When Mahatma Gandhi visited Britain in the '30s, he was asked in a rather superior way, 'what do you think of western civilisation?'

Gandhi paused and then replied, 'it would be a good idea'. He was suggesting that civilisation meant more than wearing coats and ties and eating with knives and forks. It is in the end, as the Guru observed, all about treating others with decency and humanity.

The war against terrorism is a war for people's minds. It cannot be won by calling Al Qaeda prisoners, 'unlawful combatants' to deprive them of rights under the Geneva Convention. Placing manacled prisoners in 6ft by 8ft cages, exposed to the elements is, by any definition, cruel and degrading. Whatever combination of words we use, 'prisoners of war', or 'unlawful combatants', the Al Qaeda captives are humans, and should be treated as such, by civilised society.

22 January 2002

Guru Gobind Singh and Positive Living

This week, Sikhs throughout the world are celebrating the birthday of Guru Gobind Singh, the tenth Guru of the Sikhs. A major thrust of the Guru's teachings was to remind Sikhs and non-Sikhs alike, of the absurdity of all false barriers of caste and the myth of race or inherent difference because of religion. Not easy because throughout history, we've all been conditioned to believe that our way of life is naturally superior to that of others.

Most Sikhs at the time of the Gurus, were converts from Hinduism, and many still retained caste names, linked to status in the Hindu hierarchy. Some, despite the earlier teachings of Guru Nanak, hesitated to mix with converts from a supposedly lower caste. To counter this, the Guru asked all male Sikhs to drop their caste name and take the common name Singh, literally lion, to remind us of the ideal of courage. At the same time, he asked all Sikh women to take the common name Kaur, literally princess as a reminder of the dignity and complete equality of women. Calling men lions, and women princesses was a much needed bit of positive discrimination!

The egalitarian teachings of the Guru, and his stress on the essentially common thrust of religious teaching, was met with uniform hostility by both the Mughal authorities, and Hindu hill Rajas. Then, as today, those in positions of power, felt, and feel, threatened by those seeking greater justice and freedom in society. The Guru and his followers were forced to fight many battles for survival, and in these, the Guru lost his mother and four sons. Yet he never became despondent, reminding Sikhs of the need for 'chardi kala' or optimism and positive thinking, however difficult the circumstances.

The Guru's insistence on the need for positive living, contrasts with the ethos of today's times, where the predictable response to moral concerns is, 'that there is no evidence that harm will result'. No evidence of the harmful influence of mindless violence on TV, no evidence of harm resulting from the use of drugs and so on. This negative thinking is also reflected in the boast of those who claim to have led a virtuous life because they have never harmed anyone, oblivious of the fact that sticks, stones and other inanimate objects, could boast a similar claim.

Guru Gobind Singh urged us to think in more positive terms about our responsibilities to each other and to those that come after us. We've been led by the negative long enough. I know it goes against conventional, 'social thinking', but no harm will result from giving the positive a try.

16 May 2002

The Queen's Golden Jubilee

There has been a long history of mutual admiration between the British and the Sikhs. It began with the Anglo-Sikh wars in the middle of the nineteenth century, when each side admired the courage, skill and dedication of the other. Following on from this, Sikhs played an important role in the British Indian Army, particularly in the two World Wars. Today, there is still considerable Sikh respect for British institutions, particularly the monarchy, for its positive attitude to changes that have brought about today's multicultural society.

Fifty years ago, it was still common to talk of 'heathens', to describe non-Abrahamic faiths, and to poke fun at the inferior ways of others. Today, in multicultural Britain, such attitudes are generally considered dangerous and repugnant. But, despite the progress, prejudice remains a potent force that can best be tackled by attacking the ignorance on which it thrives.

This week, the Network of Sikh Organisations is sending out letters to all Sikh institutions on ideas for celebrating the Queen's Golden Jubilee. Recognising the urgent need to counter ignorance about our different religions, the main thrust of Sikh celebration, will be support for the Prince of Wales', recent initiative on 'Respect', not to be confused with Ali G's use of the same word.

'Respect', urge people of one religion to work together with those of different religions, in combined service to the local community, a concept close to the Sikh teaching of 'seva', or service. The hope is that this working together, will in a small but lasting way, increase tolerance, respect and understanding between those of different faiths.

At the launch of 'Respect' a couple of weeks ago, while a number of us were chatting informally, I was asked by the broadcaster, John Snow, to sum up Sikh teachings in a single sentence. I said something to the effect of 'belief in one God and a dedication to tolerance, respect and active concern for others'. He went on to ask the same question to people of other faiths. He then came back to me to say, 'you religious people are all saying much the same thing'.

His remark reminded me of a verse by Guru Gobind Singh in which the Guru says:

God is in the Temple, as He is in the Mosque
God is in the Hindu worship, as He is in the Muslim prayer

The Guru taught that we should respect genuine religious difference, while recognising the essentially common thrust and common values of different religious beliefs. It's these common values of tolerance, service and respect for others, highlighted in the Jubilee celebrations, which can inspire us to a truly cohesive society.

23 May 2002

Rising Tensions on the Kashmir Border: Responsibilities of Those Abroad

Tensions are again rising on the Kashmir border between India and Pakistan. A million soldiers, armed to the teeth, face each other in a show of mutual hostility that could, by design or accident, easily erupt into armed conflict and the horror of nuclear war.

At a time of similar tension in the first weeks of the New Year, I was contacted by a national newspaper, with almost eager anticipation, about the possibility of conflict arising between the Indian and Pakistani communities in this country. My obviously disappointing response was that it was unlikely, because people here were too busy in trying to establish themselves, and in looking to the education of their children.

While it would be clearly wrong, for people of Indian or Pakistani origin settled here, to get involved in the politics of the sub-continent, it's my view, that both communities can, and should, help the peace process. Geographic distance, and distance from emotional involvement, provides us with a fuller perspective to identify common interests, and focus on ways of reducing tension.

At a distance, we can see with compelling clarity, that both subcontinent neighbours have a largely similar way of life, and a shared cultural heritage. Those of us involved in interfaith dialogue have come to recognise, often to our surprise, how much our different religions have in common. Here, it is much easier, than in the charged atmosphere of the sub-continent, to recognise the truth of Guru Gobind Singh's words about the oneness of the human family. Those of us living abroad, can see, all too clearly, that armed conflict between the two countries, would be disastrous for both nations, and how a ratcheting up of tension for factional political gain, can have dangerous long-term consequences.

In short, far from mirroring sub-continent tensions, Hindus, Muslims and Sikhs in this country have a clear responsibility to urge and even broker dialogue, and some of us from different faiths have made a start in this in a combined letter of concern to the presidents of both India and Pakistan.

Sikh teachings about a false emphasis on difference, are a timely reminder that the route to peace is to focus on that which unites us with our neighbour.

30 May 2001

Addressing the Underlying Causes of Conflict

Few would disagree that the world now seems to be a more dangerous place than at any time since the Cuban Missile Crisis of the '60s. The very real possibility of war between India and Pakistan, both nuclear powers, has pushed the Israeli-Palestinian conflict out of the news, as if it were no longer an issue of concern.

With God's grace, and a little bit of luck, the odds are that India and Pakistan will move back from the brink, and we'll turn to other national issues, like the state of readiness, or otherwise, of David Beckham's foot. Until we lurch into the next major international crisis.

To me, two things are self-evident: firstly, in our smaller inter-dependent world, war in one region, is more and more likely to have repercussions on other more distant lands, if only in the fallout of refugees and displaced persons. Secondly, new conflicts are a certainty in a world of widespread constraints on religious and political freedom, and gross disparities of income and opportunity. We cannot rely on calls for sanity every time. To expect every international crisis to resolve itself, is like playing Russian roulette. The gun chamber may not be empty next time round. The real danger is that macho posturing has its own momentum that can sometimes be difficult to reverse.

At a time of intense religious conflict, the Guru wrote:

O Lord, save our world on fire with conflict and strife
Let the healing kindness of Your blessings
Save us through any way You choose

The Guru's emphasis on 'any way' acceptable to God, takes us away from the conflict producing mindset of 'my way right, your way wrong'. It helps us recognise that there may be truth in other ways and other views. It takes us away from the naive thinking of my Saturday morning cinema days when, in our innocence, particularly in cowboy films, we saw only good guys or crooks.

Our different religions all remind us that for real and lasting peace, we need to look at the causes of conflict referred to earlier: gross disparities in wealth, opportunity, freedom and justice, and the readiness of the power hungry to exploit these inequalities. Today, in the language of my Saturday morning cinema days, we are still talking in terms of goodies and baddies or 'the free world and the terrorists'. We'll get nowhere with such thinking. The only way to true and lasting peace is a now urgent pursuit of a fairer world for all its inhabitants.

23 July 2002

Limits of Top-Down Approach in Enhancing Community Cohesion.

It's common knowledge that people from different backgrounds tend to keep together, and there is generally, no harm in this. The danger occurs when this isolation is reinforced by ignorance and fear, which can all too easily lead to hatred and violence. This is what happened in last summer's riots in Bradford, Burnley and Oldham, between mainly deprived Muslim youth and their white counterparts.

Last week, I attended a conference to discuss several government and local government reports, on how to prevent such occurrences in the future. The root cause of conflict between communities; prejudice that thrives on ignorance, got little mention at the conference. It was, however, something that was well-recognized by the founders of our different religions.

Jesus Christ pointedly reminded us, in his parable of the Good Samaritan that good can exist in other communities as well as bad in our own. Guru Nanak, with a Hindu and Muslim companion, visited Mecca and Hindu holy sites to show his respect for other religions. This same message, that no one community has a monopoly of goodness and truth, is underlined by the inclusion of verses of Hindu and Muslim saints in our holy book, the Guru Granth Sahib. The thrust of religious teaching is to make tolerance and respect for others, a norm of human behaviour, rather than a belated cure.

Today, in our cleverer times, this simple, grassroots approach to higher standards of behaviour is often ignored. Instead, when faced with any social problem, we seem to feel, we are not getting our money's worth unless we have lengthy Committees of Inquiry, producing ponderous reports peppered with numerous acronyms and a host of recommendations. In just one of the reports on Community Cohesion we discussed last week, there were forty-three recommendations, and references to strategies, and subsets of strategies.

The problem with such, undoubtedly well-meaning, top-down approaches, is that they virtually ignore the many excellent on the ground faith-based initiatives to remove prejudice and enhance respect for other ways of life. My hope is that the new Archbishop of Canterbury to be announced later today, will make greater support for this valuable work, an important priority. It may be my own prejudice, resulting from years in the construction industry, but I believe that, for lasting results, it is always better to build from the bottom up, than from the top down.

30 July 2002

Media Gossip is not News

More and more people are showing serious reservations about threatened American action against Iraq. Imminent famine on the scale of the Ethiopian famine of the '70s, today threatens much of sub-Saharan Africa. But neither of these items dominates the news. Instead, the headlines in yesterday's Times and other newspapers, and in much of radio and television broadcasting, were all given to news that a senior member of the Conservative party, had declared himself gay!

To me as a Sikh, it should never have made the news, let alone the headlines. It's about as relevant as me declaring I wear size ten shoes, or that I am left-handed. What difference should such things make, and what business it of others?

What concerns me is that we are rapidly, dumbing ourselves down into an intensely voyeuristic society, always looking to the foibles, lifestyles and perceived peculiarities of others, rather than living our life in a more positive way. It's this voyeurism that guarantees the success of such demeaning programmes as Big Brother. It says much for our sense of values that the programme's winning contestant, is today described as the most popular twenty-two-year-old in Britain.

I'm often asked what Sikhism has to say about gays and lesbians and other lifestyles. The answer is, not a lot. Sikhism started at a time in India, when many believed that marriage was an impediment in the search for God. Guru Nanak, on the other hand emphasized the equality and importance of women, and the sanctity of marriage. Husband and wife, he taught, should act as one, to look to the needs of their family and those around them; one spirit in two bodies.

At no time however, did the Guru condemn other lifestyles or suggest that any shame should be attached to those who do not fit man-made norms. At the same time, I'm sure he would not have been too impressed with today's attempts to portray alternative lifestyles as matters of particular pride to be paraded as such in public.

Sikh teachings make clear that false distinctions between people of different religions, social backgrounds or lifestyles that do not cause harm to others, are of no concern to God. They are man-made distinctions, coloured by popular prejudice. Guru Nanak emphasised that we are all different and that we all have unique opportunities to serve God and our fellow human beings.

6 August 2002

HM the Queen's First Visit to a Sikh Gurdwara

Last Thursday, I had the rare privilege to accompany Her Majesty the Queen in her visit to a Sikh gurdwara in Leicester where she was received with typical Sikh warmth and hospitality. It was her first visit to a Sikh place of worship in this country, but you wouldn't have guessed it from her relaxed and confident manner. A police van full of posies of flowers spontaneously presented to her by little children, testified to the popularity of her visit.

The previous day, the Queen had gone to a mosque in Scunthorpe. The importance of these visits showing respect for other faiths cannot be sufficiently stressed. It was a clear message from the Queen that showing respect for other ways of life, in no way compromises one's own religious identity.

The Queen, in these Jubilee celebrations, has also made clear that she is queen of all her people, and believes that our different religions show that God's love extends in equal measure to all humanity, a sentiment that is echoed in the lines of the poet Kabir found in Sikh scriptures:

From the Divine Light all Creation sprang
Why then should we divide human creatures into the high and the Low?

Today, we constantly talk about the globalisation of trade and commerce, but often forget the most important aspect of this irreversible globalisation process; the increasing movement of people, and the greater interaction of different religions and cultures.

Until recently, we could afford to look at the quaint ways and beliefs of those in more distant lands, in a superior academic way that perversely added to a sense of national identity by superficially differentiating between us and them. Now, the same attitudes can lead to disastrous social consequences.

Laws, in themselves, cannot ensure good behaviour. All they can do is define the boundaries of unacceptable behaviour, which is not the same thing. Good or considerate behaviour requires a genuine respect for the rights and beliefs of others, as emphasised in our different religious texts. Mere tacit recognition of fundamental truths is not enough, we have to love them. As Guru Nanak taught:

Truth is high, but higher still is truthful living.

To me the importance of the Queen's visits to other places of worship, is that she translated belief into action, in this very visible demonstration for respect for other faiths. Her initiative is a powerful lead to us all, and will I'm sure, be the most important legacy of this Jubilee year.

24 September 2002

Moral Smugness Should Not Feature in Our Response to Saddam Hussein

Today's recall of Parliament, and the publication of a dossier on Saddam Hussein's military build-up, will help focus minds, on the wisdom or otherwise, of possible military action against Iraq.

The debate will be held against a backdrop of the new, 'American National Security Strategy for the twenty-first century', presented to Congress by President Bush over the weekend. It is an important statement of American intentions and resolves that has far reaching implications. In it the President reveals with crystal clarity, America's readiness to act alone if necessary, using pre-emptive action, to defend 'freedom and democracy', from terrorists and rogue regimes.

I don't for a moment doubt that Saddam Hussein has much to answer for, and the Americans have the military capacity to destroy him with little real effort, but it's the somewhat glib use of words like 'democracy' and 'freedom', that leaves me with a distinct sense of unease.

I experienced this same sense of unease, at a conference that I attended in Siena in Italy over the weekend, on 'identity in a rapidly changing world'. Words like democracy, Western values, civilised values and the rule of law, were used interchangeably to define the mores of Europe and the USA, as opposed to those of the rest of the world.

A century before the French revolution, the Sikh Gurus also addressed the same issues of freedom and democracy, but, through word and deed, they gave these ideals, more precise meaning by insisting on governance that looked beyond vote counting, to a democracy underpinned by necessary and absolute acceptance of the equality of all human beings, freedom of belief, a commitment to social justice and, an even-handedness in political dealing, clearly missing in the world of today. The last of the founding Gurus, went on to emphasize equality in democracy by insisting that he too was to be regarded as an ordinary member of the community.

Today, it is undoubtedly true, that Western democracies provide much better forms of government than those found under many other regimes. But democracies that do not look at the rest of the world in an even-handed way, or, those in which one has to have huge amounts of wealth to run for high office, are still flawed democracies, and a little humility will not go amiss in the world's acknowledged superpower, and in today's deliberations in Parliament.

1 October 2002

The colour Grey

With the increasing number of television channels, we are constantly being promised more adult programmes, which being translated, means more and more programmes pandering to our ever-growing obsession with sex.

An increasing number of television comedies are about a husband or wife cheating on their partner, and it's all a bit of a giggle, with the person doing the cheating often portrayed in a favourable light. We are rarely shown the emotional hurt caused to a trusting partner, or to the children of the marriage.

It's much the same in real life. In some of the weekend papers, John Major was admired for being less grey than we had thought him, and, not to be outdone Edwina Currie boasted an earlier liaison, guaranteeing continuing press coverage. It's difficult to get our heads around the complex issues of real concern, like a probable war against Iraq, but we can all have an opinion on the rights and wrongs of political soaps.

To me, there seem to be two main attitudes to the question of infidelity. The first is what can loosely be called the Middle East approach. This assumes that man is so weak and helpless, that it is necessary to encourage or pressurise women to cover up, to curb the lustful passions of men. Even this is sometimes not considered enough. A young Saudi Arabian interviewed on this programme a few weeks ago, complained about the provocative behaviour of a woman walking alone down the street. 'But she is wearing a chadhur, you can only see her eyes', replied the puzzled BBC man.

Back came the reply, 'Yes but you know that she has breasts underneath, and that's very hard for a man!'

The West's approach has become one in which infidelity is seen as normal 'adult' behaviour, initiated by both men and women, with the pressure on women to wear ever-more revealing clothes.

The Sikh Gurus, like other religious teachers, emphasised a middle way based on restraint and respect. Lust is considered one of the five deadly sins and marriage vows emphasize equality, faithfulness and trust. The Guru taught the importance of spiritual union:

They are not truly husband and wife
Who join in physical union
They are truly wedded
When two bodies have one soul.

Sikh men are asked to look on other women as sister, mother or daughter. It's all a bit grey by today's standards, but what's wrong with grey? I like the colour.

15 October 2002

Praying for Peace and Plenty

I've just come back from a short visit to Bihar in India. It's a state steeped in religion; the place where lord Buddha received enlightenment; the birthplace of the tenth Guru of the Sikhs, Guru Gobind Singh, and it's also holy to Jains, Hindus and Muslims. In any league table of prayers per person per day, Bihar would score high, and, if God reciprocated, Bihar would be a land of plenty. Yet, despite its mineral wealth, it's one of the poorest states in India, with heart-rending poverty, suggesting that prayer alone cannot prevent injustice and suffering.

It's worth reflecting on the power and purpose of prayer in this Week of 'Prayer for World Peace', In the opening verse of the Sikh scriptures, Guru Nanak reminds us that God, the Creator of all that exists, is not influenced by self-centred or ritual prayer. At the end of the verse the Guru asks the question: 'How then can we find the peace that we all desire?' and concludes with the words 'abide by His will and make it thine'.

Most of us feel deeply about the suffering of others in Kashmir, Israel, or in other areas of active, or threatened conflict. Prayer can strengthen this compassion, and our different religions give clear guidance on the direction in which we must move if we are to abide by God's will. But we must make the journey.

The ethical imperatives for true peace are also clearly stated in the Preamble to the United Nations Charter, the UN Declaration of Human Rights and various other protocols. Sadly, these admirable sentiments are almost universally ignored in the pursuit of national or strategic interest and short-term economic gain. One statistic says it all. 80% of all arms sold in the world today that sustain horrendous conflict, are supplied by the five permanent members of the Security Council. All too often when we question these things, we get the fatuous reply, 'if we don't supply them, others will'. Or, perhaps worse, 'jobs will suffer in the defence industry if we reduce weapons sales.' A response from a line of a Christian hymn comes to mind:

They enslave their children's children who would compromise with sin.

To pray for world peace without an active commitment to move towards a fairer world order, is like asking God for sticking plasters, to cover unsightly consequences of greed and double standards. We need to walk the talk, and live the prayer.

14 January 2003

Ethical Imperatives in Sport: The Ultimate Umpire Sees All

As we've just been hearing on this Programme, arguments over whether or not England should pull out of the cricket tournament in Zimbabwe next month, are expected to come to a head at a meeting of the England and Wales Cricket Board later today.

In an interesting discussion on Radio 4's Sunday Programme this week, one of the arguments used to justify continuing with the tour, was that of consistency. There are plenty of countries with equally bad or even worse human rights records, why not take sporting action against all of them? Well yes, ideally it might be helpful for other sportsmen, and their governing bodies, to demonstrate greater concern over the wider abuse of human rights; but the argument that if we cannot tackle every evil, we should do nothing about a specific evil is, to my mind, not a very good one.

The England and Wales Cricket Board have belatedly acknowledged a moral dilemma, by issuing an instruction against the shaking of hands with President Mugabe, while, at the same time, sticking to their line that further action on moral grounds, is conditional on the government covering any resultant financial loss.

The response of some of the cricketers themselves, to borrow a different sporting metaphor, simply kicks into touch, even the need for moral consideration. 'We are professional cricketers, we are not qualified to look at ethical issues; it's not up to us to take a stand.'

Not the view of religion. Guru Nanak, in a famous verse reminds us of the need to put principle before expediency. Two of his successor Gurus sacrificed their lives in taking an active stand against the evils of the day. Centuries earlier, Jesus Christ gave his life for teachings that placed ethical imperatives above wealth and position in society.

I know times are a changing. But it was not so long ago that we could suggest that something was not morally acceptable by saying 'it wasn't cricket'. It is a measure of how far we have moved from the same guidance of our religious teachers, and the high esteem we had for sport, that cricketers today, can say moral decisions are nothing to do with cricket.

In their meeting at Lords today, the ECB might usefully reflect on the Sikh view, that cricket, is simply a game within a wider game, the game of life, which we are urged to play in a way that recognises the imperatives of ethical and balanced living. The ultimate umpire sees all.

21 January 2003

Respecting Places of Worship

Yesterday's early morning raid on the Finsbury Park Mosque in North London, was by no means the first such entry into a place of worship in recent times. Nineteen short years ago, Sikhs throughout the world, were outraged when armed soldiers of the then Congress government in India, chose one of the holiest days in the Sikh calendar, not only to enter the Golden temple in Amritsar, but also to destroy much of the complex using mortars and helicopter gunships. Then after capture, the historic library was burnt to the ground. The repercussions of anger and mistrust of a now different government continue to this day.

No deliberate sacrilege took place in the raid on the Finsbury Park Mosque, but in entering any place of worship, there is a clear need for sensitivity. Anything less gives out a message of contempt for the rights and beliefs of others, an important consideration at any time, but doubly so when the real battle against terrorism, is for the hearts and minds of men.

Many listeners to this programme yesterday will have been taken slightly aback to hear Iqbal Sacranie, Secretary General of the Muslim Council express his concerns over the footwear of officers in the context of this need for sensitivity. Removal of shoes in a place of worship is however, the norm for Hindus, Buddhists, Sikhs and followers of Islam. Nor should it come as strange to Christians or Jews, who will recall that when Moses went up the mountain to receive the Ten Commandments, he was asked to take off his shoes because he stood on holy ground.

The Sikh view of place of worship is very much a utilitarian one. A place to read, hear or reflect in the company of like-minded people, on the teaching of Sikhism in a calm and serene atmosphere. There is also a need for space for Sikhs and non-Sikhs to meet and share a meal together to emphasise our common humanity. There is little requirement for either artefacts or elaborate decoration.

Most followers of major faiths believe that religion is more than the simple recitation of sacred texts. True/reflection on our teachings leads to a view on the good and bad in secular life, and it is right to discuss common concerns in say the Sikh gurdwara, or Muslim mosque. It would however, be wholly wrong to use a place of serenity to ferment violence and discord. Today, it is more important than ever before to ensure that our holy places of worship are used positively to teach us the need for responsibility, tolerance and sensitivity to our fellow beings, of all faiths and persuasions.

27 January 2003

Understanding the Causes of Terrorism

Whenever we're confronted with new threats to life, like Sars, or more recently bird flu, we take urgent steps to understand the nature of the threat and the way it multiplies and spreads, as a way to ultimately defeating it.

In much the same way, terrorism is also a threat to life that can, as we know, all too well, also cause the death of thousands. Common sense suggests that to fully eradicate it, we need to consider how and why it manifests itself. We need to know something of the factors that impel, often educated people, with young families, not only to take their own lives, but also to murder wholly blameless innocent men, women and children. Is it a perceived sense of injustice? Outrage at the death or suffering of one's kith and kin, a warped sense of religious duty, or a lethal combination of these factors?

When cholera was first attributed to unhygienic living, no one suggested that this was an irresponsible and insulting comment on their way of life. Instead, active steps were taken to improve sanitation leading to the dramatic eradication of a killer disease. Yet when Liberal Democrat MP Dr. Jenny Tonge suggested, in a similar way, that harsh refugee camp conditions experienced by many Palestinians, might contribute to terrorism, much of the media descended on her like a ton of bricks.

There are two concerns. The first is the right to express genuinely held views. This is considered so important in Sikhism that our Gurus, while stressing the independent path of Sikh belief, constantly underlined their respect for Hindu and Muslim teachings.

The second concern is that our narrow and emotional response to what we term 'global terrorism', makes it difficult for us to see, that although terrorism in the Middle East, Chechnya and other parts of world manifests itself in similar ways, its cause is often quite different. It simply doesn't help the peace process in Israel in this instance, to talk of global terrorist conspiracies.

Instead, we should be looking to the real concerns of Israelis fearful of the future, and the Palestinians traumatized by the present with over-reaction by both communities with bombs, bulldozers and suicide bombing. Dr. Tonge may have erred in her choice of language but recognizing the strength and depth of genuine concerns is essential for terrorism's eventual defeat.

29 April 2003

Fiftieth Anniversary of the Discovery of DNA

Fifty years ago, a group of eager young scientists at Cambridge, set out, in the words of Dr. James Watson, (the youngest member of the team), 'to understand the meaning of life without reference to God or religion.'

Dr. Watson was speaking at last week's Guildhall dinner to celebrate the achievement of the team, which in 1953, succeeded in unravelling the structure of the DNA molecule that carries the instructions for the functioning of all living cells. It was one of the most important scientific discoveries of the twentieth century with far reaching consequences.

DNA identification is now a powerful weapon in the fight against crime, and we are all aware of the potential for genetic modification, of plants, crops, and animal and human life. Now, thanks to the ground-breaking work of Dr. Watson, Professor Francis Crick and others, we are on the threshold of a new ability to conquer long feared diseases.

But to understand how a small part of creation works, does not explain away the existence of a Creator, unless we argue in an unscientific way, that it all began by accident, without cause and out of nothing. For me the discovery that a mind boggling two metres or so of DNA genetic code is contained in each of our trillions of cells simply increases my sense of wonder and awe in much the same way as Guru Nanak was struck by the infinity of God's creation. He wrote:

There are no bounds to His Creation
How many vex their hearts to know His Limits
But seeking to explore infinity can find no bounds

The study of our genetic make-up is a bit like exploring infinity. There is still a long way to go, particularly in the interaction between genes and, between genes and the environment. Knowledge of our genetic make-up will be of enormous benefit in our fight against cancer, Parkinson's disease and similar conditions. The same discoveries however, also carry the possibilities of human cloning, designer children and the grotesque marketing of human vanity.

Far from being able to do without religion, as Dr. Watson suggested, we need the guidance of religion as never before to tackle the complex ethical dilemmas on how to use new discoveries without demeaning life itself. Religion also reminds us of the need for a little humility, to shield us from the downside of our undoubted cleverness.

6 May 2003

Creating God in Our Own Image

The philosopher Voltaire was once asked if he believed that man was created in God's image. He thought for a moment and said, 'What I am sure of is that man creates God in his own image'.

I thought of Voltaire's comment as I read a weekend report that claimed up to fifty young British Muslims were ready to follow the path to martyrdom chosen by Asif Mohammed Hanif, who blew himself up in a bar in Tel Aviv last week, killing three people and injuring more than fifty others. Not only do we create God in our image, but we also distort the compassionate teachings of religion to justify the killing of innocent civilians.

The main thrust of our different faiths is to move us to more compassionate and considerate behaviour, but the problem is that such teaching go against the grain of our baser instincts, so we readily bend religion to fit and justify our human weaknesses. It's all done in easy imperceptible stages. First a belief that our way to God is the only true way. Then, God, in recognition of this, has an exclusive and favoured relationship with us, making others lesser beings. It's an easy move from this to claim that anything done to further the influence of our God must have his blessings and be pleasing to Him. We can see all too easily how this warped logic can descend to the oppression and killing of innocents.

Guru Nanak was very concerned about this arrogance of belief. He taught that God had no favoured relationships. It is the way we behave that counts. He was particularly critical of the hypocrisy so called religious leaders who played on the ignorance and prejudices of their followers. He wrote:

They utter God's name but condone injustice
Shielding their actions – with religious texts

Words that ring true today. Last year we saw 2000 Muslims massacred in the Indian state of Gujarat in the name of religion. Today it is the killing of Jews to protect Islam and Jewish revenge incursions into Palestinian territory. Tomorrow it might be Christians or Sikhs. This grotesque merry-go-round of killing in the name of religion will undoubtedly continue until religious leaders have the courage to point out the real threat to our various religions lies, not so much in the behaviour of others, but in our distortion of religious teachings to justify our human failings.

15 July 2003

Tower of Babel in Religious Dialogue

Perhaps it's the weather, but there seems to be a lot of misunderstanding and heated opinion about these days. It hasn't all been peace and tranquillity at the General Synod, and it wasn't much better at an inter-faith conference that I attended last week.

It took place in the picturesque Austrian town of Graz, to mark its designation as this year's cultural capital of Europe. The celebrations also included a fascinating exhibition called 'the tower of Babel', referring to the biblical story in which God punishes humans for trying to build a tower to reach the heavens, by making it difficult for us to understand one another.

I thought of the story as I listened to a number of cross-purpose exchanges in different languages, without synchronised translations, and Power Point images conspiring to further reduce understanding. But these were minor problems compared to differing national perceptions of religious dialogue. For many, inter-faith dialogue meant closer cooperation between the different Christian denominations to meet an impending 'clash of civilisations'.

I joined a workshop on 'religious identity in public places', hoping to learn something about European initiatives for greater public respect for different faiths. To my amazement, the French and German delegates spoke with concern and passion about the danger to national identity, of allowing religious symbols like the Muslim headscarf in public places. The general consensus seemed to be that all would be well if religion was kept safely locked up in the home.

There was an air of incredulity when I explained that in Britain, the move was to encourage people of different faiths to engage with government and local government in initiatives such as urban regeneration, health and welfare. When pressed for the Sikh view of dialogue, I said that this required us to look beyond external superficial differences to our common identity.

I mentioned some words of Guru Gobind Singh:

God is in the Hindu temple as he is in the mosque
The Hindus and Muslims are one, though they appear different
Having each the customs of different environments.

But I might as well have been speaking Punjabi!

We in the UK are clearly far ahead of the continent in looking to good inter-faith relations. But there is still a long way to go. The Tower of Babel effect is probably more evident in religious dialogue than in any other form of human activity, and it will continue to be so until we are able to see our common humanity in the beliefs and practices of others.

24 July 2003

Winning Hearts and Minds in Iraq

Few will mourn the death of Saddam Hussein's wayward sons, Uday and Qusay, killed in a gun battle with American soldiers. They were without doubt, sadistic psychopaths who routinely tortured and killed on mere whim. Their death is a welcome boost to American and British efforts to bring peace and hope to the long-suffering people of Iraq. But there is still a long way to go.

Winning the war was the easy bit. Winning the peace, with British and American troops still coming under fire, and no real enthusiasm for foreign troops on Iraqi soil, will be a lot harder. 'Taking out' evil people does not in itself tackle the religious bigotry and sense of injustice in which tyrants climb to power.

Today, one of the greatest threats in Iraq is mounting evidence of a desire of some in Iraq's persecuted Shia community, to exact revenge on their Sunni oppressors. Nothing new in this. A couple of centuries ago, the charismatic Sikh ruler, Maharaja Ranjit Singh, was faced with similar pressures from Sikhs to curb the rights of their former Muslim oppressors. Ranjit Singh would have none of it citing Guru Nanak's teaching of respect for all faiths. His rule saw all communities thrive and prosper in an atmosphere of religious freedom for the first time in Punjab's turbulent history. It will take a similar gesture of forgiveness and respect to prevent Iraq's descent into brutal factional conflict.

But there are also other challenges. The United States has declared its hand against the Baath ruling party with images of playing cards showing Iraq's most wanted men. Equally, it now needs to produce a similar pack showing ethical values central to the search for true peace. While combating religious bigotry should be high on the list, there should also be an absolute commitment to visible and equal justice for all people.

Here the news that two British nationals held in Guantanamo Bay will not face the death penalty and may be given access to lawyers, welcome though it is, will undoubtedly raise questions about the rights of other detainees. Closed courts, death penalties and a lack of even-handedness, traditional tools for dictatorships, have no part to play in the search for a better world order.

It all sounds a bit harsh, but, if we are to win the battle for hearts and minds, tolerance and even-handed justice must remain the most important cards in the pack.

7 October 2003

Leaving God Out of the New European Constitution

It seems that God and religion will not get a mention in the new European Constitution being debated in Rome. I doubt if the Creator of all that exists will be too bothered by this, but some Christian groups are clearly upset about the absence of any reference to Europe's Christian heritage.

It's true that many beautiful churches, fine paintings and a wealth of music and verse is linked to Christian worship, but I'm less convinced that European history with its inquisitions, world wars, the Holocaust and more recent genocide, or its aggressive empire building, have anything to do with Christian teachings. It's a pretty dismal record, and the only thing that can be said in its favour, is that it is probably a lot better than that found in many other lands.

Most national constitutions are couched in grandiose language about inalienable rights, and at the same time, more than half of the members of the United Nations carry out cruel torture and a systematic abuse of human rights on their own people. Nothing new in this. Guru Nanak was moved to describe kings as butchers and religious leaders as assassins in religious garb. He taught that a truly religious person was one who looked on all as equals. He was equally critical of rituals like bathing at supposed holy waters, fasting and pilgrimages.

References to God or religion in national or regional constitutions are in many ways rituals in words. Like other rituals, they can easily induce a sense of smugness or superiority, and the dangerous belief that has carried into our twenty-first century, that God is on our side.

For me as a Sikh, it doesn't matter one bit whether or not the final constitution of the European Union carries a reference to God. Guru Nanak observed that God was above and beyond our human desire to be acknowledged or praised. As he put it, *'our collective praise neither adds to nor diminishes His worth'*. What is important is that the Constitution emphasises human rights, freedom of belief, gender equality and equality of opportunity. If it also shows commitment and concern for those economically and socially disadvantaged in other lands, it will be to my mind a constitution couched in religion, couched in Christian values and the common values of other world faiths.

14 October 2003

Bowing and Chanting

Some years back, I suggested to an East London local authority, that they should make a greater effort to understand and work with different religious communities. The reply was swift and sharp. 'We want nothing to do with all that bowing and chanting'.

Times have changed, and later this morning, I'll be going to a multi-faith conference organised by the Local Government Association. Last week the Foreign and Commonwealth Office had a day-long seminar on the impact of overseas conflict on religious communities in this country, and tomorrow a government-led Steering Group will discuss the interface between faith communities and the government.

It's all a bit too much for Britain's newer faith communities. We'd just got used to being ignored. Now we are being told to get involved in life around us. As a Sikh, I can't really grumble at this, because Guru Nanak told us to do much the same thing.

Guru Nanak was concerned about the bigotry surrounding religious belief and in perhaps the world's first main thrust to interfaith understanding he travelled vast distances to places as far apart as Mecca, Baghdad, Sri Lanka and Tibet to urge respect for different beliefs and the need to work together to build a fairer world.

It's a measure of how far we've slipped over the centuries, that 500 years ago Guru Nanak could speak openly about bigotry and dubious social practices masquerading as religion. The Guru was undoubtedly helped by his obvious sincerity and spirituality. Similar discussion in today's world however would almost certainly lead to accusations of bias, blasphemy and religious phobia.

My concern about interfaith dialogue is that it's becoming stuck in a grove of being superficially nice to one another; with western faiths accepting tasty ethnic snacks, and providing tea and a digestive biscuit in return. We now need to go beyond this superficiality and talk about real or imagined differences seen as impediments to a fairer and more cohesive society.

My hope for today's conference and similar ones that will undoubtedly follow, is that they will help us to build confidences to talk openly and honestly about the need to disentangle questionable cultural practices from religious teachings, and to discuss issues like gender equality, religious conversion, and the relevance of marriage and the family in today's fast changing society. Who knows, we might even learn from one another and recognise common goals of balanced and responsible living.

21 October 2003

The widening Gap Between the Haves and Have-Nots

While millions have watched David Blaine's, self-imposed fast of forty-four days, recording the number of times he waved or scratched himself, millions more face the spectacle of continuing starvation, leading to death in a world of plenty. Every year, in this 'one world week', we remember their plight and the urgent need to close the gap between rich and poorer nations, in a world in our destinies are inextricably entwined.

The President of the World Bank, Dr. James Wolfensohn, reminded us of this in a meeting last month of the World Bank and International Monetary Fund. He said, 'my generation grew up thinking that there were two worlds – the haves and the have nots – and they were for the most part separate. That was wrong then, and it is even more wrong today'.

Dr. Wolfensohn is right in saying that we in the West, cannot distance ourselves from the plight of the poor. It is however, also true that the division of the world between, the haves and the have-nots, has never been greater.

What makes the world a more dangerous place, is that for the first time in human history, the have-nots, are aware of the full extent of their deprivation, and are increasingly reluctant to accept huge disparities in life's opportunities.

There are many reasons for these inequalities, like prohibitive tariffs and subsidies. Agricultural subsidies in the developed world are, for example, a staggering 850 million dollars a day. Arms exports further enrich the West at the expense of poorer nations, fueling debilitating conflicts with equally impoverished neighbours.

Today, wars, oppression and economic instability in seemingly distant lands, create economic and refugee problems for the affluent and more secure West. Even this security is now threatened by hatreds that know no border, and terrorism that parasitically grows and thrives on social and political injustice.

Self-interest then, dictates that we redouble our efforts to move to a fairer world. But it would be wrong to look at self-interest alone. The world's great religions have long reminded us to look in a more enlightened way to the needs of our neighbours and to our common identity. As Guru Gobind Singh put it *'manas ki jaath sab ek he pachanbo'* – recognize the oneness of the human race. Today, the enlightened self-interest of the West, adds a new urgency to this age-old, moral imperative.

13 January 2004

Added Suffering in Air Travel

The Punjabi word for travel is pronounced 'suffer' and no word is more appropriate in describing the hazards of air travel in the twenty-first century, particularly to the east coast of the USA. With my usual exquisite sense of timing, I'm committed to speaking there at a conference in New York next month.

Before 9/11, we simply had to weigh up the chances of getting deep vein thrombosis. Now, we have the possibility of endless delays while passenger lists are checked and re-checked for dodgy sounding names like mine, while a real terrorist with a name like John Smith walks through. And then there is the dubious protection of possibly trigger-happy sky marshals and the added 'inconvenience' of not being allowed to queue for the toilet. On landing, there is more interrogation and now finger printing. And there's an additional hazard for Sikhs. In the immediate aftermath of 9/11, one Sikh was shot dead and others brutally beaten up in the States because Bin Laden also happened to wear a turban.

If Al Qaeda's aim was to create panic and disruption, they have, at least in part, succeeded. But what really concerns me, is that western reaction to the events of 9/11 is creating an ever-more polarized world of them and us, of rogue and friendly states, and the goodies and baddies of comics and computer games.

Constant utterances from the USA on the need to protect western interests and uphold western values, implies that the rest of the world do not share these values. Not the best way of making friends and influencing people.

Sikh teachings suggest that we urgently need to move away from what others see as a growing arrogance of culture and belief. At the time of the Sikh Gurus, different religious groupings also arrogantly referred to the inferior ways of others. The result was inevitable conflict. Guru Gobind Singh, whose birthday Sikhs have been celebrating this past week, urged that we look beyond bigotry to underlying commonalities. He taught:

Some call themselves Hindus. Others call themselves Muslims
Among these are the Shias. There are Sunnis also
And yet man is of one race in all the world.
All men have the same form. All men have the same soul.

Enhanced security at airports might reduce the threat of terrorism but emphasizing our respect for those of different cultures and beliefs is a necessary step to its ultimate defeat.

20 January 2004

Religious Symbols in France

Last weekend's demonstrations against a proposal to ban the wearing of all religious symbols in French public institutions from next September, brought to mind my visit to the French Embassy a few weeks before Christmas. I had been invited to meet a delegation appointed by the President, Jacques Chirac, to look at the British experience of working with faith communities.

The delegation was led by Bernard Stasi, an affable man with a lively sense of humour. They listened attentively, as I and colleagues from the Inner Cities Religious Council, told them that the problems currently faced by the French government, existed in Britain in the '50s and '60s, with pressures to ban Sikh bus drivers from wearing turbans, and similar attitudes in other fields of employment. We explained how successive British governments and the courts came firmly down on the side of tolerance, and how today, turbans are worn by Sikhs in schools and colleges and all government institutions. I suggested that the French should be similarly relaxed about the turban and the headscarf worn by some Muslim women.

The French delegation was clearly concerned that any display of religious affiliation in public institutions might compromise secularity and questioned why Sikhs regarded the wearing of their symbols as important.

I explained that our distinctive dress arises out of an incident in Sikh history when one of our Gurus, knowing the danger, gave his life defending the freedom of belief of another religion. The turban and other symbols, simply remind us of a readiness to be identified with this total commitment to speaking up for tolerance and the rights of others, however daunting the circumstances.

Monsieur Stasi was visibly moved. Despite this, perhaps under political pressure, when the Commission returned to France, it recommended the proposed ban. When asked about France's estimated ten thousand Sikhs, Monsieur Stasi said no one had told him that there were any Sikhs in France.

To my mind, French government policy, based on a narrow view of secularity simply panders to majority prejudice, and will prove counterproductive in promoting a harmonious society. In the Sikh view, true secularity calls for increased tolerance, understanding and respect for all ways of life.

11 May 2004

Indian General Elections

Yesterday saw the final round of voting in India's general election and early results are expected later this week. After all the hype of electioneering, the winning party, or coalition will have the responsibility of looking to the welfare of a billion people with a variety of religions and cultures, and immense problems of poverty and health in a country where the number of people suffering from HIV infections is now set to exceed that of South Africa.

Compared to its immediate neighbour, Pakistan, beset with military coups, India is a success story. One measure of the health of a democracy, is the ability of voters to throw out a government that loses their trust; something that has happened several times in the half century of Indian independence.

There is however a less happy side to India's experiment with democracy. This is the increasing awareness of politicians that votes can be won by appealing to the baser instincts and religious passions of the majority community, at the expense of minorities. As with Germany in the 1930s, it's been a tried and tested formula for achieving political power the world over.

Just twenty years ago, a Congress government, trailing in the opinion polls at the start of the year, ended it with the largest majority in Indian history, after the systematic killing of thousands of Sikhs throughout Indian cities in what a former Chief Justice of India described, as the 'greatest carnage since Partition'. Since then, Christians and Muslims have sadly been targeted, with similar electoral gain.

True democracy is much more than simple majority rule. It is also about ensuring freedom and opportunity, and importantly, respect, for other ways of life. This wider view of responsibility, is the main thrust of Sikh teachings, on gender equality, social justice and respect for other religions. It was a total commitment to these beliefs that led to our nineth Guru, Guru Tegh Bahadur, giving his life defending the right of the Hindu community to freedom of worship.

Today, majority prejudice remains a clear threat to the future of the world's largest democracy. Equally worrying are the problems of the world's most powerful democracy, the United States, faced with accusations of undue arrogance, as it tries to export its values to other parts of the world. Pandering to majority prejudice, or a messianic belief in the superiority of our way of life does nothing for democracy. Respect and visible concern for others, will take us a lot further.

1 September 2004

Religion is not an Exclusive Franchise

I must say that, as a Sikh. I found it a little disconcerting to read a piece in the Times a couple of days ago, in which Dr. Rowan Williams, the Archbishop of Canterbury, firmly declared that no one comes to the Father except through Jesus. When asked about Muslims going to heaven, he did however concede the possibility of 'God's spirit crossing boundaries. I'm not sure if that is a yes or a no; but at least Muslims are in with a chance.

The Sikh scriptures, 400 years old today, take a different view and maintain that there are no rigid boundaries between faiths, and that God is not in the least bit interested in our different religious labels, but in how we serve our fellow beings, and how we cherish and value the wonder of Creation.

Guru Arjan Dev, the main compiler of the Sikh holy Granth, included in it, not only teachings of the Sikh Gurus, but also verses of Hindu and Muslim saints to show that no one religion has a monopoly on truth. Earlier, the Guru showed his respect for Islam, by asking a Muslim saint Mia Mir, to lay the foundation stone of the famous Golden Temple, which has doors on four sides to emphasize a welcome to people from different spiritual and geographic directions.

Today, and for the rest of the month, Sikhs throughout the world, will be celebrating the first reading of these scriptures in Amritsar 400 years ago; teachings that emphasize: respect for other faiths and a balanced and socially responsible attitude to life. An early celebration has already been held in the unlikely venue of the White House in Washington and, later this month, among the many celebrations in this country, there will be a major commemoration in London's Royal Albert Hall.

My problem with all such celebrations is that we easily forget the significance of what we are celebrating. And we Sikhs are no exception here. In our celebrations we can easily forget that Guru Arjan, the compiler of the Sikh scriptures, gave his life in the cause of religious harmony. Today, Sikhs have a clear obligation to work as catalysts for greater interfaith understanding and help show that different religions are not rigid barriers between people, but gateways to a greater understanding and enrichment of life itself. Having said that, the one certainty is, that following this talk, I'll get another letter from a concerned lady in Devon, reminding me of the terrible fate in store for me for not wearing her religious label.

8 September 2004

Use and Abuse of Language

Today I'm told, is international literacy day; an appropriate time to reflect on the way words are sometimes used in a way that blurs understanding.

We are all too aware that there are groups of people willing to resort to killing, maiming, and even the cold-blooded murder of innocent children to achieve political objectives. We rightly refer to them as terrorists.

When national governments, however, do the same sort of thing with heavy weapons that kill indiscriminately, and when torture and rape are used to subdue civilian populations, as, if Amnesty International and other human rights groups are to be believed, has happened in Chechnya over the last ten years, we do not talk of terrorism, but simply of preserving law and order. Today, autocratic rulers engaged in repression only have to describe it as 'fighting international terrorism', to get an approving nod from major powers.

But as we all know, heavy-handed repression gives rise to anger and resentment and all too often, terrorist atrocities, leading to even harsher repression; continuing a vicious circle of violence, in a war, that as President Bush recently conceded, that we may not win.

The Sikh Guru, Guru Ram Das urged us to forsake dubious alliances and moral compromises in our quest for a fairer and more peaceful world. He famously reminded us of the impermanence of questionable strategic alliances, writing:

All these human powers men make pacts with
Are subject to death and decay

The Guru was warning us, that evil results, when we sacrifice our religious or ethical principles for short-term gain. A Christian hymn also reminds us that we harm our children's children when we compromise with sin. Blurred language, and tacit support to governments known to abuse human rights, do not help us focus on ways in which we can rid the world of the scourge of terrorist atrocities. Terrorism breeds and thrives on a real, or perceived, sense of injustice. The use of force may be a necessary short-term expedient in curbing its worst effects, but its ultimate defeat can only come when those in power and authority show a total commitment to civil and political rights in all parts of our troubled world.

26 November 2004

Embracing Difference

If you can't see God in all, you can't see God at all. This has been the theme of a number of celebrations this year, of the 400th anniversary of the first reading of the Sikh scriptures, the Guru Granth Sahib. To emphasize this respect for other faiths, the Guru Granth Sahib contains writings of Hindu and Muslim saints, as well as those of the Sikh Gurus.

This reaching out to others, is central to the teachings of Guru Nanak, whose birthday Sikhs celebrate tomorrow. The Guru saw different faiths as different paths to an understanding of life, and a highlighting of our common responsibility to our fellow human beings. The Guru emphasised the importance of tolerance and respect. At a time when different religions and different religious factions were at each other's throats, Guru Nanak urged us to work together in looking to the wellbeing of all in God's creation.

I was reminded of this Sikh teaching on the common thrust of our different faiths, at a Prison Chaplaincy Conference that I attended yesterday on the theme 'Embracing the Difference'. It was an opportunity for chaplains from different faiths to share attitudes to the pastoral care and the rehabilitation of those in prison. What was remarkable was that the absence of any significant difference in concerns and attitudes. Instead, we saw the capacity of different religions to work together for common ends. As the Chaplain General reminded us, encountering the views of others, can enhance understanding and help religions re-appropriate the role of religion in tackling questions of right, wrong and responsibility.

For me, the conference was a powerful reminder of the true role of religion in wider society. In every Queen's speech, we are told of new and ever tougher laws to help us cope with growing violent and criminal behaviour. But laws and punishment cannot in themselves, improve behaviour. Religion does have the potential to help us curb greed and violence and move us to more responsible living, but all too often it is only seen as a cause of conflict.

The conference reminded me that if religion to is to play its potential healing and uniting role in our world of conflict and blurred morality, it is important that it embraces difference, instead of continually focusing on divisive claims of exclusivity. As Guru Nanak reminded us, responsible living and respect for others is the essence of true religion. If we can't see God in others, we can't see God at all.

9 December 2004

Martyrdom of the Children of Guru Gobind Singh

This month, Sikhs commemorate the 300th anniversary of the martyrdom of the two younger sons of the tenth Guru, Guru Gobind Singh. The two boys aged only eight and five, were bricked alive for their refusal to disown their Sikh religion.

If the children of the Guru, out of fear, or through the lure of riches, had changed their religion, it would have dealt a mortal blow to the tiny Sikh community. In the event, widespread revulsion at the murder of the two innocents steeled the resolve of Sikhs and hastened the end of Mughal rule in India. An outcome that reminds me of a line of a Christian hymn that: *'with faith, the weakest arm can turn the iron helm of fate.'*

I thought about this episode in Sikh history while taking part in the recording of a TV programme called the New Commandments, earlier this week. I was asked to comment on the top twenty new commandments, selected through an opinion poll. Most fell into the categories of 'don't do naughty things', or 'try to be good'.

The difficulty with religion, is that different faiths give us lots of guidance on responsible living, which is easy to state, but difficult to live by. So, we forget the teachings and focus on customs and rituals. It doesn't really matter whether we have ten commandments, or (in our inflationary times) twenty if we don't live up to them. That's why I singled out, one of the new ones (that is closest to the thrust of Sikh teachings) as my favourite. 'Be true to yourself', or practice what you believe, whatever the cost. Not easy.

The Sikh teaching on tolerance and respect for other religions, for example, led to the nineth Guru, the grandfather of those two martyred children, giving, his life for the freedom of worship of those of a different religion. His brave example almost certainly underpinned the resolve of the two infant martyrs.

Their courage and commitment to being true to themselves, reminds us all, Sikh and non-Sikh alike, that if we are true to the ethical imperatives of our different belief systems, we can all make a difference, be it in the office, the workplace or in standing up to the school bully. As the poet reminds us: while 'we cannot choose battlefields,' but like those infant children, we can 'plant a standard, where a standard never flew.'

9 March 2005

Getting to the Roots of Religious Bigotry

The growing concern over the threat of terrorist activity is seen in both in the parliamentary debate over the relative powers of the executive and the judiciary, and in this week's Madrid conference of some twenty nations, meeting a year after the Madrid bombing that cost more than 200 innocent lives. There is little doubt that those who see nothing wrong in killing innocent people to advance a political cause, pose a real threat to civilized society, and what makes the threat more dangerous, is a warped motivation that God will applaud and reward their killing of innocents.

The added threat to civilized society is the danger of over-reacting to shadowy dangers. The impassioned debates in Parliament, remind us of the difficulties of striking a balance between increased vigilance on the one hand, and the protection of civil liberties on the other. When the threat comes mainly from a particular community, I see nothing wrong in looking more closely in the direction of that community, but it is both wrong and counterproductive to label whole communities as extremists. I can understand the real pain of many Muslims who feel singled out in this way.

Sikh suffered it in 1984, following the assassination of Indira Gandhi and the mass killing of Sikhs throughout India. Anyone who protested against the carnage in India was labelled a fundamentalist, in a pejorative way, although paradoxically, the very fundamentals of Sikhism emphasize social justice, equality, and tolerance and respect for others.

While we need to maintain our guard, it is a commitment to such ideals that can provide the death knell for terrorist activity. We can only defeat terrorism by looking at its causes and, I hope the Madrid conference will look beyond short-term considerations to underlying causes that fuel and sustain terrorism.

The first of these is religious bigotry. This, in its milder form, talks of God being on our side, and this easily descends into the creed of the suicide bomber. As Guru Nanak reminded us, God, the creator of all that exists is not in the least bit interested in our religious posturing , but in how we behave. Equally, I hope the Madrid conference will also look at combating, both real and perceived sense of social and political injustice in which the evil of terrorism thrives and multiplies.

16 March 2005

Free Speech v Incitement to Religious Hatred

There's a lot of anger and passion about in Parliament these days. After last week's marathon debate about anti-terrorist legislation, the House of Lords, turned this week to impassionate debate over the proposed law on incitement to religious hatred.

Overt incitement to religious hatred should clearly be condemned. Some however were concerned about the looseness of the term and its possible interpretation to curb legitimate discussion and free speech. It is a fear that has been expressed by comedians, like Rowan Atkinson, and to judge from my own postbag, by many other people, mostly on the grounds that the proposed law will curb our right to debate, or even ridicule, particular religious practices. The government on the other hand, stoutly maintains that law is designed and drafted in a way that will curb the worst excesses of incitement to hatred against people of a particular faith, while allowing robust discussion on religion itself, including the thrust of challenging humour.

As a Sikh, I certainly hope the government proves right. Much of the content of our holy scriptures, the Guru Granth Sahib, is couched in often critical comment on religious practices of the day, which in Guru Nanak's view, were taking people away from basic ethical teachings. His criticism was robust, often made with humour, and, although he made enemies in the religious hierarchy, both Hindus and Muslims regarded his teachings as a breath of fresh air. On his death, a popular Punjabi couplet described him as both the Pir, and religious leader of the Muslims, and the Guru, or religious teacher, of the Hindus.

Guru Nanak believed that the core teachings of our different religions are easy to state, but extremely difficult to live by; so instead we resort to questionable rituals and even oppressive social practices as surrogates for true belief. The Guru felt that discussion and debate on religion could help us understand the extent of this easy drift.

If Guru Nanak had lived in the Britain of today, I'm sure he would have been impressed by our healthy freedom to criticize both religious and secular institutions, and individuals, at the highest level, without fear of repercussion. The Sikh Gurus took a bold and consistent stand, for the right to speak up against oppression and injustice. But this freedom has nothing whatever to do with the freedom to incite hatred against religious or other minorities.

6 September 2006

Culture and Religious Teachings

This week, we learnt that a survey of young Asian Hindus, Muslims, Sikhs and Christians found that 10% felt that so called honour killings, that mostly target women, could be justified in certain circumstances. It's a highly disturbing statistic. But is it right to link religion with dated and perverse social attitudes to justice and honour? Any examination of Hindu, Muslim, Sikh and Christian teachings will show that they, in no way support or condone such murder.

In today's sensitive times, I believe it's important to differentiate between dubious cultural attitudes, and religion, that condemns such practices. The Sikh Gurus, for example, were strident in their criticism of rituals and social practices that demeaned or gave a less than equal role to women. They condemned infanticide, which generally meant the killing of infant girls, and forbade Sikhs from associating with the then common practices of sati, that is widows, under pressure of society, throwing themselves on a deceased husband's funeral pyre. In a further move, the Gurus gave Sikh women the name or title 'Kaur', literally princess to emphasize their elevated status.

Culture reflects the norms of a community, while the purpose of religion is to lift us to higher planes of responsibility and behaviour. The reality however is frequently different. Questionable cultural practices often attach themselves to religion, distorting or blurring true religious teachings.

I think it's particularly important that we differentiate between religion and culture in the current debate over how to make ours a more cohesive society. We can have all the commissions of inquiry we want, producing impressive reports, but we will never make real progress until we disentangle culture from religion, ditching the nastier bits, like so-called honour killings. I feel that a useful first step would be to get rid of the ugly word 'multiculturalism' which unhelpfully lumps religion and culture together as something we should be for, or against. Difficult when you don't know what it means.

When we remove the distorting overlay of culture from religion, we see our different religions as they really are, beliefs having much in common. Taking culture out of the equation will also help us see areas of religious difference in a fuller perspective and develop strategies to promote integration, based on genuine understanding and respect.

13 September 2006

Losing the War on Terror

An opinion poll this week suggests that most people in this country feel that we are losing the war on terror. I don't know about that, but I do feel that since 9/11 we've been losing the fight for clarity of language. Soundbites well, sound fine, but they don't do much for discussion and action.

If doctors wish to contain a new and virulent illness, they first try to identify and isolate its exact cause, and then go on to look for cures. We would feel less than reassured if doctors and scientists went on and on, year after year vaguely talking about their determination to fight 'nasty germs'.

Five years after 9/11, I suspect many of us feel the same way when we hear talk of 'fighting global terror', as if suicide bombers in Iraq, Tamil Tigers in Sri Lanka, Chechnyans, and countless others all have the same aims and objectives.

To me, the real struggle is between the political power of the West, and what some see, as a brash smugness about the superiority of its way of life, facing a long dormant, resurgent Islam, itself deeply divided by religious and factional differences, trying to come to terms with itself and the realities of the twenty-first century.

It's a struggle for hearts and minds, and as a Sikh, I believe that it's not one that can be won either by terrorism, or with bombs and bullets.

Of course, it's necessary to respond to and be vigilant against terrorist attack, but detention of suspects for years without trial in Guantanamo Bay, torture at Abu Graib, 'extraordinary rendition' and talk about an axis of evil are not ways to win friends, and simply add fuel to the spiral of hatred and violence. By the same token those that believe that killing innocent people in the name of religion will take them to paradise, insult their own religion, and worse, God himself.

Despite the gloomy findings of the opinion polls, I feel that we can move forward to peace by showing a little more humility about our own way of life and focussing on values like democracy and freedom of speech and belief; values that resonate with hearts and minds. I'm sure that many in moderate Islam, deeply unhappy about bigots twisting their beliefs to justify hatred and killing, would welcome any move in this direction.

20 September 2006

Religious Retreats

There is a Punjabi joke, probably made up by Sikhs, that the only culture that Sikhs know anything about, is 'agriculture'. This stems from the fact that many Sikhs in Punjab are farmers, in an area recognised as the granary of India. I was reminded about this supposed lack of culture among Sikhs, when recently asked to take part in a BBC programme about gardens associated with places of worship. They wanted to do an interview in 'the tranquillity of a beautiful garden around a Sikh place of worship'. But there was a problem. Such places are few and far between.

The fact is that Sikh gurdwaras are generally plain functional buildings. The explanation lies mainly in Sikh history, which has been one of persecution almost from the start. Sikh opposition to the whole notion of caste, and the Guru's teaching on the equality of all human beings didn't win us many friends among those in power and authority. Our places of worship were repeatedly desecrated, and at times, a price placed on the head of every Sikh caught dead or alive. In such circumstances, it's difficult, and pointless, trying to build grandiose places of worship in beautiful garden settings. In this country, we haven't done much better either, and feel really pleased with ourselves if we can get a couple of parking spaces near a gurdwara.

Beautiful places of worship and a tranquil environment undoubtedly enrich our lives and help us in our reflections, but they also have their downside, in that they can easily suggest that we have to get away from the challenges of daily life to find God. The teachings of Guru Nanak, Jesus Christ and others are all about engagement with all aspects of life.

While a beautiful garden can, as the poet observed, take us a little nearer to heaven, we can also glimpse the divine in the actions of those, who like the Sikh water carrier Bhai Kanaya, ministered to friend and foe on the battlefield, and was applauded by the Guru for his actions.

Man-made retreats may sometimes be helpful, but, as Tennyson reminds us, we can also see Him in the shining of the stars and the flowering of the fields, and Sikhs believe, in the actions and example of countless people like the Sikh water carrier who, in an age of deep cynicism, still devote themselves to the service of their fellow beings outside the walls of temples, retreats and shrines.

28 November 2006

Stand Up and be Counted

Over the last few days Sikhs have been commemorating the martyrdom anniversary of Guru Tegh Bahadur, the ninth Guru of the Sikhs who was publicly beheaded by the Mughal rulers for defending the right of Hindus to worship in the manner of their choice even though he personally disagreed with many of their teachings. His brave stand later had its echo in Voltaire's famous words, 'I may not believe in what you say, but I'll defend to the death your right to say it.'

I think it's helpful to reflect on the Guru's brave stand in the light of current concerns over freedom of speech and the equally important right of freedom of belief. From the Sikh point of view, freedom of speech is the right to state genuinely held views without fear from those in power or authority, including religious authority. Like all freedoms it has its limits and the giving of gratuitous insult or the targeting of the weak simply harms this all-important freedom,

Sikhs believe that our different religious practices should be fully open to criticism and debate. The Sikh Gurus themselves challenged religious practices like the caste system which divided people at birth into the high and the low. They also questioned the wearing of the veil on the grounds that it tended to hide women from mainstream society, and impeded the recognition of their full equality. But, at the same time, as shown in the Guru's martyrdom, they also defended the right of all people to practice their faith free from harassment.

At the time of Guru Tegh Bahadur's beheading, Sikhs had no recognisable appearance linking them to Sikh teachings. When the Mughals challenged Sikhs to come forward and claim their master's body, Sikhs, concerned for their own lives, hesitated to do so and eventually the body was removed under cover of darkness.

The turban and other Sikh symbols were chosen by Guru Gobind Singh, the last of our founding Gurus, as a constant reminder of a commitment to the egalitarian teachings of Sikhism however daunting the circumstances. Today, these same teachings remind us that a commitment to freedom of belief and frank questioning of religious practices are not mutually exclusive but essential if religion is to give a positive direction to society.

4 December 2006

The Arms Trade

A report in the Sunday Times claimed that MPs are to send a delegation to the Prime Minister demanding that he intervenes to save the £10 billion Saudi arms deal threatened by a corruption inquiry. The concern is that the inquiry could put 50,000 British jobs at risk.

Besides the obvious ethical dilemma of possibly condoning corruption to save jobs, other questions also come to mind. Does the supply of billions of pounds of weaponry to Saudi Arabia, by no means a democracy, really extend the cause of world peace? What will it do with its existing weapons? If 50,000 jobs are tied to supplying arms to Saudi Arabia, how many other British jobs are there involved in supplying other countries with sophisticated means of mass killing?

Echoes of the same concerns are found in news that Boeing, one of the largest defence contractors in the United States is seeking orders from India for the supply of fifteen billion dollars' worth of military hardware. And that India, the land of Mahatma Gandhi, now spends twice as much as China on arms.

If we extend this glimpse at just two participants in major arms deals, and recognise that other exporters of arms include China, India, Russia and France, as well as many less scrupulous nations, we can easily understand why we live in a world awash with arms, which all too easily seep into and fuel horrendous regional conflicts, often in the poorest parts of the world.

What particularly concerns me is that attitudes to defence and the notion of friendly and unfriendly countries have hardly changed in the last fifty years, although the nature of threats to peace and security are now quite different. Today the threat to security is not so much from nation states as from smaller groups exploiting a real or perceived sense of injustice, and there is now an urgent need to be more subtle and focussed in our response.

The Sikh Gurus warned that the way to peace lay not in simply wishing it or even praying for peace with elaborate rituals to please God, but by tackling underlying injustice and standing up to the arrogant pursuit of power, with as a last resort, the minimal use of force. Tying world economies to the mass production, sale and resale of ever more sophisticated weapons cannot help in this

12 December 2006

Treating Symptoms Rather than Underlying Causes

Yesterday's report by the Social Justice Policy Group for the Conservative Party, sees family breakdown as the cause of many of today's social ills. Impressive statistics show that the risk to children of couples falling apart is far greater among cohabiting couples than married ones, with half of cohabiting relationships breaking up before their child is five. It also shows that children from broken homes are far more likely to leave school with little education and fewer job opportunities. I think it would be wrong to dismiss such findings with cries of 'not back to basics again'.

The most widely reported way of strengthening the family unit has been a reference to tax incentives for married couples. As a Sikh, I find this disappointing, and feel that monetary incentives will do little to combat the underlying social malaise: an increasing selfishness that blinds us to wider responsibilities. In the Sikh marriage service, a married couple are required to see themselves, not so much as individuals, but as a team of equals in mutual support, and in joint care and commitment, not only to the family, but also to wider society.

Tinkering with tax incentives is, to me yet another example of the current trend in modern society of looking for cures to social ills through the wrong end of a telescope. For instance, concern over increasing crime is met by 'let's build more prisons'. The problem of increasing shoplifting to fund drug habits is met by a call to reduce this by handing out free drugs. Problems of binge drinking? Change licensing hours to stagger the incidence of drunken or loutish behaviour.

Let's extend this line of thinking to little junior who greets visitors to the house by kicking them in the shins. Solution: issue said visitors with shin pads as they enter the front door.

This constant looking at superficial remedies, rather than underlying causes reminds me of my own do-it-yourself efforts. When I get in a mess, it's then and only then that I turn to the instructions. In seeking stability in relationships, we need to look beyond current emphasis on the importance of the individual, to our different books of instructions, which like Sikh scriptures remind us of a need to look beyond ourselves to the needs of the family and, through such commitment, to the wellbeing of wider society.

27 February 2007

Every Child Matters

Later this morning I'll be going to a conference organised by the Qualification and Curriculum Authority, the QCA, on changes that are needed to the National Curriculum to fine tune it to the fast-changing world of the twenty-first century.

The theme of the Conference is 'every child matters'; that the education system must meet the needs of every child irrespective of disability, or social or cultural background. The aim is not only to equip children to earn a decent livelihood, but also to help them develop a sense of self-esteem and become responsible members of society. It's a timely initiative, particularly in light of the alarming rise in youth gun crime, and statistics showing children in this country are bottom of the European league in their sense of self-esteem and wellbeing.

Can our schools meet the challenge? To me the answer is not without help from the rest of us, particularly parents. Parenting isn't easy and particularly difficult for single parents who may themselves require support. But we still have to recognise that children spend more time out of school than in it, and the importance of good role models and giving time to children cannot be overstressed.

The aims of the QCA initiative, are strikingly similar to those of our different faiths in trying to move us to more ethical and responsible behaviour. The Sikh Gurus advised us to start the day by reflecting on uplifting teachings in our holy scriptures, the Guru Granth Sahib, and to keep these to the fore in all we do. At the same time, they reminded us of the importance of looking to the needs of others.

I thought of this when I was volunteered to look after my six-year-old granddaughter Harleen for half a day during the half-term break. When my son-in-law came to rescue me a few hours later, I was lying on the floor having my first ever ballet lesson, repeating 'good toes up, bad toes down', with my teacher smiling indulgently when I got it wrong! She was clearly having the time of her life. But she wasn't the only gainer. Giving time to children broadens our own vision and helps us see life in all its fullness and wonder.

Today, it has become distinctly old fashioned to say, it's better to give than receive; but it beats a sad pandering to ourselves, and it's a sure way to move to more responsible living, and help our children do the same.

6 March 2007

Rules of Engagement

Last weekend saw the Sikh festival of Hola. It's a variant of the Hindu festival of Holi, in which people joyously throw coloured water on each other to celebrate the coming of spring. But Sikhs, being Sikhs, do things more robustly and use Hola, the day after Holi, for mock sword fights, archery contests, displays of martial arts and colourful processions.

The festival of Hola began at a time when the infant Sikh community was constantly under siege from both the Mughal rulers and the Hindu Hill Rajas who saw the egalitarian beliefs of the Sikhs as a threat to the caste system and to continuing power.

Over the years Sikhs have developed a highly sophisticated system of checks and balances to ensure that their response to threat or attack was always just and proportionate. Force should only be used as a last resort, and that it should be the minimum required to redress injustice. There is also the requirement that force should never be used for personal or political gain, and that non-combatants, particularly women, should always be treated with dignity and respect.

Today many of these ground rules are routinely ignored, in conflicts across the world with a response to real or perceived threat being considered in narrow military terms with glib talk of collateral damage and pre-emptive strikes. It is bad enough when such remarks come from the military or politicians. But over the weekend, in a newspaper article on the ethics of just war, a leading Anglican Bishop suggests that a pre-emptive strike against Iran might, in certain circumstances, be justified. Such a suggestion must cause us to take serious note.

What really bothers me about a lot of such talk, is the underlying assumption that we in the West are morally superior to others, and that we have a God given right to act in such ways. At the end of the very same spectrum, suicide bombers share the same certainty of belief.

For me, pre-emptive strikes meet none of the criteria mentioned earlier, and, as commentator on this programme yesterday, observed, belligerent noises from the West simply give added support to a perverse leadership in Iran. We have to remember that many Iranians oppose the direction being taken by the present Iranian government.

Religious teachings on criteria for the use of force should be an important brake on suspicion, resentment and anger that propel us to questionable conflict; a brake that is particularly necessary in the powder keg that is the Middle East.

13 March 2007

Looking Beyond Superficial Difference

Yesterday's Commonwealth Service in Westminster Abbey had as its theme, 'Respecting Difference, Promoting Understanding'. The Bollywood actress, Shilpa Shetty, was there to speak about her experience of living with difference. More a bit player, I was invited to give a brief response.

Miss Shetty spoke movingly about her experience of growing up in multicultural Mumbai, with its different religions and cultures. She referred in passing, to her time in 'Celebrity Big Brother', arguing that despite negative experiences, we all have to learn to live with difference.

Although subjected to crude comments about her ethnicity and culture, Miss Shetty has consistently refused to attribute her ordeal to racism. I can understand why. Racism is an overworked and emotive word used to describe a broad range of behaviour. At one end, we have comments that though hurtful, are simply rooted in ignorance or insensitivity, like the 'poppadum' type name calling experienced by Miss Shetty. For Sikhs, it's having the turban compared to a bandage with remarks like 'hope your head gets better soon'. To my mind the best response to such silly comments, is a slightly thicker than average skin and good sense of humour.

Our different religions, and the experience of recent history, remind us of how ignorance and petty prejudice, relatively harmless in themselves, can all too easily be manipulated by unscrupulous people in a way that leads to fear, hatred and active violence.

Her Majesty the Queen referred to this in her address, in which she spoke of a 'difficult and divided world' in which we need to look beyond simply living with difference, to respecting and understanding it. It's a sentiment common to most religious teachings. Today there is an urgent need for us to look beyond superficial difference to, as the Sikh Gurus put it, a recognition of the overriding oneness of our human family, and our obligations to it.

When Guru Tegh Bahadur, our ninth Guru, gave his life defending the right to freedom of worship of another community, the Hindus, in the face of persecution by the Mughal rulers, he poignantly reminded us of the need to stand up for the rights of others. It takes courage, but for true community cohesion, we need to look well beyond mute tolerance, and bring this higher vision of respect for difference to the fore in schools, the workplace and in all we do.

28 May 2007

Playing with the Building Blocks of Life

Genetic research is always in the news these days, and the weekend papers were full of it with two very different stories.

The first concerned news of a new 'trawling technique' to identify rogue genes that cause inherited cancers. An exciting discovery that could in ten to fifteen years' time, lead to a full screening programme. The second item, much further down my list of useful research, was the news from New Zealand that scientists are trying to breed cows that can produce skimmed milk; not earth-shattering news for people in India who have long complained about the skimmed quality of milk from cows in the sub-continent.

The ethics of altering the physical characteristics of animals, or limiting their space to move, to suit our tastes and fads, and desire for cheap food, has always bothered me. Poultry cooped up in a way in which they can hardly move, constantly pecking at each other to relieve the boredom and tedium of life, or cattle so heavy that they can hardly stand; and now cows being bred to give skimmed milk. Next, we'll probably get chocolate or strawberry flavoured milk straight from the cow! I'm sure that calves won't be too happy with their enforced slimming regime and we'll probably end up boosting their diet with added nutrients.

Science has always been central to our quest for a better life, but it can also take us in questionable ethical directions. Perhaps more so in genetic research than in any other field of science. While most of us welcome the use of genetic research to conquer life destroying conditions like Alzheimer's disease, there are real concerns over research that simply panders to what I see as shallow want, like babies with blue eyes and other must haves. We also need to remember that despite impressive research, we still have little knowledge of the effects of the interaction of genes on each other, or the effect on genes of environmental factors like pollution.

Sikh teachings remind us that, nature, including all forms of life, reflects God himself and we have a responsibility to cherish it. We are reminded that all human behaviour, including scientific research carries either gurmukh (positive or uplifting) or manmukh (negative or demeaning) potential. We need to constantly bear this in mind in deciding where and how far to go in playing with the very building blocks of life itself.

5 June 2007

Danger of Generalisation in Confronting Prejudice

A few days ago, I was reading a story to my little granddaughter about a kind and pretty mermaid who was constantly teased and bullied by other mermaids because she had red hair. Such stories, including that of the ugly duckling, are written to teach children about the absurdities of prejudice.

But we don't learn too easily! The very next morning, I read about the real-life experience of a family from Newcastle on Tyne, who fled two homes because of constant taunting about their red hair. All too often, others receive similar treatment because of colour of skin, or other difference.

It reminds me of distant school days in Sutton Coldfield, where four Singh brothers were the only non-whites in a school of more than six hundred. We were regarded like creatures from another planet. Initially there was a lot of teasing and taunting, but, when the Singh's made up more than half the school boxing team, hostility turned to judicious respect, and warm and enduring friendship.

Today, in our 'love of labelling society', some would describe our treatment as discrimination against Sikhs, just as many learned academics describe the adverse treatment experienced by Muslims as 'Islamophobia'. But the one thing in common in those acting out such discrimination, is that generally, they haven't the faintest idea of either Sikhism or Islam. To my mind, the danger in such labelling is that it shifts the focus from underlying irrational prejudice, to suspicion against whole communities or categories of people, and a response of equally negative 'victimhood'.

The Sikh Gurus saw this danger in the culture clash between India's different religious communities. Guru Gobind Singh, the tenth Guru wrote:

God is in the Hindu Temple, as He is in the Muslim mosque
He is in the Hindu worship as He is in the Muslim prayer
The Hindus and Muslims are all one
Each with the culture of different environments
But all men have the same eyes; the same body
The one Lord made them all.

Prejudice towards others, often has a perversely unifying effect on those showing prejudice, be it in the classroom, or in the adult world against the inadequacies of foreigners. In today's world when we daily rub shoulders with difference, we need to be far more careful in looking beyond superficiality, to what the Guru saw as the essential oneness of our admittedly flawed human family.

12 June 2007

Trafalgar Square Commemoration of Guru Arjan's Martyrdom

Sikhs are about to commemorate one of the most important days in the Sikh calendar: the martyrdom of the fifth Guru, Guru Arjan, who gave his life in promoting understanding and respect between India's religious communities. His martyrdom four centuries ago, is a reminder that religious fanaticism has always been with us.

In Guru Arjan's time, society was totally polarised, with the majority Hindu community subjugated by cruel Mughal conquerors. There was virtually no resistance to forced conversion; only resentment and hatred. To work for inter-religious understanding in those difficult times required exceptional courage and commitment. Guru Arjan possessed both in abundance.

To show his respect for Islam he invited a Muslim saint to lay the foundation stone of the famous Golden Temple, or Darbar Sahib in Amritsar, with its four doors welcoming people from any geographic or spiritual direction. The Guru was also the main compiler of the Sikh holy scriptures, the Guru Granth Sahib, in which he included verses of Hindu and Muslim saints to show different religions often shared similar guidance.

All this proved too much for the bigoted Mughal Emperor. The Guru was arrested and tortured to death in the searing heat of an Indian June. Every year, Sikhs remember the Guru's suffering by heat and thirst by setting up stalls outside homes and gurdwaras to give cool refreshing drinks to passers-by.

Last year was the 400th anniversary of the Guru's martyrdom and British Sikhs decided to involve the wider community. Visitors to Trafalgar Square in London, were astonished to see turbaned Sikhs and senior clerics from other faiths joining together in handing out thousands of free cans of juice and soft drinks to passing tourists. Of course, this example of faiths working happily together never made the national news.

Today, bigotry of belief is still with us. There are real problems of prejudice, misunderstanding and potential terrorism, and we can't afford to be complacent. But constant talk of entirely divided communities simply adds to suspicion and hostility. I personally know of many initiatives by individuals and organisations, in the spirit of those taken by Guru Arjan, that are quietly building bridges of understanding between different communities. Skewed reporting of only doom and gloom makes their task that much harder.

22 August 2007

The Partition of India

I've just got back from holiday to a pile of mail that includes an invitation to a dinner on Friday organised by the Indo-Pakistan Friendship Society. It's to celebrate the sixtieth anniversary of the partition of the sub-continent to form the new states of India and Pakistan.

To me, it's a bit like a couple separated in a bitter and acrimonious divorce getting together to celebrate an anniversary of their parting. In this case the parting cost more than a million lives with millions more, including members of my own family, fleeing homes in which they had lived for generations. Previously friendly neighbours turned on each other in fear and politically induced hate. Overnight, Sikhs found that many of their holiest places of worship, including the birthplace of their founder Guru Nanak, were now in what seemed to be, an alien and hostile land.

On what might be termed the plus side, Britain found a convenient exit strategy to leave a difficult to govern sub-continent, and ageing Congress and Muslim League politicians got the power they had long craved. As India's first Prime Minister, Pandit Nehru wrote in his memoirs, 'if we hadn't taken power at that time, we might not have had another opportunity in <u>our</u> lifetime'.

To me the partition of the sub-continent was one of the most shameful peacetime acts of the twentieth century whose reverberations are still being felt today, as are the fall outs from the arbitrary division of other lands in the cause of political expediency.

Even worse is the argument used to justify partitioning countries: that people of different religions cannot live peacefully together. The actual thrust of religious teachings is in the very opposite direction of showing respect to others. In the parable of the Good Samaritan, Jesus reminded Jews of the goodness that can be found in neighbouring communities. The Sikh Holy Scriptures, the Guru Granth Sahib includes uplifting writings of Hindu and Muslim saints to illustrate the same truth, and Guru Gobind Singh taught that we should look beyond labels like Hindu or Muslim or Shia and Sunni to an understanding of the oneness of our human race.

The tragic lesson of history is that people of different faiths all too easily allow themselves to be manipulated by the power hungry or in the cause of political expediency. It's a lesson well worth remembering in looking at today's turmoil in Iraq and other parts of our suffering world.

29 August 2007

Statue of Nelson Mandela in Parliament Square.

Later this morning, I'll be going to the unveiling of the statue of Nelson Mandela in Parliament Square. We all have our heroes. People who inspire and give a lead to us lesser- mortals. For me, Nelson Mandela has long been such a person on a number of scores, the most important of which, has been his readiness to forgive and work with those responsible for his twenty-seven years of imprisonment.

In a famous speech at his trial he courageously spoke of the lack of human dignity experienced by Africans and, in a short and memorable sentence, challenged the iniquity of apartheid with the words, 'white supremacy implies black inferiority'. Words strikingly reminiscent of a verse by Kabir, a non-Sikh some of whose writings are included in Sikh Scriptures because they parallel the Guru's teachings on the equality of all human beings.

Addressing Brahmins, a supposed higher caste, Kabir cuttingly writes:

What makes you a Brahmin, and me a mere untouchable
If blood runs in my veins, does milk flow in yours?

After more than a quarter of a century in prison, it's easy to be vindictive, but Nelson Mandela's greatness is that he has never allowed personal suffering to stand in the way of a determination to ensure that all people, black and white, in South Africa enjoy equal treatment and opportunities. But for his lead, South Africa could easily have descended to the horror and turmoil of its neighbour Zimbabwe and other African nations.

In his readiness to forgive, Nelson Mandela reminds me of Mahatma Gandhi, whose statue is not too far away in nearby Tavistock Square. He also shares something of the impish sense of humour of Gandhi, as shown when Archbishop Tuto jokingly criticised Mandela's taste in shirts. Back came the laughing retort, that's rich coming from a man who goes around wearing a skirt!

Sikh teachings state that it's not who we are, or what religion we belong to, but what we do in our lives that is all important. Today's honouring of Nelson Mandela's commitment to human rights reflects the same sentiment, and to me, is a mark of a mature and tolerant society; something worth reflecting on at a time of self-flagellation over social issues like youth crime. Yes, we have a lot to do, but in tolerance and recognising the worth of others, I believe we have much to teach the rest of the world.

5 September 2007

Combatting a Negative Image of Religion

Religion has come in for a bit of a hammering in the last few days. According to an opinion poll published in the Sunday Times, nearly half of the people in this country feel that religion is harmful. And Guardian journalist Polly Toynbee, the newly appointed President of the British Humanist Association, speaking on the BBC Sunday Programme, expressed anger at the influence of religion on public life.

It's all pretty strong stuff, but I believe there's reason for the unease. The track record of religion in power or authority is not very good. It's been more about preserving or extending power than working for a just and peaceful society. Unthinking allegiance to power structures rather than teachings has often led, and still leads, followers to behave like fanatical supporters of a football team, bent on vocalising their inherent superiority.

The problem is that ethical teachings of religion are easy to state but extremely difficult to live by. It's much easier to believe that we are simply the best and God is on our side, no matter what we do. As for the actual teachings of religion, we put them in ornate books; and set them to beautiful music. We build and adorn beautiful places of worship and engage in rituals to please God. It's all a bit silly really. As Sikh Scriptures remind us, God the creator of infinite universes and all that exists, is hardly likely to be impressed by such shallow flattery.

The Sikh Gurus were fully aware of the danger of the religion falling into the hands of those who put power before principle, so they decreed that the Sikh faith should have no priests, no hierarchy of religious leadership and no power structure, only the abiding guidance of the Sikh scriptures.

Like some teachings of other religions, our Scriptures remind us of core values for responsible living: to look beyond self to the needs of others; to work for social justice, to look after the weak and vulnerable, to put principle before expediency and to stand up to injustice whatever the cost.

Sadly, the word 'religion' today has been debased almost beyond repair, but I'm sure if an opinion poll were to ask if such values should influence public debate as well as our individual lives, the response, even from those who say they have no time for religion, would be far more positive.

16 October 2007

Looking Beyond Bland Declarations of Cooperation Between Faiths

The recent letter sent by Muslim clerics to Christian leaders on the need for greater cooperation to avoid conflict between their followers, was both positive and welcome. But I have doubts about what this well-meaning initiative will really achieve. At best, Christian leaders will respond with similar sentiments, leading perhaps to a common statement on the need for continuing cooperation.

The problem, recognised by most of us, is that it's often easier to talk to moderates in other faiths than to hotheads in one's own; people who continually preach superiority, with a warped logic that justifies changing the ways of others, by force if necessary. And it's not only religious extremists who think in this way; it also carries into the language of politics with slogans like 'those not with us are against us'.

While it's important to emphasize commonalities, I believe it's not quite enough. Focussing on the uncontroversial can give a false sense of progress that papers over seemingly irreconcilable, doctrinal differences that are all-too-easily manipulated to promote active hatred. Given such difficulties, we need to move further and examine the underlying obstacles to fuller dialogue.

From a Sikh perspective, the biggest challenges to active cooperation between faiths are the conflicting claims of superiority of belief and special relationships with God. Today, we urgently need to find ways of tackling rigid stances on dogma that invite conflict. We all have the right to believe what we like, but in today's climate, is it really helpful to push our opinions on others?

It was in response to such conflicting claims of superiority of belief by Hindus and Muslims that Guru Nanak stated that the one God of us all, the Creator of all that exists, is hardly likely to be interested in our different religious labels, but, in what we do. The Guru also taught:

Religion is not simply about mere talk
Those who look on all alike, and consider all as equals
Are truly religious

Well that's a Sikh view of religious difference, and of course it doesn't have to be accepted by others. But to my mind it does help us to focus on the almost forgotten role of all our different religions: namely to make the world a better and a fairer place; and, in the process, make ourselves better human beings.

23 October 2007

Why Ten Gurus?

It's sometimes said that whenever we humans get in real trouble, God sends a prophet or messenger to help sort us out and put us back on an ethical track.

When God looked at the Punjab in the middle of the fifteenth century, He saw people immersed in ritual who had lost all sense of self-esteem; people who looked the other way as their wives and daughters were carried off to captivity in frequent invasions from the north, rumour has it, God said: 'one prophet won't be enough for this lot; I'll send ten!' And, so it came to pass that Sikhism had nine spiritual successors to the founder of the faith, Guru Nanak.

A more earth-bound reason for Guru Nanak's nine successors, lies in the wisdom and astuteness of Guru Nanak. He realised that it was relatively easy to set out simple principles of ethical and responsible living, but far far harder to change human behaviour to challenge injustice, and work for a fairer society. So the Guru started a system of succession to show that the teachings of Sikhism, with their emphasis on justice and compassion were a practical way of life in different social and political climates. The task of the successor Gurus was to protect and nurture Sikh teachings until they had taken root in popular psyche.

This week, Sikhs throughout the world are celebrating the anniversary of the tenth Guru, Guru Gobind Singh's declaration in 1708 that the mission had succeeded and the community was now mature enough to stand on its own. He declared that in future the Guru Granth Sahib, the book containing the teachings of the Gurus should be regarded as the eternal Guru of the Sikhs.

Unfortunately, some of us take this too literally and place greater emphasis on looking after and adorning the holy Granth with fine coverings, than looking to the guidance within it. It's much the same with rituals found in other religions that divert us from focussing on actual teachings.

We live in a world that throws up daily reminders of the damage caused by irresponsible and selfish living; global ones like damage to the environment and climate change, and more locally, harm to our social environment as seen in family breakdown, rising crime and a culture of greed. Our different religions give excellent guidance to help us to more responsible living, but unless we follow it, ten times ten Gurus, messengers or prophets, will never be enough.

30 October 2007

Celebrating 40 Years of the Today Programme -Focussing on Priorities

As a Thought for the Day presenter, I'd like to congratulate the Today Programme on behalf of all of us who work on TFTD on this week's fortieth anniversary of presenting news and comment in an attractive and informative way. It's been a huge success.

It's difficult to say which has been the most frequently discussed topic over these years, but the state of the Health Service must be near the top of the list, and, as someone whose father was a GP in Birmingham at the start of the Health Service, I've always had more than a passing interest in the subject.

That's why I was moved by an article I saw in the British Medical Journal over the weekend. It was by a London GP Iona Heath. In it she warns that the new system of payments to GP practices encourages them to think of themselves as 'businesses' working to maximise profits for the partners running the surgery, often to the detriment of patient care and the career development of lower paid salaried doctors.

Her views, backed by impressive statistics, make compulsive reading and will sharpen debate on how far we should go in looking at the Health Service and other public services as businesses that in her words leave little room for altruism to flourish.

Sadly, it's not only in health care that narrow pursuit of profit distorts and skews life. We see it in sport in the buying and selling of both clubs and players; we see it in cheaply produced media programmes that frequently passes for entertainment, and we see it in many other walks of life.

Guru Nanak was never very impressed with the pursuit of profit for its own sake. Asked by his businessman father to invest money for a good return on capital, he spent it looking to the sick and hungry. Invited by a rich businessman to stay with him on one of his travels, he declined and instead stayed with a poor carpenter.

Sikh teachings argue that it is important for us to live positively, working and earning by honest effort. But, like teachings of other religions, Sikhism reminds us to be wary of the blind pursuit of wealth for its own sake. In the end the only real value of money is the way we use it to help others. It's a message that's doubly important to today's times in which greed has not only become such a powerful motivator, but also a widely accepted way of life.

23 January 2008

The UN Security Council

In his visit to India earlier this week, Prime Minister Gordon Brown was urged to back India's bid to become a permanent member of the Security Council. A perfectly reasonable aspiration.

Permanent membership would undoubtedly give India real clout in international affairs, but, with Germany, Brazil and Japan also pressing for similar status, it's not a bad time to pause and reflect on the role of this elite and privileged body, formed in response to the devastation of the second world war; more than half a century ago.

At that time, Security Council membership was understandably based on military strength in the belief, or hope, that the strong would work together to protect the weak. As we know, it hasn't always worked that way, with the veto being used again and again simply to protect regional and factional loyalties.

In looking to today's role for this lead peace-keeping body, I am reminded of the lines of an English hymn:

New occasions teach new duties, time makes ancient good uncouth
They must upwards still and onwards, who would keep abreast with truth

The lines remind us that in looking to the future, we should not be too rooted to the past. Today's new political realities and challenges, question the very concept of a permanent few deciding on right or wrong, often through a lens of vested interests

Guru Ram Dass, the fourth Guru of the Sikhs warned us of the danger of looking to so-called 'strategic interests' in furthering global peace. He criticised all alliances made for worldly gain and taught the alliances worth making were those made the pursuit of equality, truth and justice.

The essence of the Guru's message was that society can only make real progress if it remains true to ethical teachings. This was also the message of the former Soviet Union dissident Andrei Sakharov who, at risk to his own life declared that for real progress in peace and human rights we must look beyond short-term alliances and be even-handed in our political dealings.

The Prime Minister rightly suggested that relations with India should be based on an equal partnership. Working together, both countries are well placed to lobby for necessary changes to make the Security Council and similar bodies more open, more democratic and a greater force for world peace.

30 January 2008

Decluttering Religion

Recent stories of people suddenly finding religion to get their children into faith schools tend to mask a very real concern in many religions over dwindling attendance in places of worship. There are inevitable calls to make religion more flexible and more attractive to needs and fashions of modern society.

Sikhs are by no way immune to such pressures. Last Sunday I attended a meeting in South London where some, seeking to make the religion more attractive argued that the Sikh marriage service should be open to include marriages between Sikhs and non-Sikhs. While there is nothing to stop Sikhs marrying outside their faith or vice versa, holding such a marriage in a Sikh place of worship becomes a bit of a charade when the service includes vows to be true to the teachings of Sikhism. Reasons advanced for change include: the bride or grooms family want it, or the phone call I received from a person of another faith wanting to get married in a Sikh service. I asked if he wanted to follow Sikh teachings and he said no, it's just more colourful.

Despite the flimsiness of some arguments for change, it is true that religion has lost relevance for some people, who see it as a collection of meaningless rituals, rather than necessary ethical guidance. Today's critics are not alone in such thinking. Guru Nanak, the founder of Sikhism was appalled at the rituals and customs that passed for religion on the sub-continent some 500 years ago. He wrote:

'All such rituals: pilgrimages penances and austerities are not worth even a grain of sesame seed if they don't move us to more godly and responsible living. They are simply chains of the mind'.

His observations are still relevant. Today there is a lot of clutter of dated and questionable social and cultural customs that have attached themselves to religion, which seem to arouse more loyalties and passion than underlying ethical teachings, and I believe it would benefit the image of religion if we did a bit of spring cleaning of outmoded and unnecessary practices.

At the same time, we have to remember that true religion is not a commodity, like toothpaste or a breakfast cereal, to be packaged to increase consumer demand. Its aim is to change human behaviour towards more responsible living; something more relevant than ever in today's interdependent world.

25 March 2008

Genetic Research

Strong criticism of the Human Fertilization and Embryology Bill by Catholic Bishops has reinforced a dilemma of conscience felt by some MPs.

I served on the BMA Medical Ethics Committee for a number of years and found discussion on genetic research unusually complex and taxing. It's like walking in an ethical minefield, blindfolded! Genetic research holds immense possibilities of conquering long feared ailments, but there can be unforeseen dangers in playing with the very building blocks of life.

What is particularly concerning about the Bill's proposals to allow the creation of part human and part animal embryos is, that while it may help in combating illnesses like multiple sclerosis or motor neurone disease, it also opens the door for research that could, particularly if used by the less scrupulous, significantly change what it means to be human.

There is also the fear that over the years, in the interest of life enhancement, we have been inching away from a previously accepted view of the sanctity of human life. If for example, the research now being contemplated had been conducted by Hitler's scientists in the 1940s, it would in all probability have been universally condemned.

Medical advances over the years have imperceptibly conditioned us to accepting that the means sometimes justifies the end, but how far do we want to go in this questionable direction? Our different religions give us some guidance on the importance of human life. Sikhs are taught that it's not how long we live, but what we do to help others that's important. And this includes our human duty to help the sick and infirm, as Guru Harkishan poignantly reminded us when he lost his life helping smallpox sufferers in Delhi.

While it's important to try to eradicate debilitating disease, we have a parallel responsibility to ensure that this is not at the cost of demeaning human life in general. Looked at in this way, those involved in such decisions must turn to individual conscience.

The words of the poet James Russell Lowell, come to mind:

We owe allegiance to the State, but deeper, truer more
To the sympathies that God has set within our spirit's core.

1 April 2008

Forget the bottled water and go straight to the well.

'Forget the bottled water and go straight to the well'. These words of Pope Benedict suggest that we shouldn't place too much store on distilled and often skewed religious writing and preaching but should go back to the source teachings.

His advice was quoted at a Vatican Education Conference last week, on the need for greater dialogue with those of different faiths to which I had been invited. The quote struck an immediate responsive chord. A number of the learned contributions seemed to me, to miss the declared aim of the conference of understanding, and rejoicing in what different communities hold in common and respecting and reconciling areas of difference. Despite this, the conference did show people in Europe are becoming increasingly alert to the challenges of living together with different cultures.

In Britain, we rightly pride ourselves on our progress in understanding and respecting the communities around us. But, in my view, and that of some other minority faiths, since 9/11 and the London bombings, we seem to have lost our sense of focus. Concerns over the activities of a small core of Muslim extremists, and an understandable wish not to offend the Muslim majority have pushed the need to understand our different faiths and cultures to the back burner. Earlier initiatives on greater understanding have given way to new thinking, based on the questionable premise that all faith communities are isolated, and there is an underlying need, in the jargon of the day, to build bridges and connect communities. Bridges from where to where? The Sikh community, for example, gets on fine with those of other faiths or none, and this year celebrates the 100th anniversary of the opening of the first gurdwara in Britain in London's Shepherd's Bush with friends from other faiths.

What worries me about political and academic maneuverings to curb extremist activity in one religious community, is the implicit suggestion that similar problems exist in all minority faiths. It's true that religion can be manipulated and packaged with dangerous rhetoric, but, as Pope Benedict observed, the best way to counter this is to go back to source teachings. The Sermon on the Mount or Sikh teachings on equality and justice, and similar teachings in other faiths cannot be open to misunderstanding and focusing on these and other values we hold in common is in my view, a sure way to true community cohesion.

8 April 2008

Symbols of Commitment

In a few days Sikhs will begin celebrating the spring festival of Baisakhi. It's a joyous time, recalling an occasion when, in 1699, Guru Gobind Singh, the last of the founding Gurus, tested Sikhs for their commitment to living up to the teachings of their faith without further living Gurus. To the Guru's joy Sikhs came through the test with flying colours. Our turban and visible identity are symbols of this commitment.

There is however a clear paradox. Identity generally looks to difference, but one of the most important teachings of Sikhism that will be heard again and again on Baisakhi is that there are no real differences between members of our one human family. Guru Gobind Singh taught:

Manas ki jath saab ek he Pachanbo
Recognize the oneness of the human race.
Looking at the exclusive and divisive claims of different religions he wrote:

Some call themselves Hindus; others call themselves Muslim
Among these are the Shia, there are the Sunnis also,
And yet man is of one race in all the world.
All have the same form; all have the same soul.

I think it's worth reflecting on these sentiments at a time of increasing pressures of globalization and a blurring of previously held attachments. We see it in repeated attempts to define British identity, and I see it in constant complaints of those from the subcontinent that 'our children are losing their culture and values'. What we forget is that culture and ideas of national identity are constantly changing.

A less justifiable but common way of reinforcing common identity is to look in a negative way at those we consider different. Looking down on 'them' is a sure way of strengthening 'our' unity. We see it in jokes about foreigners or those of different faiths. It takes a more serious form in unity based on manufactured hatred of whole communities as occurred in during the Holocaust, and sadly, many times since.

To me, in our increasingly interdependent world we can no longer afford the luxury of supposed unique identities that derives their strength and cohesion on the supposed inferiority of others, or a righteous belief that often pervades religion that we alone have the whole truth.

We live in a world of shared problems of global warming, scarce resources and fragile economies. We can only solve these by looking beyond a false mirage of difference, and, as the Guru reminded us, recognizing our common humanity and shared destiny.

23 June 2008

Empire Windrush

For centuries, Christianity has played a central role in the history and culture of Britain, and this should be recognised in <u>any</u> discussion on the shape and direction of British society. It's true, that at times, there have been, and continue to be, conflicts between the different strands of Christianity, but these are in the nature of family feuds, with shared history and culture providing necessary social cohesion.

Sixty years ago, this month, all this changed, when the Empire Windrush arrived at Tilbury with some 500 Jamaicans, mostly ex-servicemen seeking a new life in Britain. This was quickly followed by others with quite different religions and cultures, seeking new work opportunities. The challenge, then and now, was how to find a new equilibrium of trust and respect to prevent ignorance, suspicion and prejudice harming community cohesion.

A similar challenge existed on the subcontinent of India at the time of the fifth Guru, Guru Arjan, whose martyrdom, some four centuries ago, Sikhs have been commemorating this past week. Perhaps we can usefully look at, and possibly learn something from the history of those times to add perspective to meeting present day challenges.

Before Muslim incursions and settlement, most people in India also shared a generally common history with a bit of a superior attitude to the rest of the world. The conquering Muslims were considered barbarians and the Muslim invaders were equally dismissive of the majority Hindu population.

It was against this background that the Sikh Gurus taught the importance of respect between different religions and cultures. Guru Arjan asked a Muslim saint Mia Mir to lay the foundation stone of the Golden Temple to show his respect for the followers of Islam. He also added verses of Hindu and Muslim saints in the Sikh Holy scriptures the Guru Granth Sahib, where these were in line with Sikh teachings, to show no one faith has a monopoly of truth.

In his own compositions he wrote of the importance of recognizing the same one God of us all, who is both, Allah and Ram, and God and Jehovah; the Creator of all that exists. He also emphasised the Sikh teaching of the equality of all human beings.

Today, respect for beliefs of others, and recognition that we are all members of one human family, remain twin pillars for harmony in our increasingly diverse society.

1 July 2008

Sixtieth Anniversary of the Start of the National Health Service

Last Sunday, the actor Richard Briars, speaking on Radio 4, made a moving plea for help for those who are both blind and deaf. The appeal was to help people, living in a fearsome existence of silence and darkness to purchase vibrating smoke alarms and similar devices to help them cope with the hazards of everyday life. Such appeals beg the question why can't we all pay a little more in taxes to meet such basic human need?

This week we are celebrating the sixtieth anniversary of the start of the National Health Service that was created to do just this by the provision of health care that was equally available to all whatever their means. Sixty years on, significant increases in funding are being outpaced by expensive new treatments and the retirement from economic activity of those born in the post war baby boom. New initiatives are clearly required to meet growing demand.

Yesterday's announcement of new proposals to improve standards of patient care and make clinically appropriate drugs equally available to all, are welcome steps to fairer and more effective provision, but these have to be complimented by additional savings. Improving efficiency can help, but there is concern among doctors that new initiatives like replacing traditional surgeries with larger polyclinics could endanger the 'family doctor concept' of knowing and helping the patient to better all-round health, rather than impersonally treating isolated symptoms.

Sikh teachings, like those of other religions remind us of the need to extend this holistic approach to looking to the health of not only the individual but the family and society in general. Prevention is better than cure and it has been estimated for example, that a pound spent on a child's health could save eight pounds in later life.

The Gurus also reminded us that a healthy personal lifestyle and active concern for those around us are essential to personal and wider wellbeing.

We can't do much about the cost of health care but can significantly reduce need, by moving away from today's unhealthy obsession with pandering to self 'because we're worth it', to looking to what Sikhs call 'seva', or active concern for those around us, particularly for the lonely and disadvantaged. Sikh teachings remind us that looking to the needs of others gives us a more balanced perspective on our own lives as well as benefiting society as a whole and it's cost effective!

8 July 2008

Continuing Antics of the Human Race,

A few years ago, I was asked to comment on a TV programme on 'what God thinks of us'. I replied that if God had human emotions, he would be angry and bewildered at the continuing antics of the human race, and doubly determined to keep us away from any truly intelligent life in the vastness of his creation.

I was half joking but continuing widespread disregard for human rights abroad and a sense of despair over self-inflicted social problems here in Britain lend support to my TV suggestion that God is not best pleased about how we on planet Earth conduct ourselves.

We too get upset by human behaviour. The reason for our anger and outrage is that we start from an assumption that decent and responsible living is normal and natural. But Sikh teachings on free will challenge this, recognizing a capacity for irresponsible behaviour in all of us. The Sikh Gurus taught we are free to move in either a positive ethical (or what Sikhs call gurmukh), direction, or in a negative manmukh direction. In the Sikh view, the true purpose of religion is to nudge us in a positive direction of respect for others and more responsible living.

Does this mean that it's only religion that can get us away from our often-self-inflicted problems? Of course not! But it does mean that a well-ordered responsible society does not come about by itself. We all have to work at it. Government and the rule of law, to which we turn when things go wrong, can do no more than curb our worst excesses. Tougher action against violent crime, harsher penalties for drug or alcohol abuse, government guidance on what we eat and what we wastefully throw away can help alleviate some of the symptoms of unthinking behaviour, but they cannot address underlying human weaknesses.

It's here that the ethical teachings of our different faiths should kick in. My fear is this won't happen unless religions focus on the actual teachings of the founders of our different faiths, rather than on petty internal disputes or aggressive claims about their uniqueness or superiority. Today there's a lot of talk of interfaith dialogue, but to me as a Sikh the only dialogue worth having is on how to work together with others, for positive or gurmukh living.

29 September 2008

What are British Values

The Conservative spokesman, Dominic Grieve, has added fresh fuel to the debate on British identity. Quoted in the weekend papers, he makes a withering attack on the way in which, he feels, new cultures are eroding traditional British values. Unfortunately, he does not define these values in detail, or explain how they are being eroded.

The reality behind this debate is that cultural and social norms have never been constant. Having grown up in this country, I see myself as British and look back nostalgically to a time when we were noted for keeping our emotions in check and being modest and self-effacing. Now we have become far more excitable, hugging and kissing like foreigners on the sports field, and far from being sporting losers, we've suddenly changed to winning ways, with hauls of gold medals in the Olympics. Our attitudes and aspirations constantly change with time.

Dominic Grieve is however right in drawing our attention to the danger of rapid social change leading to extremist and intolerant behaviour. We humans are not very good at adjusting to change, and instinctively react to apparent difference in a way that can, and often has in the past, led to active hatred of whole communities. We saw this in the Germany of the '30s. It also occurred in the India of Guru Nanak's day some 500 years ago where religious tensions between the Hindu and Muslim communities frequently resulted in active conflict.

It was against this difficult background that Guru Nanak bravely set out his vision for a just and enlightened society that went beyond race, religion or national boundary. He emphasised the oneness of all humanity, reminding us that the one God of us all, was not interested in the names of our different beliefs and notions of exclusivity, but in our actions; our concern for the weak and disadvantaged, and our tolerance and respect for the beliefs of others. Interestingly, different faiths meeting at Lambeth Palace at the turn of the millennium came up with a similar list of imperatives to carry us forward to a more peaceful twenty-first century.

I believe that instead of looking nostalgically to, what was in reality, an ever-changing past, we in Britain should give a lead to the rest of the world, in embracing and promoting values that stress our common humanity and the need for tolerance and respect for others in an increasingly complex and interdependent world.

7 October 2008

Measures of Success

Continuing turmoil in the world's economic markets and headlines like 'market mayhem' in this morning's papers provide a disturbing reminder of a global financial crisis that just won't go away. While rescue packages may cushion the effects on those with money, they do little to help growing child poverty, the unemployed, or the elderly experiencing increasing difficulties in heating their homes.

It all seems such a mess And yet it's less than twenty years since we rejoiced in the demolition of the Berlin Wall and the triumph of capitalism and free market forces over the freedom-stifling economies of the former Soviet Union. Today we have the capitalist world frantically nationalizing failing banks and financial institutions to avert greater economic collapse, while billionaire oligarchs in Russia flaunt their new-found capitalist wealth.

Greed seems to have become the prime motivator in all economies. Perhaps it was always so, but today, it resonates and grows on itself with more deadly effect in our smaller interdependent world. We blame dodgy financial institutions and greedy speculators, but there would have been no irresponsible lending without some equally irresponsible borrowing that has become the norm rather than the exception.

Ever the optimist, I'm sure that our new National Economic Council and similar bodies and agencies throughout the world will be able to stick the right size sticking plasters on the right places, and the current crisis will eventually subside.

All our different religions have long offered us advice on putting the pursuit of wealth in its proper perspective. As a young man, Guru Nanak was given a sum of money to invest in the city to give a profitable return. To the exasperation of his father, he spent it feeding and clothing the hungry.

On another occasion he upset a rich businessman by refusing his invitation to a banquet and chose instead to stay at the house of a poor carpenter and share his simple food, In the same way we know how Jesus Christ valued the widow's mite above the silver of the rich man.

I believe that we are suffering two separate but related crises; and that beneath the credit crunch, there is a deeper and more serious crisis of values by which we measure success. Something we should tackle with equal determination.

14 October 2008

The Perils of Building a Do-It-Yourself Society

Sikhs throughout the world are preparing to celebrate the 300th anniversary of Gurgaddi, the day when our tenth Guru, Guru Gobind Singh decided that the infant Sikh community was now strong enough to stand on its own without the guidance of further living Gurus.

Many question the need for successor Gurus. After all, key Sikh teachings on the importance of religious tolerance, emphasis on gender equality in our one human family, and a commitment to social justice, were all put forward by the founder of the religion: Guru Nanak.

Guru Nanak was a realist. He wasn't interested in simply putting forward impressive sounding ideals, but in permanently changing attitudes and aspirations of people trapped in the rigidity of caste for whom religion had become ritual and superstition. He saw the difficulty of bringing about real change in a single lifespan and instituted a system of succession. The task of succeeding Gurus was to show the practicality of Sikh teachings in often difficult and dangerous circumstances which cost two of the Gurus their lives.

By the time of the tenth Guru, Sikh teachings had taken strong root, and Guru Gobind Singh gave his followers one final command: – follow the guidance of the Sikh scriptures as you would those of a living Guru. It is command that will be the main focus of our celebrations next week. In lectures and services in gurdwaras we'll be reminded to constantly focus on the instructions for responsible living detailed in our holy scriptures.

But following instructions doesn't come easy to any of us. They seem boring and unnecessary and get in the way of what we want to do. In self-assembly I dive straight in, proud of my DIY skills. But as I step back to admire my handiwork, I find it all skewed and ready to fall apart. Only then do I turn to the book of instructions.

In much the same way, we've become a bit of a clever-clogs society. We don't need old fashioned religion to shape the way we live. Look at what we've achieved without it. Well these last few weeks we've been looking, not in admiration but horror at our attempts to build prosperity on debt and greed. Perhaps it's time for us all to go back to the drawing board and look again at the guidance of our scriptures on our collective responsibilities to wider society.

21 October 2008

Religion and Secular Society Working Together

Yesterday's visit by the Prime Minister to the Christian Organisation, Faithworks, to talk about 'the Role of Faith in Britain' set off predictable alarm bells. The fact that senior figures in other political parties have also addressed the Group, simply adds to the concern of people who believe religion should be kept separate from political life.

Speaking on this programme yesterday, for instance, MP Alice Mahan expressed her fear over proselytising and the promotion of bigotry. I understand what she means, but I'm not sure that secular life is totally free of bigots, and, as for proselytising, politicians are not entirely reticent in drawing attention to the merits of their cause. Of course, religion has its fair share of nutters, but it also has much to offer.

For example, last weekend I attended a fundraising dinner for a proposed Sikh school in Slough; a large donation was made by the local Muslim community. The following day I attended the launch of a sponsored cycle ride at the Neasden Hindu Temple, to help deprived children in Africa, and, such charitable activities are routine in most Sikh gurdwaras. The campaign to make 'Poverty History' is being led by religious communities.

Sikhs see our different religions as guidebooks to help us get the most out of our journey through life. Each lay different stress on things to do, and what to avoid, but the general thrust is toward more responsible and peaceful living. It is for this reason that the Gurus taught that all such guidebooks should be respected. When pressed as to which was the best religion, the Guru responded:

Of all religions the best religion
Is to remember God and work for a fairer and more peaceful world.

Of course, we can get by without religion. We've done it for years, consigning religious teaching to the margins of life. If, all was peace, harmony and responsible living I'd say, let's keep it that way. But, even a glance at our daily paper reminds us of the problems of violent behaviour, unfaithfulness, drug abuse, binge drinking and much else at home, and horrendous conflicts abroad. Surely, we need all the help we can get!

Our different religions teach wholesome values like putting others before self, looking to the needs of the less fortunate and much more. The trick is to welcome these values into daily life, while isolating those who manipulate religious sentiment to promote superiority and hate.

6 January 2009

Looking Beyond the Gloom of Recession and Conflict

As we peep out from our collective hangover of 2008, and take our first glance at the year ahead, it seems that 2009 may not be any better. Many start the year without work, and the threat of redundancy hangs over others.

Sales in shops have an air of desperation, and, looking beyond our personal problems, we see appalling suffering in Gaza following Israeli retaliation for daily rocket attacks. In many parts of Africa, famine and disease continue to take their toll in both man-made and natural disasters. We start the year then with a distinct sense of unease about what might be in store for us and how we should react to new challenges.

For Sikhs the beginning of the New Year coincides with the birthday of our tenth Guru, Guru Gobind Singh which we celebrate this week. In our celebrations we remember the courage of the Guru who devoted his life working for religious tolerance and a fairer society in difficult and dangerous times.

It was a stance that was bitterly opposed by those who believed in the concept of caste, or superior status for some at the expense of others. Sikh teachings on freedom of worship, also drew the anger of the powerful Mughal rulers bent on a policy of forced conversion in Kashmir and other parts of India. In the inevitable clash with authority, the Guru's two elder sons were killed in battle and the younger two were captured and killed.

Despite these personal setbacks, the Guru never wavered in his attitude to other faiths, insisting even in battle, Sikhs should look to the needs of the enemy wounded. The Guru also taught that whatever the setbacks, Sikhs should always maintain a positive mindset, a teaching encapsulated in the words 'chardi kala', optimism in all circumstances.

The Guru also reminded us that over-focusing on the trappings of material wealth, can skew our values and divert us from real priorities. In a famous hymn composed when he was driven into the jungle wilderness, weary and hungry, he composed some memorable lines of how palaces, luxury clothes and other trappings of wealth can be an impediment to true contentment if we don't live true to our principles and values.

It's a powerful teaching that, with a little 'chardi kala', can help us understand and negotiate the many challenges that we all face in the year ahead.

13 January 2009

Prince Harry Uses the Word 'Paki'

The row over Prince Harry's use of the word 'Paki' reminds me of a wonderful cartoon I once saw of a jolly monk saying, 'speak in words that are soft and sweet, for tomorrow you might have to eat them'. I'm sure that as a result of media coverage over his lack of sensitivity, the Prince must have experienced a little indigestion over the weekend. But he's said sorry and should be allowed to move on.

This in no way justifies his use of inappropriate language; a prince of the realm should know better, but extensive media coverage suggesting that the army is the last bastion of racism, is taking things a little too far. The army is a part of wider society in which language is often used to belittle those that are not 'us'. The word heathen, with its clearly negative connotations, was common currency until quite recent times. Its dictionary definition is 'someone who is not a Christian, Moslem or Jew'. So, you can see where that leaves me! Today, some of those papers that scream loudest over the indiscretion of Prince Harry, have at times in the past, like the football world cup, referred to other nations in terms that would make most people squirm.

The word 'Paki' is simply an abbreviation of Pakistani. We consider it offensive because of the way in which it's used to draw negative attention to difference, at a time when we are struggling to provide respect and cohesion in society. The multi-racial nature of modern society means that we need to be much more careful to avoid language that gives undue offence to others.

The real problem though, is not so much with the Prince or the army, but with a general decline in respect and consideration for others. Although overtly racist language is now much less common, a decline in respect for others is all too evident, particularly in relations between parent and child and teachers and pupils.

A couple of years ago, I was asked to do an RE inspection of Guru Nanak School in Hayes. The pupils, from what would be described as a deprived background, were clearly top achievers, and one Ofsted inspector put this down to the Sikh ethos of respect for others prevalent throughout the school, which made teaching much easier.

The Sikh Gurus taught that we harm ourselves by rough and rude language, and Guru Nanak appropriately observes that if we lose by speaking, it's often better to stay silent.

20 January 2009

President Obama Assumes Office

We Sikhs are very democratic. We all consider ourselves all equals, and those who find themselves in authority are given constant instructions by one and all, as to what they must do.

Multiply this a thousand-fold and we get a small measure of the challenges Barak Obama faces today as he assumes office as President of the United States. He begins his term at a time of doubt and uncertainty over conflict in the Middle East and Afghanistan and the response to terrorism. He also faces a global economic crisis that dwarfs anything seen in the last half century.

Today, not only America, but the whole world will be looking to the new President with near impossible hopes and expectations. The cartoonists capture this mood perfectly, with the one Sunday paper showing Barak Obama as superman flying through the air holding the world aloft, in the palms of his hands.

The new President also face the reality of powerful lobbying groups that have long dominated the American scene, trying to pull him in different directions, and there will be the constraining influence of long-established policies at home and abroad. The challenge for the President will be to react to these in a way that is consistent with his eloquent promises of a more prosperous America and a fairer world order.

I see hope in the inspiration that he will derive from the rich diversity of his upbringing in different cultures. This broader vision will be of immense help in harnessing the energies of people of different faiths to work together for the common good, an important thrust of Sikh teachings. As Guru Nanak reminds us:

Religion consists not of mere Talk but service to those around us
Those that look on all alike and consider all as equals are truly religious.

There are encouraging signs that Barak Obama is moving in this direction. He has already had meetings with different Christian denominations and people of other faiths, and it has been reported that he will visit a Muslim country within his first one hundred days of office.

It won't be easy to change the perception of religion being a cause of conflict, but if Barak Obama succeeds in getting our different faiths working together in this way, he will be tapping an important resource, and his 'yes we can', may well become a reality.

14 April 2009

Baisakhi

Today Sikhs throughout the world are celebrating Baisakhi: a popular spring festival in India. For Sikhs, Baisakhi has added significance as it was the day chosen by Guru Gobind Singh to announce an end to the line of living Gurus and the creation of a new community of equals pledged to live true to the teachings of Sikhism.

The Guru was the last of the nine that followed Guru Nanak. Their task was to show, by the example of their own lives, that it was possible to live true to the teachings of Sikhism, whatever the challenges.

It wasn't easy and two of the Gurus were martyred for their emphasis on religious tolerance, and a third died serving the sick in a smallpox epidemic.

On Baisakhi day in 1699, Guru Gobind Singh decided that the Sikh community was now sufficiently established to stand on its own. He declared there would be no more living Gurus, and that henceforth Sikhs should pledge allegiance to Sikh teachings as contained in our holy scripture, the Guru Granth Sahib, rather than to any individual.

The teachings are clear and unambiguous; belief in one God, the equality of all members of our human family including the full equality of women; respect for other faiths and responsible living with a commitment to redress social and political injustice. In a last moving act of true leadership and humility, the Guru declared that he should no longer be seen as the leader, but as an equal member of the new Sikh community.

It was a rare and inspiring sacrifice of power that underlined a total commitment to Sikh teachings.

I thought of the Guru's disdain for the trappings of power as I listened to a discussion on religious leadership on this week's Sunday programme. We all know that throughout history, those in a position of faith leadership have often succumbed to playing to the baser prejudices of their erstwhile followers. It is a path that can lead, and sadly has led to religions becoming competing factions rather than the inspiring guidance for positive and responsible living, taught by the founders of all our different faiths.

We all have the guidance of our different faiths. If we live true this guidance, each one of us can make a significant contribution to the true purpose of religion: the betterment of the world about us.

21 April 2009

Indian Elections

India's general election, spread over a month is now well under way. The logistics are awesome with 700 million voters, many illiterate, spread over thousands of square miles, often in remote villages with voters sometimes facing the threat of insurgency and terrorism. Whatever the outcome, it is a credit to the people of India that the country has been largely able to stick to democracy since independence.

The election this year coincides with the twenty-fifth anniversary of the highly organized mass killing of thousands of Sikhs throughout the length and breadth of India in the wake of the assassination of the Prime Minister Indira Gandhi. Several Commissions of inquiry subsequently condemned the massacre and named some of those thought to be responsible, but not a single ringleader has ever been brought to justice.

At a recent press conference organized by the Union Home Minister, a young Sikh journalist repeatedly asked why a prominent politician thought to be responsible for incitement to murderous violence in 1984, was again being put forward as the Congress candidate. When the minister refused to answer, the journalist gave vent to his frustration in Iraqi style by lobbing a shoe in the direction of the minister. The shoe missed but made a huge impact on Indian public opinion leading to an official apology for the party's lack of sensitivity and the withdrawal of party support for the candidate Jagdish Tytler. The incident was another reminder of the power of public opinion in the world's largest democracy.

India then, has reason for pride in its democracy, but no matter where we happen to live, the mere placing and counting of votes in a ballot box does not guarantee fair and effective government, human rights or the protection of minorities. We see this today in many countries throughout the world.

The democratic ideal is firmly embedded in Sikh teachings with particular emphasis on what Sikhs call Miri Piri. Miri relates to practical or secular considerations and Piri to attached ethical implications. The Sikh Gurus taught that all of us, particularly those in authority, should look to ethical as well as practical implications in all we do, or fail to do. It is sound advice not only for those involved in distant elections, but for all of us, much closer to home who aspire to see a fairer and more tolerant society.

28 April 2009

Banning Questionable Interrogation Practices

Following his banning of questionable interrogation practices, President Obama has authorized the publication of classified material on their earlier use. He has also indicated that no action should be taken against those involved, in moves clearly intended to draw a line under a difficult past.

But far from bringing closure, his action has sparked an acrimonious debate, with many demanding exemplary action against those responsible, and others, including former Vice President Dick Cheney, angrily asserting that robust interrogation techniques, like water boarding and sleep deprivation, helped safeguard the security of America, and were therefore justified.

Growing up in the aftermath of the Second World War, I used to believe that torture was mainly a thing of the past, only used in more recent times by exceptionally evil people in Nazi Germany. Years later, particularly as a member of an Amnesty International Awards Panel on the reporting of human rights abuse, it became all too clear, that given the slightest veneer of justification, like preserving OUR way of life, ordinary people all over the world can all too easily become torturers and killers.

Our different religions are as one, in saying that which is morally repugnant can never be politically justified. A line from an English hymn puts it perfectly. 'They enslave their children's children who would compromise with sin'. Sadly today, nominal adherents of different religions frequently ignore the uplifting teachings of their faith and unleash atrocities on others, even members of their own faith, in the name of religion. We saw an example of this in last Friday's suicide bombing outside a Shia mosque in Bagdad causing sixty deaths.

The Sikh Gurus taught that ill-treatment of others only takes place when we are persuaded to see them as lesser beings. It was because of this that they criticised all notions of racial difference and emphasised that different religions, are paths to the same one God. As Guru Gobind Singh taught:

God is in the temple as he is in the mosque
All men have the same eyes, the same body
The one Lord made us all.

Sikhs firmly believe that we will continue to enslave our children's children with hate and prejudice, unless we learn to see others, not as lesser beings, but as reflections of our common humanity.

21 July 2009

Age determining Suitability

Fifty-nine-year-old Tom Watson's weekend performance in the Open Golf Championship thrilled us all. Although a missed 8ft putt at the last hole eventually robbed him of victory, it was still a tremendous achievement for a player who won his first Open thirty-two years ago – before some of his fellow competitors were even born. The irony is that if he was a year older, he wouldn't have been eligible to even take part in the tournament.

Tom Watson's performance illustrates the absurdity of rigidly using age to determine fitness for purpose in sport, and in many other walks of life.

In religion, bias has traditionally been in favour of older people. In India, conventional wisdom was that young people were expected to spend their time in education or in domestic life and leave any substantial involvement in religious practice to later in life.

Today the pendulum has swung a bit the other way with young people being courted as an important sector of the commercial market and their involvement sought in all activities. The importance of getting young people involved in religion, is always high on the agenda of faith and inter-faith meetings.

Sikh history and experience however, remind us that age is irrelevant to the true practice of religion. One of the successors of Guru Nanak who did so much to increase the involvement of women in society was more than seventy when he assumed the Guruship, whereas it was the courage of the two young children of Guru Gobind Singh in resisting forced conversion that steeled the resolve of the tiny Sikh community to stand up to the might of the Mughal rulers.

To my mind it's a fallacy to generalize that most young people have no interest in the problems of the world about them. In my talks to schools and colleges I find many acutely concerned about issues like third world poverty; about the way earlier generations have harmed the environment and about the need for a fairer and more compassionate society.

Twice a month, young people from a London gurdwara take food to the homeless in different parts of the city and get involved in other faith driven activities. They may not be too keen on formal worship but share values and priorities that are central to Sikh teachings. They and others like them, together with the ever young like Tom Watson, remind us that we can all achieve much in life, whatever our age.

28 July 2009

Getting Rid of Unnecessary Clutter

In California, of all places, there's a growing movement against unnecessary personal clutter. Many people including Hollywood stars such as Reese Witherspoon and Leonardo DiCaprio have signed up to what is known as, 'the 100 things challenge', which says we should limit our personal possessions to no more than 100 items. Some latitude is allowed, with underwear being collectively considered as one item and shoes, no matter how many pairs, also being counted as a single item.

While many people around the world would consider it the height of luxury to own even a dozen or so personal possessions, most of us would readily confess to buying on impulse and holding on to things we don't really want because one day, they might come in useful. Only a couple of days ago, I finally gave away a virtually unused leather jacket that had been hanging in my wardrobe for years. I'd been persuaded to buy it by my wife and two daughters while on holiday in Kashmir because 'leather things were much cheaper out there', but whenever I tried to wear it back in London, my family would simply dissolve into uncontrollable laughter at my appearance.

Our different religions are as one in constantly reminding us that obsession with unnecessary material possessions hinders our spiritual progress. But what of the clutter we find in the practice and presentation of religion? Over the years religions have accumulated all manner of rituals, customs, and questionable social practices that have little relevance to core belief.

Guru Nanak famously declared that rituals are 'chains of the mind' and he spent much of his life questioning obscure practices that had, over the centuries, grafted themselves on to religion, stifling true teachings. Fortunately for Sikhs, our religion is only some 500 years old and we've had comparatively little time to acquire such clutter but believe me, we are doing our best to catch up!

Today there is an added need to look afresh at religious teachings and discard spurious practices that give sustenance to extremism. Despite millions spent on inter-faith dialogue we haven't got much further than promoting acceptance of often dated customs and practices. A little of the discipline of the '100 things challenge' in discarding such clutter would help provide a clearer view of core beliefs and help true inter-faith understanding.

4 August 2009

Positive Discrimination

The papers are full of Harriet Harman's weekend comments that men and women have different abilities and, because of this, one of the two top posts in her party should always be filled by a woman. It's a curious comment coming from someone who has spent a lifetime campaigning for the equal treatment of both men and women.

It would be foolish to argue that there are absolutely no differences between men and women on attitudes to decision making on different aspects of life. Most of these differences have arisen as a result of generations of discrimination and social conditioning.

In our family, I still retain a central role in decision making, although this has been progressively reduced. When we go out shopping, and my wife and two daughters have narrowed the choice of a dress to say, a red one or a blue one, they turn to me for advice. I sagely pronounce 'the red dress', at which they look at each other, smile and say, 'we'll take the blue one!'

Against this, there are many men who can give good advice on the choice of clothes. In schools and colleges, girls often outperform boys only to find that they are often denied fair employment opportunities. It's the pigeonholing of aptitude on the basis of gender, race or colour that is objectionable.

The Sikh Gurus raised similar concerns over the rigid stratification of Indian society on the basis of caste, with women being placed at the bottom of each caste. Guru Nanak taught that all, men and women, are equal members of our one human family. Men and women from different social backgrounds were encouraged to take part in all walks of life. Women not only worshiped alongside men, but also often led worship. And women played a central role in resisting persecution of the community for its egalitarian ideals. Today, the only Sikh chaplain to the British armed services is a woman, chosen not on the basis of gender, but on ability.

If suitability of a person for high office is, as suggested, to be determined by gender, there is a parallel argument for appointments on the basis of colour, race or disability rather than in selecting the best person for the job in hand. Whatever gloss or spin we put on it, so-called positive discrimination is a bad thing, and I've got the permission of my wife to say so!

27 October 2009

The Trial of Bosnian Serb leader Radovan Karadzic

The trial in The Hague this week of the Bosnian Serb leader Radovan Karadzic will bring to mind one of the worst atrocities seen in Europe since the Second World War. Tens of thousands of Bosnian Muslims had been herded together in the town of Srebrenica by UN peacekeepers. Some 8,000 men and boys were then taken from this supposedly safe haven, tortured and then shot by Serbian militia.

For Sikhs, the trial strikes a resonant chord because of the events that followed in the aftermath of the Indian army attack on the Golden Temple in 1984. It was stormed on the grounds that it was sheltering armed Sikh militants. The attack took place on one of the holiest days in the Sikh calendar with a huge loss of life and the resulting sense of outrage led to the assassination of the Prime Minister, Indira Gandhi by her Sikh bodyguards twenty-five years ago this month.

What happened subsequently has its parallels with Srebrenica. Thousands of Sikhs in Delhi and other large cities were dragged from their homes, beaten and burnt alive. To their credit, many Hindu families sheltered Sikhs risking their own lives; but many of those in authority stood by and watched.

While Sikhs today would like to see a Truth Commission type inquiry, to look at all the events of 1984, including charges of extremism levelled against Sikhs, this in the India of today is unlikely, despite an apology to Sikhs by the present government.

Sikh teachings remind us that though we should learn from history, we should not live in the past but work for a better future. Guru Nanak himself was a witness to barbarities carried out by invading armies and he and successor Gurus though saddened by such savagery, were equally critical of Indian rulers at the time who rather than protect their subjects, themselves abused human rights. The Sikh Gurus lived their teachings, and the ninth Guru, Guru Tegh Bahadur gave his life defending the rights of Hindus, those of a different religion to his own, giving a higher meaning to the concept of tolerance.

The lesson of Srebrenica, the killing of Sikhs in 1984 and similar mass killing of others simply because they have a different faith or culture, is that this will happen again and again until we are all prepared to stand up uncompromisingly for those superficially seen as different.

3 November 2009

Resetting Moral Satnavs

This week Sikhs are celebrating the birthday of Guru Nanak, the founder of the Sikh faith. Celebrations take the form of colourful processions, and services in gurdwaras on Sikh teachings. We will be reminded of the Guru's stress on the equality of all human beings including gender equality, the need for responsible living and a commitment to always stand up against social or political injustice.

While teaching respect for different religions, the Guru was forthright in his criticism of rituals and superstitious practices becoming substitutes for ethical teachings. Some of his observations on religious practice would have been deemed politically incorrect today, but in those more difficult times, they were a breath of fresh air equally welcomed by both Hindus and Muslims. When he died, a Punjabi verse relates how he was acclaimed as both a guru of the Hindus and a pir, or religious leader of the Muslims.

In reflecting on the Guru's teachings, I wonder how he would see today's times. In some ways he'd note that things haven't changed much. Emphasis on rituals still dominates our attitude to religion. We set religious teachings to beautiful music, sing and chant those teachings, but forget to carry them into our daily lives.

The Guru would certainly have welcomed today's tentative steps towards an Arms Trade Treaty, as he would current discussions at Windsor Castle and talks in Copenhagen next month on the threat from global warming. But he would also have warned that grandiose declarations of intent are not enough, unless we also walk the talk.

It doesn't take Guru Nanak, however, to tell us that we've made a bit of a mess of things with our skewed priorities that ignore the consequences of selfish living. We live in a world in which so-called defence industries in wealthier nations help them to grow even richer by exporting the means of mass killing to poorer countries where Kalashnikovs are easier to buy than basic food; a world of undreamt prosperity for some, while tens of millions of others face starvation, made more imminent by the way we have allowed greed to damage our environment.

The Gurus advice to us today, would be that we won't get far on our journey to a fairer world unless we reset our moral satnavs and follow the direction of more responsible living; the underlying message of all our different faiths.

10 November 2009

Hopes for Inter Faith Week

When a building is demolished in a city redevelopment, we see the surrounding streets and structures in a new light. It was, as we were reminded yesterday, the same with the demolition of the Berlin wall when East and West Europe saw each other for the first time for decades, as fellow human beings with similar aspirations and concerns.

On Thursday of this week, some of us will meet at the Queen Elizabeth Conference Centre in London, to launch the first National Inter-Faith week in England and Wales. The idea is to break down barriers of suspicion and prejudice in the hope this will enable us to see sister faiths in a more positive light.

It's a move central to Sikhism. Some 400 years ago, Guru Arjan the fifth Guru of the Sikhs included some Hindu and Muslim verses in our holy scriptures the Guru Granth Sahib, to show that our different faiths, while different in some beliefs and practices, have much in common. In another move, the Guru asked a Muslim saint to lay the foundation stone for the historic Sikh Golden Temple at Amritsar to show Sikh respect for the teachings of Islam.

Unfortunately, history has shown that attempts to increase tolerance and understanding are sometimes met with hostility and persecution. Two of the Sikh Gurus lost their lives in their attempt to build bridges between different faiths.

Today, there are still some who would like to see such barriers maintained and strengthened by claiming an exclusive franchise with God, a God who is on their side, while dismissing others as heathens, infidels or kaffirs. Such people are entitled to their view. My objection is that this is not the best way to win friends and influence people in our shrinking and interdependent world where harmony and respect between our different faiths, and between religions and those in wider society is now more important than ever before.

My hope for Inter-Faith Week is that it will move us from the usual polite exchange of pleasantries, to actually looking to ways of replacing, what I believe to be false barriers of misunderstanding and prejudice that divide our different religions, with sympathetic understanding and true respect for different ways of life. Demolition of false barriers of belief are every bit as important as removing false political teachings that seek to perpetuate political division.

23 February 2010

Déjà Vu on British Values

Tomorrow I'll be going to central London for a meeting on British values. It'll be with a real sense of déjà vu. It's been a recurring theme in both political and religious discussion for many years.

At the start of a new millennium, some of us from different religions, meeting at Lambeth Palace reflected on the century we were leaving behind; a century in which man had killed more of his fellow beings than in the rest of recorded history put together. We debated long and hard about common ethical imperatives necessary to carry us to a more peaceful future and produced a short paper on Shared Values for the New Millennium. Fast forward a few years. Another meeting in Lambeth Palace and an American evangelist speaking on his new idea: the need for common values! For many, the earlier consensus in the very same room had already been forgotten.

The problem is that it's easy, even among people of different faiths, to draw up a common list of ethical imperatives for a fair and just society, but much harder to change our wayward human behaviour. Guru Nanak was acutely aware of this and, as he neared the end of his life, he instituted a system of succession, with the task of the nine successor Gurus being to live his teachings and embed them in the infant Sikh community. It wasn't easy and three of the Gurus lost their lives being true to their ideals.

Today in Britain, we have an added difficulty with some, instead of looking to the shape of future society, wishing to return to a rosy past when we never had today's problems. In a discussion I attended recently on a possible written constitution, two of the essential attributes of Britishness were listed as a 'stiff upper lip and a commitment to orderly queuing!'

The reality is that though change was slower in the past, cultural norms have never been constant, or necessarily good. Today, relationships, commitments, aspirations and, the background and faith of those around us, are now changing at a bewildering rate. We obviously need common values to tackle new social challenges, and ensure community cohesion, justice and peace as we move to an uncertain future. Perhaps we need to dig out, dust down, and look again at the values identified at Lambeth.

I remember one of these being 'tolerance and respect for different ways of life'. It would be top of my list today.

2 March 2010

Murder of Two Sikhs

At a recent conference on 'Religion and the News', I complained that the media always seemed to look to the sensational rather than to objectivity in their coverage of religion. I grumpily suggested that the news we get about religion was often processed information which, like processed food, bears little resemblance to the source material and is simply designed to meet the tastes and prejudices of a targeted audience.

Media reporting about the murder of two Sikhs in different parts of the country have made me think again about such generalizations. The first was the murder of thirty-one-year-old Sukhvinder Singh a few weeks back by two men he chased when he saw them mugging a young woman and stealing her handbag. The media reaction was one of overwhelming sympathy and support. In an item on this programme, a reporter reminded listeners that the young Sikh was probably inspired to help the woman by the teachings of his faith which emphasize helping the weak and vulnerable. An English doctor, moved by the piece, emailed to help pay for the funeral costs of a local hero.

Last weekend, the Times carried a warm two-page tribute to Gurmail Singh, a sixty-three-year-old grandfather who ran a corner shop in a village on the outskirts of Huddersfield. He was stabbed to death by two intruders as they stole from his shop. A local resident was quoted as saying 'he was a wonderful chap who worked really hard but was so gentle and quietly spoken and went out of his way to look after the older people in the village'. The piece took the opportunity to give readers helpful information about the essentials of the Sikh religion.

Sikhs, long used to being virtually ignored by the media, or, with appalling and widespread ignorance, being called Bin Laden and worse because he too wore a turban, have welcomed these reports on Sikh internet sites, as examples of how the media can help combat ignorance on which prejudice festers and thrives. It is a welcome departure from the usual stereotyped reporting on newer faith communities which suggests that religion and extremist violence are one and the same thing. As Sikhs we don't always get it right, but in the Sikh view the essence of true religion is concern and respect for others. Responsible media reporting can, as shown, play an important role in promoting this more balanced image of Sikhs and other religious communities.

9 March 2010

Limiting Personal Freedom

A hospital in East London has introduced a new initiative to limit the amount of alcohol taken by pregnant women in an effort to reduce the danger of serious birth defects caused by excess drinking. A pregnant woman will be urged to have blood alcohol levels tested to give a picture of how much she has to drink while related urine tests could show evidence of occasional binge drinking.

The logic of such testing is faultless, and some midwives have welcomed the scheme. But other voices have expressed concern that it's an unnecessary intrusion into the privacy of responsible mothers-to-be; another example, as they put it, 'of the nanny state curbing the freedom of the majority to tackle an irresponsible minority'. They could have a point. The downside of such measures is that they generally do carry some degree of encroachment on personal freedom.

In some ways the use of such control measures, is bit like some supposed treatments for physical ailments. They can often appear to be quite helpful, but sometimes they can also carry side effects not always immediately apparent.

For me, the most dangerous side effect of such imposed behaviour, is that it nudges us away from a sense of personal responsibility and the importance of looking beyond ourselves to the needs of others – a central teaching of our different faiths. Guru Nanak was particularly critical of those who left social responsibilities in the search for God. He also advised against the use of drink or drugs to try to escape stresses of everyday life. In a memorable passage, he taught that serving God through looking to the needs of others gives a much more lasting sense of wellbeing than the consumption of any amount of insipid alcohol.

Laws and regulation have their uses in setting boundaries to unacceptable behaviour, but in themselves they do little to make us more responsible people. Speaking as a Sikh, and keeping to the medical analogy, we should also consider the more holistic approach found in our different religions and reset our moral satnavs to a direction of more responsible living, not only for our own health, or that of the unborn child, but also of generations to come who will be affected by the priorities in life we chose for ourselves today.

19 May 2010

Claims to Uniqueness in Religion and Culture

My wife and I have just got back from a cruise holiday to historic places in the Mediterranean.

Our first stop was Egypt, and, at the Cairo museum we were constantly reminded by a bright and likeable guide, that virtually anything worth inventing, from writing to medicine to board games, had been invented in Egypt. In Athens we were told that it was the Greeks who were first in everything, and in Ephesus in Turkey we were reminded that theirs was the earlier civilization!

The reality is that these early civilizations, far from being unique, had much in common, and traded extensively in both goods and ideas, even borrowing and re-branding their gods and heroes with new takes on their often-amorous exploits, and views on life, death and the afterlife. In Cairo we saw a beautiful painting of two recording angels noting the deeds, good and bad of one of the pharaohs. Similar imagery is found in the Abrahamic faiths and even in Hindu and Sikh scriptures.

I thought of these similarities while attending the funeral of the Hindu leader Om Prakash Sharma a couple of days ago. We first met more than twenty years ago when we were both involved in setting up the Interfaith Network, now the leading body for interfaith dialogue in the UK. I will always remember his moderating influence at times of fraught discussion.

The funeral service was in essence, not very different from a Sikh or Christian funeral service in which we all commiserate with the family and friends of the bereaved, stress the impermanence of life and reflect on the life and contribution of the departed. In this, all echo the Sikh teaching that a person's worth is measured by what he or she does for others.

To me, it seems different religions, instead of recognizing important commonalities, all too often act like those over-enthusiastic guides on our Mediterranean trip by over stressing the uniqueness and primacy of their religious message.

Guru Nanak, concerned by the constant focussing on difference, taught that our different religions were essentially one in ethical imperatives. My late friend Om Parkash Sharma recognized this truth and the need for different faiths to work together for the common good, and at a time when even politicians are expressing the same sentiment, we should give it a real go.

26 May 2010

Rights and Responsibilities' in Freedom of Speech

Lord Lester's bill to reform Britain's libel laws reported in the Times yesterday, will strike a particularly responsive chord in two people each bearing the name Singh. Despite successfully defending recent libel actions brought against them, strict rules on costs left them both thousands of pounds out of pocket.

First it was the well-known science writer and broadcaster Dr Simon Singh who won a case brought by the British Chiropractic Association. Last week in another case, Hardeep Singh, a young Sikh from Slough, found himself in court for expressing his concern over a rich and powerful figure in Punjab, whose activities he alleged, were, causing divisions in the Sikh community in Britain.

Reformers argue that it is not just the cost of defending such libel actions that concerns them, but the very principle of freedom of expression in the internet age where we all have much more access to information and opinion.

The philosopher Voltaire underlined the importance of freedom of speech when he declared 'I may not believe in what you say, but I will defend to the death your right to say it'. Throughout the centuries, many brave people have lost their lives in pursuit of this important ideal. In India, the Sikh Guru, Guru Tegh Bahadur, was publicly beheaded for courageously defending the right to freedom of expression of the Hindus even though theirs was a different religion to his own. It's because of the courage and sacrifice of such people that we today enjoy the right to freely criticize those in power and authority and hold them responsible for their actions.

While there are those who argue that libel laws need updating to guard such hard-won freedoms, it is equally important to ensure that freedom of speech is not used to cause gratuitous insult and offence, particularly to the weak and vulnerable or smear whole communities as happened in the Holocaust.

The Sikh Gurus reminded us that the right to free speech, like all other rights carries an attached responsibility. Guru Tegh Bahadur, the Sikh Guru who gave his life for freedom of religious expression also taught that while we should never yield to those that seek to intimidate us, we must also strive to ensure that we do not cause hurt or fear in others. It is a balancing responsibility to freedom of speech that we sometimes forget.

2 June 2010

Jassa Singh Ramgharia; a charismatic Sikh Leader

This week Sikhs are celebrating the birthday of Jassa Singh Ramgharia a charismatic and talented Sikh leader who lived in the first half of the eighteenth century. It was a turbulent time in Indian history that has important implications for us today.

It began with the tiny Sikh community challenging Mughal persecution of other faiths with enlightened teachings on the need for tolerance and respect. The response of the authorities was brutal repression. Repeated incursions by Afghan invaders added further to suffering.

Gradually, Sikhs, with leaders like Jassa Singh, began emerging from their forest hideouts in guerrilla bands, attacking the rear of Afghan convoys going back to Kabul, recovering loot and freeing captives being taken for sale in the slave markets of the Middle East. Incredibly, in the space of a few years, Sikhs then went on to finally overcome both Mughals and Afghans to become sovereign rulers of Punjab.

Naturally in celebrations like those this week, Sikhs applaud the leadership of people like Jassa Singh, but the reality is that they would have achieved little without the active shelter and support of the people of Punjab. After suffering repeated looting and crippling taxes, towns and villages welcomed the fairer rule of the Sikhs with its respect for all faiths. Even the Afghans, who in the language of the day referred to Sikhs as 'dogs', wrote of Sikh chivalry, and fairness to all communities. This grudging admiration eventually led to a sizeable and well-respected Sikh community settling in Afghanistan until the recent rise of the Taliban.

I thought of this Sikh experience as I read of today's convening of a meeting of tribal leaders by President Karzai, to consider ways to peace. The meeting coincides with news of British troops in Helmand being placed under American command, and the 1000th death of American soldiers.

The dilemma is how to beat the insurgents without increasing further military commitment. Here the Sikh experience of the mid-eighteenth century helps to remind us that winning the hearts and minds of the people of Afghanistan by providing security and self-esteem can lead to true progress in even the most daunting of conflicts. It's not easy but, as history shows, it's well worth re-doubling efforts in this direction.

24 August 2010

Floods in Pakistan

Yesterday, Brenden Gormley, Head of the Disasters Emergency Committee commented that generous donations by the British public to flood relief in Pakistan were shaming politicians across the world. His words remind us how political concerns, like those over terrorism or corruption, can all too easily trump basic humanitarian considerations.

The suffering evokes poignant memories for many Sikhs. The floods are in the land of the birth of Guru Nanak, the founder of the Sikh faith; a land that saw the forceful expulsion of their grandparents during the partition of the sub-continent sixty-three years ago this month in a frenzy of religious hate. Despite this, most Sikhs see it as their basic religious duty to help. Many Sikhs like others have contributed generously to the aid effort, while others are helping in Pakistan. But for some, the hurt of the past remains. So how do we break the chains of history to look to the needs of the present?

For Sikhs, the answer lies in two incidents. The first occurred a little over 300 years ago, when the infant Sikh community was defending itself from attack by the Mughal rulers. In a particularly fierce battle, a Sikh water carrier called Kanaya was seen supplying water to the enemy wounded. Angry Sikh soldiers dragged him before Guru Gobind Singh. The Guru asked if the charge was true. The bewildered Kanaya replied that it was and said that he was simply doing what the teachings of Sikhism required him to do: look to those suffering whoever they might be. The delighted Guru embraced him, calling him 'bhai' or brother and gave him medicines and bandages to continue his good work.

The second incident lies in the experience of the war between India and Pakistan in 1971 when Punjabi Pakistani prisoners of war and their Punjabi Sikh captors embraced each other and swapped stories like long-lost brothers. The incident showed the utter absurdity of man-made borders drawn on maps to divide communities on the basis of politically induced communal fear and hate. Yet this has been done over and over again and is still being done around the world today.

Helping those in need is not only a basic human duty, but here it can also play a small part in boosting confidence, trade and prosperity. More importantly, it can give a lie to the myth that people of different faiths cannot live together.

31 August 2010

Decluttering

The Communities Secretary Eric Pickles has declared war against scruffy signs, bossy bollards, patchwork paving and much else that clutters our streets, confusing motorists, hindering pedestrians and impeding those with disabilities. His comments touch on a more general aspect of human behaviour: our infinite capacity to cause clutter in much of what we do. My desk is a prime example.

It's certainly true in religion, where cultural and ritual practices easily attach themselves to, and distort religious belief. With time, such clutter becomes so entwined with core belief that it becomes difficult to decide where one begins and the other ends.

A linked problem is that some of the commentary embedded in religious texts refers to specific circumstances in history which may not have relevance today. Such ambiguities can all too easily be exploited by fanatics with their own agenda.

Tomorrow, Sikhs celebrate the work of a remarkable man who faced these problem head on: Guru Arjan fifth Guru of the Sikhs and compiler of the first version of Sikh scriptures. With tact and persistence, he retrieved the original writings of Guru Nanak and successor Gurus. To these, he added his own compositions and, in a remarkable gesture also added verses of Hindu and Muslim saints to show that no one faith has a monopoly of truth, giving us the first version of our Holy Granth. It is this achievement that Sikhs will be celebrating tomorrow.

Guru Arjan, was conscious of the morass of customs rituals and other practices that passed for religion in the India of his day and he took pains to ensure that the Holy Granth contained only reflections on God the Creator, and principles of responsible ethical living that cannot be dated by time.

So, with such clear guidance, is all well with Sikh practice today? Well, no! While the teachings of religion are easy to understand, they are harder to live by. It's much easier to focus on customs and rituals that supposedly make us more holy. For Sikhs these ironically, include rituals around the reading and care of the Holy Granth, and other areas of worship.

Yes, it would be great to have clutter free streets, but perhaps society would gain even more if we remove harmful clutter from religious belief and focus on the essential ethical thrust of our different religions: how to rein in our wayward human behaviour and become more responsible human beings.

7 September 2010

Plight of the Roma

Today's demonstrations over the retirement age in France remind me of parallel demonstrations over President Sarkozy's forced repatriation of more than eight thousand Roma to Eastern Europe. The European Commission, the UN and the Vatican have also expressed concern. Here, France is not alone. Italy evicted thousands of Roma in 2008 and Germany plans to repatriate 12,000 this year.

The plight of the Roma is part of a deeper problem. Easier travel, particularly in the EEC and changing economic and trade realities have resulted in people, often different in appearance and culture, disturbing the equilibrium of previously close communities. We have it in our genes to be wary of difference, but unfortunately our knee-jerk reaction is to exaggerate the fear and vilify the stranger, as is now happening with the Roma.

And they are not alone, particularly in Eastern Europe long isolated from different cultures. Sikhs arriving at Polish airports for example, while appreciating the needs of security, are dismayed by negative attitudes to their turban. Only yesterday, a Sikh businessman, on arrival at Warsaw airport was excitedly told to remove his turban and throw it on a tray for inspection as if it would explode at any moment: treatment that is in marked contrast to the culturally sensitive security checks in the USA and much of western Europe. The irony is that the Sikh turban is an important religious symbol of a commitment to respect the rights and beliefs of others.

Such displays of hostility to supposed difference were seen in the Britain of the '50s and '60s as a reaction to new arrivals from the Commonwealth. Fortunately, a strong British sense of tolerance and fair play prevailed, and European politicians could do well to look to British experience.

Our different religions teach us to look beyond superficial difference to more important commonalities. Guru Gobind Singh, our tenth Guru, concerned about religious conflict, taught that superficial differences of religion and culture between our different faiths should not mask the fact that are all members of the same one human family.

Today the focus is on the Roma; tomorrow it will be others as people exercise their increased rights to freedom of travel and settlement. Somehow, we have to bring ourselves to look beyond superficial difference and see others as fellow humans with a common destiny.

18 November 2010

The Shirt of a Happy Man

In the current economic gloom and the risk of one country's woes affecting others, a little bit of good news, like the announcement of the royal engagement is doubly cheering. As a Sikh, I also welcome the government's initiative to help us see our economic concerns in a fuller perspective of individual and national wellbeing. The founders of our different religions have long reminded us that there is much more to life than the pursuit of material prosperity. I'm less sure however, that the Office for National Statistics will ever be able to come up with a meaningful measure of individual and national wellbeing.

In this search for happiness and wellbeing, I'm reminded about a poem that I used to read our children, called 'The Shirt of a Happy Man'. It tells the story of a king obsessed with his health, who'd fly into a rage when doctors told him there was nothing wrong with him. Eventually, a wise and perceptive doctor told him that he would be restored to full health if he slept one night in the shirt of a happy man. The king sent messengers throughout the land to find such a man, but all they found were people with real concerns. The reports of the suffering of his subjects made the king ashamed of his imagined woes, and as he began to look to the needs and concerns of his subjects, he experienced true contentment for the first time in his life.

In many ways we've become a bit like the king, a little over-obsessed with our own wellbeing. We are not helped by the media and adverts that constantly pander to our greed and vanity. Guru Nanak urged us to look beyond ourselves when he taught: 'Where God exists there is no self, where self exists there is no God'. And a Christian theologian put it in even blunter terms when he said 'it's the 'i' in the middle of sin, that makes it sin'.

Sikh teachings remind us that there is nothing wrong with material comfort, but for a true sense of wellbeing we need to look beyond ourselves to the needs of others, as we will be reminded in this week's Children in Need Appeal. Contentment may be difficult to quantify in an index, but as a Sikh I believe our own sense of wellbeing is directly proportional to the amount of our life we devote to helping those around us.

24 November 2010

Announcement of Wedding of Prince William and Kate Middleton

The news that Prince William and Kate Middleton are to marry in Westminster Abbey next April is doubly welcome to Sikhs, particularly as it comes at a time when Sikhs are celebrating the birthday of Guru Nanak.

In a refreshing change to the background of his times, Guru Nanak in the India of the fifteenth century taught the complete equality of women. Marriage in Sikhism is seen as the coming together of two equal partners in mutual love and support, and importantly that they should act as one, in common service to the community. The equality is seen in the important positions occupied by women in worship, where women often recite from the scriptures and occupy positions such as secretary or president of the local gurdwara.

Unfortunately, culture sometimes trumps the teachings of the religion and Sikhs still have to work within the community to ensure the equality taught by the Guru trumps culture.

In the past the roles of men and women in the family were quite distinct with the man being the major breadwinner and the woman the main carer. The welcome move to greater equality in society has resulted in a wider acceptance that both roles are important and there is nothing demeaning in men playing a greater role at home, even though women believe men still don't do enough.

In our family, I am often the hunter-gatherer, frequently braving the charge of supermarket trolleys as I hunt for food. However, I also put the washing out and chat with the neighbours while I'm doing it. At the moment, my wife is doing school inspections in Abu Dhabi and I find myself in charge of all departments, cooking and washing all the plates—both of them.

Of course, in future, Kate and William won't have to bother about such things. They'll have a few people to help them. But they will have even more difficult challenges, particularly a press, watching and speculating on their every move, what they wear and where they go. My plea to the media is to allow them some breathing space to get on with their own lives.

It will be particularly hard for Kate coming into what is familiar to Sikhs as an extended family. I'm delighted that they are getting married in Westminster Abbey. The Abbey has been host to the Annual Commonwealth Service, always an interfaith event since the '70s. The setting will be an excellent start to what I'm sure will be a happy married life.

1 December 2010

A Nudge Towards More Healthy Living

Yesterday's launch of a new health initiative by the Health Secretary Andrew Lansley, will strike a responsive chord in many Sikhs. He announced that responsibility for public health would be transferred from the NHS to local councils who would be expected to nudge us rather than nanny us to healthier lifestyles.

The nudge approach is commonly used in Sikh religious teachings. For example, the Guru's advice on drink and drugs is that 'we should refrain from that which harms our body and dulls our senses', and instead look to the greater sense of wellbeing that comes through spiritual reflection and turning this reflection to positive and purposeful living.

The Sikh Gurus also taught their followers that it was their basic duty to defend people against frequent invasions of Punjab, and they encouraged physical fitness through wrestling competitions, horse riding and similar activities to go alongside spiritual learning. The result was the community soon became known for their physical endurance and strength. In the '50s and '60s of the last century, Sikhs formed half of India's gold medal winning Olympic hockey teams.

But, times are a changing and for Sikhs, as with the rest of us, questionable lifestyles are proving a more subtle and insidious threat to wellbeing. Last week I attended a Sikh prison chaplaincy training event in Rugby where the common experience of the Sikh chaplains was that most members of the community serving custodial sentences had grown remote from religious teachings and were there for drink or drugs offences.

Even among those attending gurdwaras there are real problems linked to the change from the more active lifestyle of Punjab to one of less physical activity and a reluctance to make changes to a tasty but calorie rich diet. A growing risk of obesity and linked threats of coronary heart disease and diabetes has now become a common problem faced by all of us irrespective of religious, cultural or social background.

Being increasingly alert to such issues, we now run regular health clinics in our gurdwaras and arrange sponsored runs and cycle races and other sporting activities. But like others in the wider community, we need to do much more. Few of us, especially Sikhs, respond to a prescriptive approach, but for me and many others in all communities, it will take a really firm nudge to move us to more healthy living.

24 November 2010

Finding Common Ground in the Three Rs of Religion

This week's much publicized debate between Tony Blair and Christopher Hitchins on 'is religion a force for good?', coincides with interfaith week. the celebrations of Guru Nanak's birthday and the festival of Eid when different religions are tentatively exploring links with each other and finding such encounters can be both spiritually rewarding and a bit of fun.

Events like meetings between different faiths and sharing in one another's festivals are a useful step in this direction, but after years of attitudes of superiority and distrust between different faiths we still have a long way to go to ensure superficial respect percolates down to, and overcomes, deeper prejudices. Many people see religion today as a cause of conflict or at best, irrelevant to the needs of society. So, what more do we need to do to bring religion in from the cold as a positive force for good?

Guru Nanak faced a similar question in the India of some 500 years ago at a time of intense rivalry between different faiths. It was a time when for many rituals and superstitions had replaced the essential thrust of religion. To put superficial differences in their true perspective. Guru Nanak chose a Hindu and a Muslim as his travelling companions and in his discussions on religion earned the respect of all. It was a time when religions around the world generally did little to help ordinary people and simply talked about punishment or reward in the afterlife.

Today, talk of punishment and reward has faded into the background, but religion still finds itself on the margins of society because, contrary to the essence of religious teachings, we seem to have separated religious worship from everyday living. Guru Nanak reminded us that spiritual reflection was important, but its main purpose was to give us a balanced and responsible attitude to life and equip us to help our fellow beings.

Guru Nanak and his successor Gurus constantly emphasized the importance of recognizing important commonalities between our different faiths, which in essence are the three Rs of religion: right wrong and responsibility, greater emphasis on these core teachings can help provide a healing balm for many of the ills in today's society.

8 March 2011

Integration, and Respect for Different Cultures are not Mutually Exclusive.

Television pictures of migrant workers fleeing the turmoil in Libya remind us that the existence of sizable minorities in many countries has now become a global phenomenon. While much of this movement of people comes from those seeking new economic opportunities, persecution and changes in political boundaries adds to the flow.

Tomorrow I'll be going to Tallinn in Estonia to Talk about British experience in accommodating minorities. Estonia, once independent, became a part of the former Soviet Union and now, independent again finds itself with a sizeable minority population, including Russians, Germans, Scandinavians and others. The government in Estonia is trying to take a generous and enlightened attitude to many, who until recently were in effect their colonial masters. Like Britain, Estonia has passed laws to prohibit discrimination and protect cultural freedom.

Despite this, there are still problems. Indigenous Estonians generally earn more and have a better standard of living than minority communities. There, as in Britain, the debate is about how to protect minority cultures while at the same time promoting a sense of national identity. I've been invited to talk about British experience in the use of ethnic minority media in meeting these twin objectives. And I've got a problem.

Minority media undoubtedly helps to give minorities a sense of cohesion and self-esteem and can also help them understand the concerns and aspirations of the wider community. But there is also a downside. There's less of an incentive to learn the language of the majority; a disadvantage in itself but one that can also create a gulf of understanding between parents, comfortable in the language and norms of their background culture, and children who are more rooted in that of their adopted country.

In Britain, this is particularly evident in religion. For Sikhs the language of our scriptures is Punjabi. But the first language of our children and grandchildren is English and their understanding of Punjabi is often poor. If as Sikhs we want our children to understand and be true to the teachings of our faith – like respect for other cultures, it's important that we make much greater use of English in gurdwaras.

Integration, and respect for different cultures are not mutually exclusive. Both are important, but require patience, adjustment and understanding on all sides.

14 March 2011

Earthquake in Japan and Damage to the Fukushima Nuclear Plant

Television pictures of the destruction wrought by Japan's most devastating earthquake in a hundred years, confirm the worst estimates of damage and loss of life. To add to the suffering, this morning's news of a second explosion at the Fukushima nuclear plant adds to poignant fears of dangerous radiation levels from damaged nuclear reactors. Japan, more than any other country knows the harm such leaks can cause to life and limb even in unborn children.

When such disasters strike they arouse predictable emotional reactions. There is huge sympathy for those suffering the loss of their near and dear ones and for the loss of homes and possessions, and concern for those still trapped in the rubble, and a general feeling of helplessness. There is also our human desire to blame someone. There will be questions on the design and siting of nuclear power stations although Japan is probably more safety conscious than most countries.

The thrust of Sikh teachings is to move us away from pointless speculation and debate about causes, to active concern for consequences. This was demonstrated when the eighth Guru, Guru Harkishan went to Delhi to give aid and comfort to those suffering in a severe smallpox epidemic when others were fleeing the city. His courage and compassion eventually cost him his life.

Although we can do much to reduce suffering in natural disasters, we also have to accept nature as it exists in all its incredible beauty and occasional terrifying unpredictability. The people of Japan knowing that they live in a region prone to earthquakes have done just this. Regular earthquake training given to children and the development of calm and orderly evacuation procedures, have, I'm sure, helped save many lives.

Sikh teachings in respect of response to both natural disasters and manmade suffering, remind me of a verse by the poet Adam Gordon:

Question not, but live and labour
Till your goal be won
Helping every needy neighbour
Seeking help from none
Life is mostly froth and bubble
But two things stand out like stone
Kindness in another's troubles; courage in your own.

In the spirit of the sentiment behind this verse, it is encouraging to learn that Britain, and other countries, including New Zealand, still reeling from its own recent earthquake, are sending trained rescue teams. The people of Japan are showing tremendous courage and resilience and deserve all the help and assistance a stunned and watching world can give.

22 March 2011

Lessons from History

History can be one of the most boring subjects as well as one of the most interesting, depending on what is taught and how it is taught. In Saturday's Times, Professor Niall Ferguson, an advisor to the Education Secretary, was quoted as favouring a much shorter curriculum with an emphasis on European and Western history and the importance of the Renaissance.

Personally, I'd like it to be a little bit wider to show how other parts of the world were, like Europe, also questioning the rigidity and oppressive conformity of belief systems at about the same time. Guru Nanak was a contemporary of Martin Luther, and like the leaders of the Reform movements of the West, the Guru was hailed as someone who brought light and open debate to the darkness that then often passed for religion.

Wider study of world history also reveals interesting parallels in scientific thinking. In the West the astronomer Copernicus is credited for the discovery that the sun rather than the Earth is the centre of our planetary system. Yet this was then common belief in India. Guru Nanak, born a few years before Copernicus, refers in beautiful poetry to the infinity of Creation and to countless universes and solar systems.

These examples show how people in different parts of our world were thinking and behaving in similar ways in a common and fascinating journey to our modern world. It wasn't always enlightened progress and one of the benefits from a study of history is its reminder of how easily we humans, given triggers of hate and prejudice, can regress to near barbarity despite an outer veneer of civilization.

Perhaps the most important gain from a study of the past, is that this should help us build a better future. I see evidence of this in our cautious reaction to events in Libya. For me the most heartening news in the last few days is not the success of air strikes stopping Gadaffi's forces in their stride, but the news that British Tornado jets on a 3000-mile return mission to attack military targets, turned back home when they saw civilians in the target area.

It is a gesture close to Sikh teaching that compassion for the innocent is more important than short-term military gain. It is a gesture that will help win the hearts and minds of the long-suffering people of Libya.

13 April 2011

Responsibility to the Elderly

This week, British Sikhs are celebrating Baisakhi, one of the most colourful festivals in the Sikh calendar. Before Sikhism, Baisakhi was celebrated in much of Northern India to mark the coming of spring and the gathering of the winter harvest with spectacular fairs and festivities.

Last weekend's mini summer helped Sikhs to bring Punjab to Britain with processions in many towns and cities, with the Sikh scriptures, the Guru Granth Sahib carried in a decorated float to the singing of traditional hymns or shabads. In the Sikh tradition, the route of the procession is inevitably lined with lots of stalls offering free food and soft drinks to spectators and passersby.

Baisakhi is important to Sikhs as it was on the festival of Baisakhi in 1699 at a time of intense religious persecution that our tenth Guru, Guru Gobind Singh announced the creation of the Khalsa – Sikhs with a visible identity pledged to stand up for freedom of belief for all people. The Guru reminded Sikhs that while they should live by uplifting ethical values that recognize the oneness of our human race, the main thrust of a Sikh's life should be to look beyond self to the needs of others. But to do so, we also need to look after our own health and fitness, and sporting contests and displays of physical fitness are traditionally a part of Baisakhi celebrations.

In recent years however, it has become increasingly clear that we are overfocussing on the wrong end of the age spectrum. A growing number of wheelchairs and mobility aids in gurdwaras remind us we are part of a population that is living longer with all the problems of old age. The media carry almost daily stories of a less than adequate treatment of the elderly, and Sikhs are not immune from such concerns.

So this Baisakhi we are working in partnership with Age UK and Sporting Equals to promote better health and fitness for the elderly, with talks on healthy diets and lifestyles, and physical activity sessions in gurdwara halls. We are also working with the Organ Donation Taskforce to encourage organ donation in the Sikh community.

When Guru Gobind Singh said we should be ready to give our all to help others, the need then was to confront oppression. Today needs have changed but the commitment to look beyond self, made on that Baisakhi of three centuries ago is more important than ever before.

31 July 2011

Maharaja Ranjit Singh

Last week I attended the re-launch of a book by the celebrated author Patwant Singh about the life of Maharaja Ranjit Singh the charismatic first, and last, Sikh ruler of the Punjab. Ranjit Singh was an astute leader who managed to unite different Sikh factions behind him to eventually become the ruler of a vast kingdom that included the whole of Punjab before its partition in 1947, and the State of Kashmir.

Ranjit Singh, blinded in one eye through smallpox in infancy, was totally illiterate. As a child he would regularly attend the local gurdwara and was moved by the stories of the bravery of Sikhs in battle and heavily influenced by the Gurus' teachings of respect for the beliefs of all people, as ruler of Punjab, he would refer to his loss of sight in one eye saying it was God's purpose that he look on at all faiths with the same eye. His government included members of all communities. It was he who put the gold on the Golden Temple in Amritsar. He also built a beautiful Hindu temple on the banks of the Ganges and gave lavishly to the upkeep of mosques in Punjab.

There is a wonderful story of some Sikh villagers complaining to the Maharaja that the daily Muslim call to prayer was too loud and disturbing. The Maharaja suggested that if the villagers took on the responsibility for reminding individual Muslims when it was time for prayers, he would consider their complaint. It was quietly dropped. On another occasion he met a Muslim with a handwritten copy of the Koran which had taken him years to produce but was proving difficult to sell. The Maharaja appreciated the man's dedicated effort and paid the astonished vendor handsomely for his work. Ranjit Singh's kingdom which brought peace and prosperity to Punjab, after centuries of invasions and religious conflict, came to an abrupt end with his death in 1839.

Times have changed, and conflicts have now become more complex with wider implications for our smaller and more interdependent world. But this brief glimpse at Ranjit Singh's respect for difference underlines the importance of aiming at the well-being of all people in resolving conflict and bringing peace and prosperity to many suffering areas of the world today.

3 August 2011

Murderous Rampage of Anders Breivik in Norway

We've just come back from a wonderful holiday exploring glacial valleys and stunning mountain scenery. We also experienced warm and kind hospitality despite our distinctly foreign appearance. It was in Norway, and we left the country on the same day that Anders Breivik launched his murderous assault. Since then, I've been asking myself how could such an outrage have taken place in such a wonderful and tolerant country?

There is a well-known verse in Sikh scriptures which says:

There is an inner light of God in all and it becomes manifest as we reflect and act on religious and ethical teachings, centered on a belief in the oneness of all humanity.

Unfortunately, the opposite is also true and we can also carry within us, ungodly concerns and suspicions about those who appear different, especially newcomers to our country, despite evidence that immigrants generally bring new skills and vigour into a community. Fear of possible economic or social disadvantage, can all too easily lead to irrational prejudice and hatred, and I believe it's this that triggered the recent carnage in Norway, as it has done in countless other hate-fueled outrages throughout history.

Travel can help us develop more enlightened attitudes to others when we see people in different lands with similar concerns and aspirations, laughing, joking, rejoicing and, grieving at the same sort of things.

But we don't really have to go very far to understand this truth; we can see it in the lives and concerns of those of different cultures who are our near neighbours—if we care to look! I remember the suspicion and stand off a few years ago when Sikhs sought planning permission to extend a gurdwara in Southfields in London. There was no dialogue between Sikhs and local residents and rubbish was sometimes thrown into the existing gurdwara premises. A few of us decided to knock on every door in the immediate neighborhood and invite the residents to discuss their concerns over refreshments. To our surprise, most came. Few concerns were raised and much of the discussion was about recipes for making chapattis and Indian dishes.

We are told that it is good to talk, and dialogue between different cultures helps understanding, but both settled communities and new arrivals need to make an effort to change prejudice and misunderstanding into mutual respect.

9 August 2011

Violence and Riots in British Cities

As we have learnt this morning, the wanton violence and looting seen in Tottenham and other parts of London over the last few days has now spread to places like Birmingham and Bristol. It has its origins in the police shooting of a member of the public in still confused circumstances. But while the mindless violence has taken the headlines there are legitimate concerns over the balance of the right to life and freedom of individuals and how far the police should go in the course of their duty.

In a different area of the balance of rights and freedoms, the Equality and Human Rights Commission chose last weekend to suggest that the banning of satellite dishes in conservation areas may infringe an individual's human right to freely practice their religion by denying the right to services beamed from abroad.

Both these examples show the importance of getting a sense of perspective on human rights. When the Human rights Act was first brought in, it was generally seen as an overdue protection of fundamental freedoms, but today many see it, and associated European legislation, as undue interference in the right of our country to its own interpretation of individual rights. I doubt if many will see access to a satellite dish as high on the scale of national priorities. Overfocusing on comparative minor infringements of religious liberty simply blurs real issues.

For many of us religion is much more than formal worship. For Sikhs and I believe for most faiths the essence of religion is responsible living. This is something far removed from, and perhaps an antidote to, what has been termed 'the recreational violence' seen on our streets over the last few days.

Religion takes us away from a narrow obsession with self and my rights, to concern for those around us and respect for our surroundings. It is because of this that I believe that it would make for a more contented society if rights were seen in their true perspective, and the proposed new Bill on Human Rights framed to encompass both rights and responsibilities.

16 August 2011

Proposed Action on Inner City Riots

Yesterday, in a sombre response to last week's riots, Prime Minister David Cameron spoke of a slow-motion moral collapse that Britain had suffered in recent decades. In a hard-hitting speech he attacked society for 'twisting and misrepresenting human rights' to undermine personal responsibility. He went on to say policies on education, welfare, parenting and drug addiction would be examined to help mend a broken society. Opposition leader Ed Milliband, in a parallel speech, drew attention to what he saw as the effects of economic deprivation and lack of job opportunities.

Curiously, religion and the role of faith communities hardly figures in this comprehensive call for action, although religion addresses many of the issues involved: such as the family, and the harm done to both the individual and society by greed and selfishness. It's a reminder that religion, at one time recognized as the main determinant and arbiter of moral values, is now seen as largely irrelevant.

For me, the riots were not only, what the Prime Minister described as, 'a wakeup call for the country', but also one for our religious communities. The problem is that there has always been a disconnect between religious teaching and living true to religious values. Living true to such values is not always easy as seen in the death of Jesus Christ, and the later martyrdom of Guru Tegh Bahadur, whose anniversary of Guruship falls this week. Even when life is not threatened it's not easy to stand up to the bully, or to look to the rights of others at the expense of benefits to ourselves.

The initiatives announced by the Prime Minister involving government departments are a welcome step in bringing sanity back to society. But religious communities also have a responsibility to translate lofty teachings on right, wrong and responsibility, to positive action to address underlying needs of society.

Today there are many initiatives by religious charities to tackle social deprivation. Sikhs have the institution of langar to feed the needy and the concept of seva or service to others. I believe there can be a huge multiplier effect if our different religions combine their individual efforts, in joint initiatives to bring respect, responsibility and cohesion back to all levels of society. In doing this we will simply be doing what the founders of our different faiths taught us to do.

28 October 2011

Divali and the Sikh Festival of Bandi Chor

The news that in a desperate attempt to end or ease the crisis in the Eurozone bankers have agreed to write off half the Greek debt, comes as a welcome sign of hope in a story of doom and gloom. The move is not so much motivated by altruism, but by a wider understanding that in our interdependent world our fortunes are linked to those of others. Here self-interest, and the religious imperative of looking to the needs of others, are not so far apart. It was greed and self-interest that led to the global financial crisis. It's responsible living that can get us out of it.

I was reminded of the dangers of neglecting a wider view, by a suggestion that as the first turbaned Sikh in the Lords I should focus on Sikh issues and concerns. To my mind simply looking to one's own community, goes against the very teachings of the Gurus who went out of their way to look to, and work for the greater good of all, sometimes at the cost of their own lives.

This looking to the greater good, is the theme of the festival of Bandi Chor which Sikhs celebrate this week. It concerns a time when the Mughal Emperor Jahngir's persecution of other faiths had made him deeply unpopular, particularly the incarceration of the sixth Guru of the Sikhs, Guru Hargobind. The Emperor, in an effort to boost his popularity decided to make a gesture of goodwill to coincide with the Hindu festival of Diwali. He ordered the release of the popular Guru.

The Guru however, refused to leave, unless fifty-two other political prisoners were released at the same time. The Emperor offered a compromise: anyone who could hold onto the Gurus cloak as he went through the narrow exit from the fort, could also leave. In the event, the Guru's followers made him a cloak with 52 tassels of varying lengths enabling each prisoner to hold onto one of the tassels on their way to freedom.

Today we are fortunate in living in free society, but there is always a danger of some, on the back of real financial hardship for many, seeing it as a free-for-all society, as we saw in this summer's riots. Concern for our neighbour as shown in the story of Bandi Chor can help ameliorate genuine hardship and add stability and cohesion to society, often at little real cost.

4 November 2011

Twists and Turns in the Greek Financial Crisis

The latest twists and turns in the Greek financial crisis, regular meetings of Eurozone ministers, a daily threat of strikes over pensions, job cuts and huge bonuses for the privileged few, all remind us that protestors outside St. Paul's aren't alone in thinking that all is not well with the capitalist system, a system in which we all live, move and have our being. But what can we do about it? A Polish friend of mine once wryly observed that under capitalism, man exploits man; under communism it is the other way around!

There is a lot of truth in what my friend says. To me, the underlying cause of our very real economic problems is selfishness and greed, our concern for our own wellbeing at the expense of that of others. A small increase in GDP is still growth. The problem is that when everyone grabs at what they can get some, often those in greatest need find themselves worse off.

Our different religions have consistently reminded us of the need to curb individual greed for the wider benefit of society. Jesus Christ famously observed that it was harder for a rich man to enter the kingdom of heaven than for a camel to pass through the eye of a needle. Guru Nanak, whose birth anniversary Sikhs will be celebrating next week, once gave a rich man who was constantly boasting about his wealth, a needle to keep with him as sort of passport to heaven. The rich miser excitedly showed it to his wife who laughed at him saying how can you take a needle with you when you die? If you'll excuse the pun, it's fascinating how needle stories in our different faiths have a common thread.

The essence of Guru Nanak's teachings are summed up in his three rules for responsible living. Reflect on religious teachings to get a wider perspective on life to help us distinguish between that which is important, and the greed and passion that so often motivates what we do. Earn by honest effort and thirdly, and most importantly, share what you have with others, particularly the less fortunate.

The Guru taught that simply amassing money is foolish and, if obtained by exploiting the weak, positively criminal; but he also taught that the true use of wealth, is to help create a fairer and more contented society. It's a message for all of us in today's turbulent economic times.

7 January 2012

Role of Faith Communities in Promoting Peace

There's a meeting in the House of Lords tomorrow on the 'Role of Faith Communities' in promoting peace. But if we look at the world about us we can hardly fail to notice that, at first sight at least, religions seem to be part of today's conflicts. When religions talk of taking the lead in working for peace, some may be forgiven for the comment: 'physician first heal thyself'.

So what should religions be doing to improve their image and make a real contribution to peace? Is peace in itself always a good thing? I'm reminded about the time when I was invited to give the annual City of Coventry Peace Lecture. I immediately started to look through Sikh scriptures for suitable quotes on the importance of peace in the usual meaning of the word; that is the absence of active conflict. To my dismay, I found nothing. It was then that I realised why Sikhism and other religions that talk so much about justice and fairness in society, and see the absence of conflict desirable, also recognise that this, in itself, does not always result in justice.

All wars and conflicts eventually end in peace, but it can be the peace of the graveyard with injustice and arbitrary rule being the true victor; a fate which with the current brutal government crackdown in the city of Homs, could be the lot of the hapless people of Syria today.

To my mind, peace without justice is simply a papering over cracks. Greater justice and a fairer society for all people must be the goal for people of religion who want to make a real difference It's a sentiment echoed in the closing line of the Sikh daily prayer, the Ardas, with its emphasis on the wellbeing of all. Its perhaps because of this that I have always been a fan of the brilliant and compassionate novels of Charles Dickens whose birth bicentenary falls today. He saw that a fairer and more peaceful society can only be built by tackling underlying hardship and injustice.

My hope is that we move to this wider understanding of peace. To do so we need to set aside energy sapping and conflict causing arguments about my religion, or my interpretation of religion being better than yours and move to a common goal of working for peace based on fairness and justice for all members of our human family.

14 February 2012

Prayers in the Council Chamber

The court ruling that councils have no legal right to hold prayers at the start of meetings has certainly created a bit of a storm. The Times headline, 'Christianity on the Rack', may be a bit over the top, but there is genuine concern over what some see as a continuing marginalisation of religion in public life.

It reminds me of a time when I approached a local authority who were giving grants to community groups for social welfare projects to do the same for religious groups only to get a curt response that religion had nothing to do with social improvement. The same authority today does include religious bodies in its grants programme, confident in the knowledge that a small grant added to largely voluntary effort is true value for money in addressing social welfare issues.

To some, brief prayers before a council meeting are simply a time-wasting imposition, for others they are an opportunity to calm moods and passions and reflect on the real priorities and ethical implications in the work before them. For myself, I see nothing wrong in attending the service of a religion that is not my own. But this was not always so. As a child my three brothers and I found out that Catholics did not have to attend the daily school assembly. We sought our parents support to opt out and get extra free time. They were unimpressed, and I remember thinking of how unreasonable parents can be, when my mother said 'forget it, it's good to learn about other religions'.

Ever since, I've been eternally grateful for her wise words which have encouraged me to study other beliefs in which I sometimes find resonant echoes of Sikh teachings. Bigotry, whether secular or religious, occurs when we refuse to look beyond the narrow horizons of our own beliefs and prejudices. This becomes unacceptable when we attempt to impose these on others.

In the past, religions sometimes used their might and muscle to promote their beliefs. Today some in secular society seem to be doing much the same thing. We seem to be losing a spirit of live and let live and becoming less considerate to the beliefs and feelings of those of other persuasions, even when the gain to us is proportionately less than the hurt to the sensitivities of others. It's this that bothers me more than the actual court ruling.

13 April 2012

Parallels between Easter and the Sikh Festival of Baisakhi

Tomorrow Sikhs celebrate Vaisakhi, a major festival in the Sikh calendar. It comes a week after the important Christian festival of Easter and there are striking similarities.

The crucifixion of Jesus Christ was followed by a rapid rise of Christianity as a force for good in the world. It has its parallel in the martyrdom of Guru Tegh Bahadur, the ninth Guru of the Sikhs who gave his life defending the right to freedom of belief. It too was a defining moment.

We all know that in the immediate aftermath of the crucifixion of Jesus Christ, even those closest to him denied their allegiance to Christ fearing for their own safety. Much the same fear gripped Sikh onlookers at the time of Guru Tegh Bahadur's martyrdom. Sikhs at the time had none of the distinguishing symbols worn by us today, and hesitated to come forward to claim their master's body.

Guru Tegh Bahadur and earlier Gurus, taught a belief in the equality of all human beings, including full gender equality, freedom of belief and the importance of looking beyond self to the concerns of others. On that historic Vaisakhi festival of 1699 Guru Gobind Singh, the tenth and last Guru of the Sikhs, aware that nominal adherence to such teachings was not enough, resolved to put the community to the test by asking for those prepared to give their lives for these ideals to step forward, and to his joy Sikhs readily did so.

Vaisakhi is important to Sikhs because it moved the community from a passive acceptance of responsible living, to a total commitment to working for a fairer and more just world, even when it is difficult or dangerous to do so.

For Sikhs and people of all faiths today, the difficulty of living true to one's principles is not so much a direct threat to life, as a more subtle one of offending the norms of some in society by pointing out long-term consequences on issues such as the erosion of family values, or that happiness is not something that can be purchased, and the dangers inherent in a society in which values are becoming skewed by an obsession with me and my rights.

The message of Vaisakhi, like the message of Easter, is one of a total commitment to live by values that look beyond self, to the needs of others, including those of generations to come. Today we need this positive commitment more than ever before.

20 June 2012

Two Important Visitors

London is a frequent host to heads of state and powerful politicians who control the destiny of millions. This week the capital extends a welcome to two quite different people, who far from having power, have suffered anger, hostility, detention and exile from those who rule their countries.

The visitor from Burma, Aung San Suu Kyi, is here following her release from detention and house arrest for more than fifteen years. Her courageous stance and refusal to bend under pressure has earned 'the lady' as she is affectionately called, the warmth and admiration of millions both in her own country and all over the world. On a short visit to Britain this week, she will meet members of royalty and address both houses of Parliament.

The other visitor to the capital this week, the Dalai Lama, will be speaking at Westminster Abbey on peace and reconciliation and also meeting members of Parliament. Forced to flee Tibet more than half a century ago, he has been the subject of continuing hostility from the Chinese rulers for daring to speak about democracy and human rights in his country and, it seems that this disapproval has extended to those that allow him a voice in other lands.

The teachings of our different faiths remind us of the importance of standing up for the oppressed, and both these distinguished visitors have shown in their own ways remarkable strength and resilience in their steadfast pursuit of democracy and justice for their people.

Guru Nanak reminded us that it was important to live true to such ideals but warned us that if we chose to tread this path, it could cost us our life. This was the fate suffered by our ninth Guru, Guru Tegh Bahadur, who when asked by Hindus to speak up against the oppression and forced conversions being suffered by their community, felt duty bound to do so. It was a principled stand for the rights of others that cost him his life.

The temptation for most of us in our individual lives, and in the political world, is to pursue questionable compromise. This week we have the opportunity to salute two remarkable visitors who, by the example of their own lives, remind us that the high ideals taught by the Gurus and other faiths have even more relevance in the different world of today.

18 September 2012

Sikh Attitude to Genetic Manipulation

Yesterday's announcement of the possibility of replacing damaged embryonic material with that from a third person to prevent inherited genetic disease has caused some alarm with calls for a rigorous ethical debate.

As I understand it, the procedure involves the substitution of a faulty power component of a cell with a healthy replacement. In practical terms however, the parents will continue to be those who nourish and care for the child giving freely of their time and resources to help the boy or girl grow up in a healthy way to be a responsible member of society.

Sikh's attitudes to the use of scientific advance fully support the use of science to promote health and healing. There is no conflict between Sikh teachings and scientific discovery, and science is viewed as a gift of God to be used for the greater wellbeing of all. To Sikhs the ethics of scientific discovery lie in the use to which such discoveries are put. As Dr. Werner von Braun inventor of the V2 rocket and the father of the American space programme put it, a knife can be used as means of killing, or as a surgeon's scalpel to combat disease and promote healing.

To some extent we all have foreign genetic material introduced in us whenever we are vaccinated to prevent disease. A person who has a lifesaving organ transplant introduces genetic material from a third person into his or her body.

Yet we should always bear in mind the possible downsides to genetic manipulation and we already see this in male child obsessed countries like India and China, where embryonic testing for gender, has in some places, led to many unnecessary abortions and an alarming disparity in boy/girl ratios.

What concerns me is not the inevitable advance in scientific discovery, but our obsession with self and what I want. This blurs our ability to use concepts of right, wrong and responsibility to make rational ethical decisions on the benefits or downside of scientific discovery. It is these imperatives, emphasised in Sikhism and other faiths that we must keep to the fore to ensure new discoveries in science and other fields are always used for the greater good.

25 September 2012

Good and Bad Culture

Aneurin Bevan, founder of the Health Service famously declared that whenever he heard the word 'culture', he immediately thought of bacteria. He was critical of questionable social practices being given legitimacy as culture.

I was reminded of this by the interview with Professor Ted Cantle on the Sunday Programme. He gave us a timely reminder that self-imposed isolation in some communities can give rise to a siege mentality, further isolation, and lead to fear and prejudice in others. Professor Cantle went on to suggest that giving public funding to cultural groups and to some faith schools can add to this isolation.

In this I believe he is both right and wrong. Some aspects of different cultures such as emphasis on individual, family and civic responsibilities promote and enhance social cohesion, but, by the same token, the word culture can also include negative attitudes towards women and those seen as different. State funding can help tackle disadvantage but its blanket use as social policy can also strengthen negative ideas of difference.

I can also understand concern about some faith schools encouraging isolation and a less than respectful attitude to others. I had similar concerns when I was invited to visit the first Sikh faith school in Hayes some years ago. As I entered the main lobby I was struck by a colourful display about the Jewish festival of Purim. The assembly covered topical festivals in all faiths with genuine respect. Teachings of all faiths were included in the curriculum and the Sikh ethos of respect and easy informality between teachers and pupils of all faiths contributed to high academic standards. The school, now an academy, has excellent links with other schools, charities and commerce.

To my mind faith schools that meet such criteria, can encourage confidence and a sense of self-worth in children of a minority faith, as well as respect for others. Without this understanding and respect for the beliefs of others, there is a very real danger of faith schools creating unhealthy segregation.

Coming back to Nye Bevan's comment about culture and bacteria, we now know that bacteria can be good or bad. The same is true of culture. In the words of the old song, we need to ensure that we accentuate the positive and eliminate the negative.

21 November 2012

Massacre in Oak Creek, Wisconsin

J.K. Rowling in her latest novel, *The Casual Vacancy*, features a Sikh family in its central plot. At the book launch last Thursday she explained that she had been deeply influenced by Sikhism because of its egalitarian teachings and stress on gender equality. She said that this had prompted her to study the religion in greater depth and was struck by its modernity.

Her generous words were doubly welcome to a Sikh community increasingly apprehensive about how it is viewed by others. Sikhs are particularly concerned that in the minds of some, the turban seems to be increasingly associated with extremism, whereas in reality it is worn as a visible reminder of a commitment to live by values such as those mentioned by the author of the Harry Potter series.

Unfortunately for Sikhs, Osama Bin Laden also wore a turban and although he is no longer with us, the image still lingers in the minds of many in the United States and mainland Europe who continue to view any turban with a degree of hostility. Even here, teasing and bullying of turban wearing children in schools and vandalism of gurdwaras seems to be on the increase.

Two months ago, a former US army veteran took this irrational dislike of turban wearing people further, when he entered a Sikh gurdwara in Oak Creek, Wisconsin and began shooting innocent members of the congregation, killing six worshippers and injuring many others. President Obama, who had lived among Sikhs in his formative years, paid tribute to the contribution of the community to the life of the USA and in a moving gesture, ordered all Union flags to be flown at half-mast.

Sikhs have two problems in explaining their religion to others. First, respect for other faiths and other ways of life in Sikh teachings, means that it is wrong for us to indulge in any form of proselytizing or pushing our beliefs on others. The second reason is less excusable; we simply do not do enough to get involved in interfaith groups, religious consultative bodies in schools, and many other areas of life in which we can and should let others know more about us and the values for which we stand. We should not expect best-selling authors and others to do this for us.

28 November 2012

Number of Arms of a Hindu Goddess.

I spent yesterday morning helping look after a poorly granddaughter. We watched a TV programme on general knowledge on a variety of subjects taught in schools; the idea being to test the knowledge of an adult against that of a schoolchild. RE was one of the subjects chosen and the question was about the number of arms of a certain Hindu goddess.

The question of course, had nothing to do with the ethical teachings of Hinduism, and, like so much that passes for RE, was about the peripherals of belief found in all religions; about the quaint and exotic; about the form of worship rather than the substance.

Today, Sikhs celebrate the birthday of Guru Nanak, the founder of the Sikh faith who urged the importance of translating rituals of worship, often seen as an end in themselves, to responsible living.

The Guru taught that pilgrimages, penances and ritual acts of giving were, in themselves, not worth a grain of sesame seed in the court of God. He said that such rituals were chains of the mind if they took us away from religious imperatives of leading an honest life in the service of our fellow beings.

Some five and a half centuries ago, the Guru in a major move towards understanding and cooperation between different faiths, taught that the one God of us all was not interested in our different religious labels, but in our attitude and behaviour to those around us. This required accepting the oneness of all humanity, gender equality and social responsibility for the less fortunate. The Guru's popularity, humanity and compassion was welcomed by people in all communities and when he died he was popularly regarded as a Pir or religious leader of the Muslims, and a guru of the Hindus.

Today Sikhs throughout the world will reflect on Guru Nanak's teachings couched in clear uplifting language. Such teachings, like those of the founders of other faiths, give meaning and direction to life but are not always easy to practice. It's much easier to sing or chant religious imperatives than to translate these into demanding living. But, as Guru Nanak reminded us, unless we live true to such teachings, unless we walk the talk, it all amounts to nothing, reinforcing a growing perception of religion as being irrelevant to the challenges of modern society.

8 January 2013

Dangers of Sex Grooming and Trafficking

Later this morning I'll be going to a conference organised by a local gurdwara and the police to alert young Sikhs to the dangers of sex grooming and trafficking. While the plight of vulnerable white girls has made the headlines, few outside the community are aware that Sikh girls, particularly those entering college and university, are also targeted.

Crimes against women and their unequal treatment have long existed in all societies throughout the world. We were reminded of this by the horrific rape and murder of a young medical student in India; a country with a long history of less than equal treatment of women. Crimes of this nature are said by some to be related to the affection lavished on male children whilst girls are treated as lesser members of the family.

Guru Nanak, the founder of the Sikh faith was appalled by the lowly position of women in Indian society. In a memorable verse he wrote women give us birth, nurture us in our infancy and give men companionship; it is women that give birth to kings and rulers. Both he and successor Gurus took concrete steps to ensure the full and equal treatment of women in religious worship, education and other walks of life.

Last Saturday Sikhs celebrated the birthday of the tenth Guru, Guru Gobind Singh who took the work of earlier Gurus further by giving Sikh women the name Kaur, literally 'princess' to emphasize their dignity and complete equality. The Guru had to fight many battles for the survival of the infant Sikh community, and insisted that even in the heightened passions of battle; Sikh soldiers treat women as sisters, daughters or mothers.

Sadly, despite such teachings, the sub-continent culture of male superiority still affects some Sikh households and gives a ready excuse to rebellion prone teenagers to seek attention and affection elsewhere. I have no doubt that today's conference will remind those attending, of the dangers of internet chat lines and predatory behaviour in pubs and clubs. But I believe the best safeguard is for parents to live true to teachings of equality and responsibility and give their children a sense of self-esteem and self-worth to help them distinguish between genuine friendship and false and dangerous relationships.

17 January 2013

Looking at a Common Problem from Different Perspectives

A favourite poem I used to read to my children begins:
Six wise men from Hindustan to learning much inclined
Went to see an elephant, though all of them were blind
Each touches a different part of elephant like the trunk, tusk or tail and comes to the instant conclusion that an elephant is like a serpent, spear or rope. The poem reminds us of the dangers of looking at an issue from too narrow a perspective.

I was reminded about this by two reports this week on the widespread use of drugs. One by a group of parliamentarians says current criminal sanctions do not combat drug addiction and only marginalise users. They want possession and personal use of all illegal drugs decriminalised and the least harmful sold in licensed shops, with labels detailing the risks.

The second report from the BMA also says that there is too much focussing on criminality and goes on to suggest that drug taking is like an illness and those with serious problems shouldn't be inhibited from seeking urgent treatment.

Both these reports look at different facets of a common problem, but they don't give us an understanding of why drug use has become a major problem in recent years. The reports focus on symptoms rather than addressing underlying causes, which, to me, are linked to lifestyles that move us away from responsibility to and support from those around us, to a more selfish and isolated pursuit of personal happiness. It's a bit like chasing a mirage; we never quite get there, and drink and drugs are sometimes seen not only as a remedy for disappointment, but as an end in themselves.

Sikh teachings and those of other religions remind us that life has both ups and downs, and of the importance of developing equanimity and a sense of resilience in balanced and responsible living. In a memorable verse Guru Nanak taught that the lasting sense of contentment in looking outwards to actively helping those around us and working for a fairer society, far exceeds the short-term buzz from drinks and drugs.

The Parliamentary and BMA reports on drug abuse are useful contributions as far as they go. But the underlying problems lie in lifestyle and expectations. These are far harder to change, but we do need to look at and reflect on the wider picture.

24 April 2013

Care in the Community

There has been a bit of a spat over the last few days between the government and the Royal College of Nursing over a new government proposal that nurses work for a year as health care assistants to teach them care and compassion. The government's suggestion is a reaction to the poor standards of care found at the Staffordshire hospital, but Dr. Peter Carter, Chief Executive of the RCN argues that it doesn't address what he sees as the real issue of cuts in resources and inadequate training budgets. Responding to this criticism, Health Secretary Jeremy Hunt accused the union of having vested interests and putting its member's interests before those of patients. It seems we have moved a long way from the cosy picture of the NHS seen at the opening of the Olympics last summer.

The reality to this growing sense of crisis in a health service, once the envy of the world, is the escalating cost of looking after a rapidly growing elderly population, the high cost of expensive new drugs and procedures, as well as growing expectations. To me, those with a stake in a satisfactory resolution of these real concerns are not only the government and health care providers, but also the rest of us.

Looking beyond ourselves to the wellbeing of others is a central part of Sikh teachings. Guru Har Rai the seventh Guru started a free dispensary for the poor and needy and expanded on the concept of langar or free food for all who come to a gurdwara. His son Guru Harkishan died while administering aid to victims of a smallpox epidemic in Delhi. Today many of our larger gurdwaras fund medical care in India and other countries.

All our different faiths remind us that a duty of care and compassion should not have to be taught in hospitals but should be an essential part of everyday life. Guru Nanak declared that looking to the wellbeing of others through giving, and in particular the giving of time, as the most important of the three pillars of Sikhism. Today, we can all do much more to make care in the community a reality rather than a euphemism for an absence of care, and, as Sikh teachings remind us, in so doing, get a more lasting sense of wellbeing ourselves than we do from our sometimes more selfish, questionable and costly lifestyles.

30 April 2013

Lessons of World War One

The First World War is very much in the news these days. Over the last week the papers have carried stories and comment over how we should commemorate next year's centenary of a war we hoped would end wars. An article in the Sunday Times reminds us that there is no clear agreement on exactly how it started and what it meant. What we do know is that the war claimed some 16 million lives, devastating the lives, dreams and aspirations of countless others, and that it ended with something of a controversial peace treaty that provided some with a warped rationale for renewed conflict some twenty years later.

It is right and proper that in the commemoration we remember with gratitude, the courage and sacrifice of British and allied soldiers including volunteers from the Commonwealth and subcontinent. Few know for example, that 83,000 Sikhs lost their lives in the two world wars. However, in the commemoration it's also important that we look to the lessons of the past in trying to prevent future conflicts.

Looking from the perspective of time, it seems that the 1914-18 war had much to do with strategic interest, with one side seeking to extend theirs and the other to defend the status quo. As a concept, defending one's strategic interests seems fine. The trouble is that such interests are not mutually exclusive, and often conflicting, at a time when more and more countries are flexing their economic and military muscles.

The famous scientist Albert Einstein was typically blunt in his view of strategic interest or nationalism, calling it 'an infantile disease, like measles'. We know that he had good reason to fear rampant nationalism, but his blunt words have relevance today as we look at continuing conflicts around us. We have marvellous international bodies like the UN and the Security Council designed to reduce conflict, but all too often see so-called 'strategic interests' of member states preventing necessary action.

Guru Ramdas the fourth Guru was similarly concerned. He wrote:

All powers men make pacts with
Are subject to death and decay
False are all factions that divide men into warring groups.

The Gurus taught that focussing on social justice and human rights is the best way of ensuring lasting peace. Something we should reflect on in next year's commemorations.

16 July 2013

Parliamentary Group for International Religious Freedom

Last week, I attended the first AGM of the newly formed All Party Parliamentary Group for International Religious Freedom, set up to look at ways of protecting basic human rights in the face of mounting religious bigotry in many parts of the world. To date it has received evidence from persecuted Bhai's in Iran, Muslims in Burma, Christians in North Korea and Saudi Arabia, and Hindus in Pakistan and many others. Little is now left of a once thriving Sikh community in Afghanistan. The list is virtually endless.

As a first step the newly formed group will continue mapping the extent of religious persecution in different parts of the world and lobby the government to take the lead in ensuring international aid is strictly tied to full observance of freedom of religion and belief as detailed in Article 18 of the UN Declaration of Human Rights. It also has the difficult task of trying to ensure that we, and others do not turn a blind eye to human rights abuses in so-called 'friendly' countries. It was the great human rights activist Andrei Sakharov who observed that there will be no peace in the world until we are even-handed in addressing such abuse.

The question we all have to ask is, why do religions which talk of peace and forgiveness, themselves promote or get actively involved in horrendous violence against those of a different faith? How can we get followers of our different religions to respect the clear teachings of tolerance and respect for others found in our scriptures?

To me as a Sikh, the answer lies in the fact that while the core teachings of religion are easy to understand, living true to them is far more demanding. We find it much easier to turn to and import negative culture into our different religions which often carries with it false and divisive notions of superiority. With the passage of time, these negative cultural attitudes to those that are different tend to obscure underlying ethical teaching.

The Sikh Gurus observed in some memorable verses how such negative and divisive culture masked and distorted true religious teachings in our different faiths and urged drastic spring cleaning of that which passes for belief, to bring uplifting ethical teachings of responsibility and concern for others back to the fore. Much the same task faces all religions today.

23 July 2013

Baby Boy for Kate and William

The long wait for Kate and William and for millions of well-wishers around the world is finally over with last night's announcement of the birth of a baby boy and welcome news that both mother and baby are doing well. All babies are special to their proud parents; all bring their own gifts of love and unique personality but this baby, third in line to the throne, will also be special to millions in many other lands. As coincidence has it, I was doing my stint on this slot at the time of the announcement of the engagement of William and Kate, and I'm delighted to offer them, and the rest of the Royal family, my congratulations and those of the British Sikh community at this joyous news.

The Sikh community in the UK and abroad have a great regard for the royal family which, given the egalitarian teachings of Sikhism and our obsession with elections, seems at first sight a little odd. Sikh admiration for the royal family is linked to the very positive lead it has given in welcoming other communities and cultures to these shores.

In many ways the British monarchy has been years ahead of the rest of society in promoting greater interfaith understanding, with the Queen herself ensuring that annual Commonwealth Day Service in Westminster Abbey for the last forty years has always been a multi-faith event, with readings from the scriptures of all the major world religions. Since then, the royals, particularly the Queen and the Prince of Wales have graced many functions of different faiths with genuine interest, charm and respect.

As with many faith communities, Sikh parents take their new baby to their place of worship, the gurdwaras as soon as possible after the birth. Prayers are said for the baby's health, and happiness, with the proud parents being reminded to bring their child up to be a credit to the community. It's not an easy task, particularly in today's fast changing social environment, and it will be even more difficult for Kate and William if they are constantly in the glare of media attention.

While wishing them and their new baby every health and happiness for the future, I'm sure many will also join me in wishing them a measure of privacy to enjoy their proud status as parents. It's something they need and deserve, and it's the best present we can all give them.

23 October 2013

Equality in the Criminal Justice System

A couple of days ago I attended a Ministry of Justice meeting looking at ways of ensuring greater equality in the criminal justice system. We were given some impressive looking statistics on hate crime and the negative treatment of minority faiths. Muslims, Jews, Hindus and Buddhists were all covered, but when I inquired why there was no mention of Sikhs, I was told that the figures were based on complaints received and Sikhs rarely bothered to complain. At the time I thought this was simply an excuse for a flawed survey, but on reflection there's some truth in what was said.

The Sikh Gurus taught that we should treat adversity as a new challenge. It's an attitude of mind that has certainly come in handy over the years, but it is not a valid excuse for a failure to highlight negative attitudes to Sikhs, which, from personal experience, have certainly increased since 9/11 with some people in this country and abroad assuming turbaned Sikhs to be Muslim extremists.

When we went on to look at future policies, it was agreed that the key lay in much greater education, particularly in early schooling. Much has been said in recent days about faith schools which fail to respect the culture of others. As a Sikh I believe that any school, faith or otherwise that fails to teach an understanding of and respect for other ways of life, is a failing school and should be treated as such.

Ignorance is a bit like a fog in which everyday objects including people from different cultures can appear frightening and menacing. Prejudice thrives on such ignorance and is difficult to remove once it becomes engrained in everyday attitudes and behaviour, making short superficial induction courses less likely to succeed.

But the responsibility for moving us to a fairer society does not just lie simply with government and bodies like the Ministry of Justice; in the Sikh view, religions too have a real responsibility to work to remove self-created barriers of superiority, difference and exclusivity which add to suspicion and distrust at home and horrendous conflict abroad. As Guru Nanak taught, we all need to work together for greater fairness and true social justice for all members of our human family.

30 October 2013

Heartening Emphasis on Human Rights in Schools

Last week, I was invited to my old school, Bishop Vesey's Grammar School in Sutton Coldfield to give a talk on the Sikh view on justice and human rights. In touring the school, I found this concern for human rights reflected in the very ethos of the school. It was very different from the one I knew in the late '40s and early '50s, when the four Singh brothers were the only ones in the school who looked different and talk of 'our' inherent superiority was all too common.

Today in a very different world, about a third of the pupils are of minority ethnic origin. Respect for different cultures and concern for justice was seen in the many posters on the school walls, including the work of human rights organizations, and moving comments on a visit to Auschwitz. At the Founder's Day service at which I spoke, as well as Christian hymns, there was also readings from the Guru Granth Sahib and the Koran. There is much to be proud about in the way we have adjusted to new cultures and different ways of life and I believe that in this we lead much of the rest of the world.

One thing that has not changed however over the years, is the tendency of children to form their own groups or little gangs which sometimes gain added cohesion by looking down on or excluding others. Sadly, religions and cultures all too often behave in the same way, exaggerating difference and emphasizing exclusivity.

The Sikh Gurus were very concerned about such claims and taught the importance of focussing on commonalities. Guru Nanak taught that the one God of us all was not interested in what we call ourselves but in what we do for our fellow beings. Guru Arjan gave practical utterance to the Sikh belief that no one religion has a monopoly of truth by including Hindu and Muslim verses in our holy scriptures, the Guru Granth Sahib.

Good academic results are important in schools, but due emphasis should also be placed on ensuring that pupils go out to the world with a sense of responsibility and care and compassion for people of all backgrounds and beliefs. It was encouraging to find my old school weaving this wider view of education into all they do.

18 November 2013

Sikhs and Interfaith Dialogue

Yesterday, Sikhs throughout the world celebrated the birthday of Guru Nanak, the founder of the Sikh faith. Guru Nanak is regarded by some as the father of interfaith dialogue, and it's a happy coincidence that his birthday falls in interfaith week; a week in which different faiths share food and pledge to work together.

Guru Nanak was acutely concerned that people at the time were ignoring the many commonalities between different faiths and instead focusing on supposed difference and looking at those of other beliefs as lesser beings. It was against this background that the Guru in his very first sermon declared that in God's eyes there was neither Hindu nor Muslim, and by today's extension, neither Christian, Sikh nor Jew. That the one God of us all is not interested in our different religious labels but in what we do to bring peace, justice and harmony to our fellow beings.

The Guru, who lived in the fifteenth century travelled widely with a Hindu and a Muslim companion constantly emphasizing commonalities in our different faiths while criticizing superstition and divisive practices that attach themselves to and take us away from underlying ethical imperatives. His teachings were widely welcomed by all communities. Succeeding Gurus elaborated on his teachings in various ways, such as including verses of other faiths which parallel Sikh teachings in our holy scriptures the Guru Granth Sahib. The following lines by the Muslim poet Kabir, resonates with Sikh teachings on equality. Kabir writes:

'The same one Divine light permeates all Creation
Why should we then divide people into the High and the low?

As we celebrate another interfaith week, I can't help wondering how little real progress we've made in true understanding and respect for other beliefs. True we've learnt to be more politically correct than Guru Nanak and not say anything that might possibly be construed as offence. Fine, but the downside is that events like Inter Faith Week can easily become a bit superficial rather than an opportunity to question, look and learn from the positive while challenging that which needs to be challenged. And looking at the religious intolerance and active persecution of minorities in many parts of the world today, there is much to be challenged.

14 April 2014

Festival of Vaisakhi

Today, Sikhs throughout the world are celebrating the spring festival of Vaisakhi; a day chosen by the tenth Guru, Guru Gobind Singh, to see if the infant Sikh community was ready to stand on its own and live true to the teachings of Sikhism, without the guidance of further Gurus.

Living true to such teachings means putting ethical imperatives before political or social expediency. It requires real commitment to human rights including, gender equality and recognition of the oneness of our human family, with a total rejection of all notions of caste or race. Another key teaching is that of freedom of worship. The Guru's own father, Guru Tegh Bahadur, was publicly beheaded for supporting the right of Hindus, those of a different religion to his own, to worship in the manner of their choice.

Such teachings are not easy to live by, and on Vaisakhi day 1699 Guru Gobind Singh decided to put the community to the test by asking for volunteers to pledge themselves to live by, and if necessary, die for these ideals. Sikhs, who then had no distinguishing appearance, readily came forward. They were called the Khalsa, the community of equals and were asked to wear the symbols by which we are recognized today, to underline a commitment to Sikh teachings.

Today despite such teachings we still see gross abuse of human rights in many countries, much of it carried out in the name of religion. A renowned scientist from former Soviet Union Andrei Sakharov, was acutely concerned how both in the East and the West, politicians would stridently denounce human rights abuse in other lands but look more benignly at the behaviour of so-called friendly countries. Sadly, religious leaders behave in much the same way and there is much truth in Sakharov's observation that will never be real peace in the world unless we are even-handed in our concern for human rights.

Despite a mushrooming of interfaith activity, we are still far from real trust and cooperative working between religions. At a recent interfaith meeting one of those present referred to this lack of even-handedness in our approach to human rights which, in turn impacts on faith relations in the UK. The disappointing consensus was that it was too political a topic for faith groups! We are still far from the principle of positive commitment, central to the meaning of Vaisakhi.

3 June 2014

Truth and Justice for Sikhs in India

In a few days' time, Sikhs will be commemorating the martyrdom of Guru Arjan; the founder of the Golden Temple and the compiler of the Sikh scriptures the Guru Granth Sahib.

Today, with the active persecution of religious minorities in many parts of the world, we are constantly reminded about the need for greater religious tolerance. Living in early seventeenth century India, Guru Arjan felt passive tolerance was not enough and taught a positive engagement in which different religions shared and cherished common insights and recognized and respected differences.

To this end, he showed his respect for Islam by inviting a Muslim saint, Mia Mir, to lay the foundation stone of the Golden Temple at Amritsar. He placed a door at each of the Temple's four sides to signify a welcome to people from all geographic or spiritual directions, and included verses of Hindu and Muslim saints in the Holy Granth, where these paralleled Sikh teachings. But the Guru lived at a time of religious bigotry and he was tortured and cruelly martyred for his beliefs.

This year's commemorations have added significance. Thirty years ago, today, the Indian army attacked the Golden Temple with ground forces, tanks and heavy weaponry to remove alleged separatists inside. There was a huge loss of life and the assault was recently described by Prime Minister David Cameron as 'a stain on the history of post-independence India'. A worse fate was to befall Sikhs in November of that year following Prime Minister Indira Gandhi's assassination by her Sikh bodyguards. According to American Embassy documents, more Sikhs were killed in just three days than those killed in the whole of General Pinochet's despotic seventeen-year rule in Chile.

In a recent talk at the Indian High Commission, I recalled how close the Hindu and Sikh communities used to be before the traumatic events of 1984 and how this had been replaced with fear and suspicion. I spoke of the desire of Sikhs worldwide for an open independent inquiry to bring closure to still grieving families. To my surprise, the then Acting High Commissioner, responsible to a Congress government, said he agreed with every word.

Today there is a new government in power in India and Prime Minister Narendra Modi has a real opportunity to win the confidence of those who question his commitment to religious tolerance by making this Sikh yearning for justice a reality.

10 June 2014

Wars to End War

Last Sunday I was invited to a memorial service for some Hindu and Sikh soldiers who died in the conflict of the First World War. It was at the Chatri memorial, a remote spot in the beautiful Sussex countryside where some who died from their wounds were cremated on the spot where the memorial now stands. They were part of a volunteer Indian army of some 800,000, many of whom received the highest decorations for bravery.

'Chatri' literally means 'umbrella', and the domed canopy of the structure is a poignant reminder of the care and affection the wounded received from British nurses and doctors in the nearby Brighton's Royal Pavilion hospital.

Many of those who volunteered did so in hope that allied victory would bring a promised measure of independence for the sub-continent. Sadly, the end of hostilities saw the passing of the repressive Rowlatt Act and agitation against repression culminating in the infamous Jallianwala Bagh massacre of 1918.

This year with a century of hindsight, we are all reflecting on the horrors of a war which it was hoped would end wars. Recent conflicts remind us that civilizing constraints are the first casualties of war and that civilians, believed to be one with the enemy, are often prime targets. We lose our focus, if in remembrance services, we forget the deliberate killing of civilian men, women and children. This week's Summit on sexual violence in conflict is a timely reminder that women and girls are often the principal sufferers in conflicts that bring out the worst in human behaviour.

Guru, Guru Gobind Singh who, was acutely aware of the horror of war, reminded us that force should only be used as a last resort to prevent greater harm to the vulnerable, and, only when all other means for redressing that evil have been tried without success. He taught that force used, must be the minimum necessary and importantly, there should be no financial or territorial gain. Sikhs were reminded to give the same respect to enemy women as they would to their mother, sister or daughter.

Standing at the Chatri memorial, I saw that the best homage we could pay those who gave their lives for others, and the best hope for future generations is to work towards a world in which all wars, particularly for economic gain, or softer sounding 'strategic interest', are finally confined to the dustbins of history.

2 September 2014

Need for Twenty-First Century interpretations of Religious Texts

Like many others, I've been trying to get my head around the plight of thousands caught up in the onslaught by soldiers of the so-called Islamic State in Syria and Iraq. Images of cold-blooded killings, and terrified and bewildered children haunt the mind. Worse, the killers, some from Britain, say they are doing this in the name of Islam. Their actions have been condemned by Muslim leaders around the world. Over the weekend some of Britain's leading Muslim clerics issued a statement calling on all Muslims to have nothing to do with what they termed a 'false and poisonous ideology'.

I am sure their views reflect the feelings of the vast majority of Muslims and I can understand the hurt felt by some in the community over the use of language that links them with the actions of a small minority. Some of my Muslim friends find it particularly hurtful to see mindless killers being described as 'Islamists'.

To my mind, neither this tarring of a whole community because of the actions of a few, nor the frequent use of the word 'Asian' to diffuse blame onto an even wider community, help us understand how some in our different faiths, justify unspeakable acts in the name of their religion.

In a thoughtful article in the Times last weekend, Mathew Syed reminds us that religious texts are often written in the specific context of a very different world of hundreds of years ago. Most people understand this and simply look to underlying ethical guidance within them. But some selectively quote passages out of context to justify clearly unacceptable behaviour. As the saying goes: the devil can quote scriptures for his purpose.

Guru Nanak was aware of the danger from the manipulation of religious sentiment. While he himself put forward key ethical teachings, such as those on equality and responsible living, successor Gurus were charged with the difficult task of keeping these to the fore in changing social and political circumstances.

Today we are naturally worried about the dangers we may face from returning British religious extremists and the need to safeguard ourselves. But due emphasis should also be given to the urgent need for people of all faiths to ensure common underlying imperatives are couched in today's terms. In so doing they will avoid the potential for harmful distortions. It will also help to make religion, what the founders of our different faiths intended, a positive force for good.

9 September 2014

Downside of Smart Technology

Media hype over this week's launch of the latest smart phone and the million ways it will help us connect to everyone and everything, leaves me a little cold. I'm a bit wary about sophisticated gadgetry telling us what to do with our lives. Admittedly I'm a bit of a Luddite about mobile phones, the social media and the internet. I envy those with the speed and dexterity of Madame Defarge who clicked away on her knitting needles while watching the guillotine in action. I can't cope with lengthy texts demanding instant replies. My granddaughter recently said she would send me an email because 'you can't text'. Determined to prove her wrong I slowly and ponderously wrote a text message signed 'master texter' – and then, inadvertently sent it to her puzzled aunt.

My relationship with the internet lurches between love and hate. I can't get over the power of the internet that gives near instant access to detailed information on the vaguest of topics—that is, when it works! At the moment we have lost our wi-fi and have only intermittent internet access due to a fault on the line. We've all had similar experiences.

My real concern is that it is all too easy to get hooked on such gadgetry in a way that takes us away from due attention to those around us. Guru Nanak too was concerned about the way people often neglected their responsibilities for more selfish pursuits. In his day, some people would leave their families and friends to go to the wilderness in search of God.

Today there isn't much wilderness left, but it is all too easy to drift into a virtual wilderness in pursuit of virtual friendships to the neglect of real people around us. I am reminded of the poet's words:

'We flatter those we scarcely know, and rush to please the fleeting guest, but heap many a thoughtless blow on those who love us best.'

Now there's a 'Thought for the Day' -in less than 140 characters!

16 September 2014

Courage in Conflict

Sikhs are often described as a martial race. Two things wrong with that. First, Sikhism is a religion open to all, and one of its basic teachings is that we all belong to the same, one human race. Nor are we particularly martial, and our Guru's teaching on responding to personal affront is, (I hope metaphorically), 'to kiss the feet of those who would do you harm'.

At the same time Sikhs are duty bound to stand up to injustice against the weak and vulnerable and if necessary and as a last resort, by the force of arms. Unfortunately, in a short history of constant persecution, we've had plenty of practice.

I was reminded of this last Friday when I attended an impressive function at the Royal Military College Sandhurst to commemorate Saraghari Day. On September 12th, 1897, twenty-one brave Sikhs holed up in a small brick and mud fort at Saraghari on the Northwest Frontier of India, held back an army of some 10,000 marauding and pillaging tribesmen, for nearly a day to give valuable time for their colleagues to regroup. Eventually they were all killed, but the thought of surrender never entered their minds. Their courage received a rare standing ovation in the British Parliament and their achievement has been recognized by UNESCO as one of eight most inspiring stories of collective bravery in human history.

I saw more modern examples of uplifting courage in a visit to the Invictus Games, the brainchild of Prince Harry. In the Games, wounded soldiers show how despite appalling injuries, they can still laugh, joke and compete in athletic activities. The Games, take their name from Henley's poem Invictus, which reminds us that however difficult or unfair life may appear, we should never give up. It ends with the immortal lines:

It matters not how straight the gate; how charged with punishment the scroll, I am the master of my fate; the captain of my soul.

I saw limbless blade runners, one with severe burns to his face, and others racing in wheelchairs enthusiastically embracing life. They and the brave soldiers of Saragarhi remind us of the importance of courage and commitment. Courage that refuses to accept the *bludgeoning's of chance*, and helps put all our petty aches and pains, and grumblings about the unfairness of life, into true perspective.

6 November 2014

Guru Nanak's Teachings on the Equality and Dignity of Women

Today, Sikhs celebrate the birthday of Guru Nanak, the founder of the Sikh faith. The Guru was concerned at the way different religions in his day, seemed to be more intent on rubbishing the beliefs and practices of sister faiths than in living the values taught by their own.

In his very first sermon he taught that in God's eyes there was neither Hindu nor Muslim, and by today's extension, neither Christian, Sikh nor Jew. He reminded us that the one God of us all has no religious affiliation, but looks to how we live and what we do for our fellow beings.

With a Hindu and Muslim companion, the Guru travelled the length and breadth of India, to Sri Lanka and Tibet and to the Middle East preaching the importance of religious tolerance and a recognition of the equality and oneness of our human race.

Guru Nanak was particularly concerned about the plight of women on the subcontinent who, as in much of the world, were treated as inferior beings. He taught that women should be given full equality with men, not simply as the wives or daughters of men, but as individuals in their own right, playing a full part in society.

Unfortunately, as we are daily reminded in the news, deep rooted cultural practices often tend to blur or subvert the teachings of religion which challenge unthinking attitudes and behaviour. I was vividly reminded of this while working as a young mining engineer in a remote area of Bihar, I had just received news that my wife had given birth to our first child, a daughter. I was over the moon and excitedly rushed to the house next door, that of a Sikh and told him the wonderful news. Contrary to clear Sikh teachings, his culturally conditioned response was 'never mind, it will be boy next time!' I was not then the gentle, easy going soul that I like to think I am today, and it took great restraint not to give physical vent to my annoyance.

Today, as we celebrate the birthday of Guru Nanak, we should resolve to do as he did and continually challenge all forms of unjust or oppressive behaviour which often masquerades as religion, and instead focus on true religious teachings of respect for and service to all members of our one human race.

17 November 2014

Need to Demolish Barriers of Dogma or Belief

Last week we were celebrating the twenty-fifth anniversary of the fall of the Berlin wall; a physical structure designed to keep the people of Eastern Europe isolated from the freedom and democratic values of the West.

This week is Interfaith week; a week in which we question equally divisive barriers of belief between religions. Barriers built on claims of exclusivity and superiority, seen in the use of language to denigrate those of other beliefs or ways of life. Today, we are all too aware of the way in which words can be used to promote active hatred and the mindless killing of thousands of innocents, as seen in the Middle East and many other parts of our world.

In the past, talking about distant religions in a disparaging way, though wrong, was fairly harmless and gave us a perverse sense of unity based on the superiority of our way of life over that of others. Today such thinking is food and sustenance to the fanatic. In our smaller and interdependent world, recognizing that we are all equal members of the same human family has now become an imperative.

Sikh teachings remind us that our different religions are different paths to responsible living and must all be respected. Religious teachings are not mutually exclusive and frequently merge in shared truths and a heightened understanding of our own faith.

A popular Christian hymn states:

To all life Thou givest; to both great and small
In all life Thou livest the true life of all
The lines have a striking parallel in Sikh scriptures
There is an inner light in all
And that light is God

The Sikh Gurus frequently used parallel teachings in different faiths to emphasize important commonalities and shared values.

Today religion finds itself confined to the margin of society as a cause rather than a cure for hatred and violence. We see this in governments focusing huge resources on programs to combat religious extremism. And yet... if religions work together to live common core teachings of right, wrong and responsibility, who knows? Instead of programs like 'Prevent', we might even have government programs called 'Enable' to embed these values in daily living as the founders of our faiths intended. Not easy, but events like Interfaith week are at least a step in the right direction.

18 March 2015

Mental Health Provision for Children and Adolescents.

Yesterday, a Department of Health taskforce published a report recommending sweeping changes in the funding and operation of mental health provision for children and adolescents. The report follows a series of Times articles on a growing epidemic of mental health problems in children and adolescents resulting in a huge rise in children resorting to self-harm and exhibiting symptoms of anxiety and depression in schools.

Many are seeking treatment for mental health problems in hospitals, or worse, ending up in prisons. In one of these articles, the columnist Libby Purves highlights the urgent need for parents, to reset their priorities and recognize the ground realities of pressures on their children.

Today, it is all too easy to spend all our time on personal pursuits or lose ourselves in the virtual wilderness of the internet to the neglect of those around. Worse, in the absence of comfort and support from parents, children may look to friendship, love and support on internet chat lines oblivious to the dangers of grooming, blackmail and the hurt that can be caused by online bullying. While yesterday's promise of enhanced provision will help, Sikh teachings and those of sister faiths suggest that the real remedy lies in the home.

Reflecting on parental responsibility, Guru Nanak reminded us that the birth of a child comes with an attached responsibility for the child's care and comfort that continues even if parents split. It is the family rather than on the internet that children should share both triumphs and concerns and receive time consuming but necessary encouragement and support. Today, obsession with personal fulfilment has replaced a search for God. Our different faiths remind us that both personal fulfilment and God can be found in looking beyond ourselves to the care and support of those around us.

2 June 2115

Plight of Refugees

The weekend news of seventeen bodies being pulled out of the Mediterranean and the rescue of more than 4000 people in just three days, reminds us of the unbelievable suffering in the Middle East. Refugees, from brutal rule in Libya, Syria and Iraq are continuing to take their chance in leaky boats to escape further persecution. Their plight is mirrored by that of the Rohingya Muslims from Myanmar, starving and adrift in ships for months at an end, because no one will give them sanctuary.

A common feature of such tragedies is the manipulation of religious sentiment to further political power, with selective quotation of religious texts written hundreds of years ago being used to justify brutal behaviour. Paradoxically, similar selective quotation is used to argue that religions teach only peace.

Most religions suffer this problem of selective quotation to justify different views. Sikhism is a comparatively new religion with the founder, Guru Nanak born in 1469. The teachings of the Gurus were couched in lasting ethical principles and were recorded in their lifetime. Sikhs were asked to follow only these recorded teachings. Despite this clarity, we still suffer from selective quotation on emotive issues such as meat eating, and more worryingly, in attempts to introduce new teachings which many Sikhs feel to be of dubious authenticity.

Today, religious leaders have the additional task of disentangling advice, given to meet the particular social or political climate of several centuries ago, from more lasting and timeless ethical teachings.

To move in this direction, it is important that our different religions work together to tackle common concerns. Sikhs believe that true religious commitment goes beyond narrow boundaries of belief and that our religious labels, or membership of different sects count for nothing in the eyes of the one God of us all. It's what we do to counter poverty and work for peace and justice that really counts.

The challenge of putting religious teachings in perspective and working together on common concerns, is not easy, but it is essential that we move in this direction to make religion what the founders of our different faiths intended it to be, guidance for responsible living, and the cure rather than the cause of conflict.

25 November 2015

What Does God Think of Us?

When invited to a radio programme on the theme 'what does God think of us', my jaundiced contribution was: 'If God had human emotions they would be of utter bewilderment and despair at the antics of the human race, coupled with a determination to keep us well away from any truly intelligent life in the vastness of Creation.' Today, in the aftermath of the religion-linked massacres in Paris and Mali, this seems to be a bit of an understatement.

Such killings are nothing new. At the time of Guru Nanak, whose birth anniversary falls today, Catholics and Protestants were at each other's throats in Europe and, in India, there was religious conflict between Muslims and Hindus. Why do our different religions with much to offer, ignore important commonalities and focus negatively on supposed difference and notions of exclusive access to God's truth?

It was a concern close to Guru Nanak's heart. In his very first sermon, he courageously suggested that the one God of us all was not impressed by our different religious labels, but by what we did for our fellow beings. The Guru devoted his life to stressing commonalities and questioning the validity of some supposed differences.

Today in our demographically changed world, while recognizing and respecting genuine difference, there is an urgent need to counter the use of difference to justify hatred and violence towards others. The concern over the capacity of those working with ISIS to persuade young Muslims to leave the UK, to join fighters in Syria highlights the need to reach hearts and minds. I can fully understand the revulsion felt by those who say we should bomb ISIS off the face of this earth, but such statements, can be cynically used by extremist as 'an attack on our religion'.

A letter in yesterday's Times by nearly 200 Muslim scholars deploring terrorism in the name of Islam gives hope. They point out that there is nothing Islamic about the so-called 'Islamic State' and no acts of terrorism, hate and violence can be justified. Distortion and misinterpretation can happen with many historic religious texts and is why, particularly in the context of today's times, it's necessary to stress the important commonalities with other faiths. In this, all who speak out in such a way deserve our full support.

2 December 2015

Imperatives in War and Peace

Today's debate about the rights or wrongs of air strikes against ISIS, will be focused on what constitutes a just and proportionate response to ISIS atrocities in Paris and elsewhere. While much has been said and written about criteria that need to be met for a just war, less has been said about imperatives for just and lasting peace.

Syria, like much of the Middle East, is a cauldron of competing rivalries, not only those of Sunni and Shia Muslims but also smaller groups: Alawites, Kurds, Christians and others. While we would all like to see functioning democracies in the region, this is easier said than done. The history of the Middle East, and many other parts of the world shows that majority rule does not always equate to just rule. Majorities insensitive to the rights of minorities can all too easily morph into tyrannies. What is important is, not so much the process of acquiring power, as the way power is exercised.

I was reminded about this at an event celebrating the birth anniversary of the Maharaja Ranjit Singh, who lived in the nineteenth century. He ruled over a vast area of northern India, including present day Pakistan. Although the Maharaja gained power through military might, he reached out to all communities winning both love and loyalty.

Totally illiterate, he spent hours as a child in the gurdwara, listening to Sikh teachings on respect for all communities. He was deeply influenced by the Sikh belief that token respect for other ways of life is not enough, and that for true respect, we should be prepared to put our own rights and freedom on the line, in support of those of others.

The Maharaja kept this teaching close to his heart. There were more Hindu and Muslim ministers in his government than Sikhs. He also gave generously for the upkeep and development of places of worship of all communities, bringing peace, stability and prosperity into a region that had been subject to factional rivalry, not unlike that seen in the Middle East today.

Yes, this is history from the nineteenth century, but it contains fundamental truths that we would be wise to learn from. Reaching out to others in this way is not easy, but is possible, and to my mind, essential for true and lasting peace. We should give our full support to any group working in this direction.

8 March 2016

Plight of Refugees

The news that Royal Navy vessels are to be sent to the Aegean to curb the activities of people smugglers has much to commend it, but for some, it masks the fact that many of those risking their lives and savings to clamber onto leaky and overcrowded boats are refugees.

Not so long ago the word 'refugees' conjured up images of innocent men, women and children fleeing terror. Today, the word refugee is sometimes interpreted as alien hordes, and tear gas and razor wire fences have been used to keep would-be refugees, including young children at a distance.

This morning's decision on agreed controls goes to the heart of the moral dilemma of deciding whether refugee applies only to those fleeing a war or whether it can also encompass those seeking a better life for themselves and their children. Ongoing violence in Afghanistan and Iraq, abuses in Eritrea, as well as poverty in Kosovo, are also leading people to look for new lives elsewhere, and not just in Europe.

As a Sikh, I applauded the initial welcome given to refugees fleeing from Syria. It was a welcome that resonated with Sikh teachings that, even in the height of conflict, we should never forget that we are all members of the same one human race and our highest religious duty is to look to the needs of others.

The crisis in Syria is linked to the wider turmoil in the Middle East following the second Gulf War. The pro-democracy demonstrations, cracked down on in 2011, were followed by the emergence of ISIS with its brutalities and beheadings and the horror of bombs raining down on the long-suffering people of Syria, from all directions, including Russia, ISIS, the coalition allies and President Assad himself. Who would not wish to leave? The inevitable exit of refugees has almost become an unstoppable tide.

The problem, now, in dealing with such large numbers is immense. The current tentative ceasefire in Syria is perhaps the best hope for their future, but there are very real difficulties in translating this to peace and stability.

Sikh teachings are not alone in emphasizing our common responsibility to help those fleeing tyranny. And I believe it's important that any agreed system of controls on the grounds of expediency should not reduce our sense of our common humanity, or blind us to the importance of our values and ideals.

15 March 2016

Role of Commonwealth

Yesterday HM the Queen, now in her ninetieth year, attended the Annual Commonwealth Day Service at Westminster Abbey. As Head of the Commonwealth, her commitment and dedication have been central to making this loose linking of fifty-three countries a tried and tested force for stability and mutual cooperation.

The Commonwealth is a fortuitous creation of recent history. The name itself is a bit of a contradiction and an odd way to describe a grouping of countries at different stages of economic development with huge disparities in wealth. Member countries also differ considerably in their adherence to human rights and freedom of worship. And yet to my mind, it is a grouping of countries that carries hope and a sense of common vision necessary in an uncertain world.

I believe there are two reasons for this. The first lies in the curious ability of British people to turn people of countries they conquered and once ruled, into friends and equals, united by a shared history of respect and understanding.

Equally important is the central role of Her Majesty as Head of the Commonwealth. Her warmth and enthusiasm has been a noticeable feature of the Commonwealth Day Service for many years, and it is also evident in her Christmas day broadcasts. The service in the Abbey always includes readings and prayers from other Commonwealth faiths.

This warm welcome to those of different faiths echoes the central Sikh teachings that we are all members of one human race and that no faith has a monopoly of truth, The Sikh holy book, the Guru Granth Sahib itself contains the writings of saints from other faiths to highlight shared core beliefs.

To me, this improbable grouping of multiple identities gives strength and inclusivity – the theme of this year's celebration – to the Commonwealth to help it meet many of the challenges of human rights, religious freedom and sustainable development facing it. It has already gently helped the Sri Lankan government set up a Truth and Reconciliation Commission to investigate alleged human rights abuses against the Tamil Tigers and it could lead to similar initiatives to address other concerns. A common ethos of respect and unity of purpose can achieve much, and in this the Commonwealth has much to offer.

6 July 2016

Repeated Lessons of History

In the recent media coverage of the bravery of those killed on the battlefields of WW1, I was particularly moved by a piece in the Times by Daniel Finkelstein about the courage of both his paternal and maternal grandfathers. Both regarded themselves as intensely patriotic and both were decorated for their heroism. However, they were on the German side of the conflict. Courage can be found in both friend and foe, and patriotism is entirely subjective.

While it is right and proper to honour the memory of those who gave their lives for their country, we will never learn from history if we fail to reflect on its lessons. This thought was in the mind of the Queen's grandfather, King George V as he looked on rows and rows of endless graves in Flanders and commented that '*we will have failed to honour the memories* of *those who gave their all, if we allow such slaughter to ever occur again.*'

Later generations, with the advantage of hindsight, need to ask questions like did the war advance the cause of peace and social justice in Europe or elsewhere? And did the punitive reparations demanded of Germany in any way contribute to the rise of Adolf Hitler?

Today, with the publication of the long delayed Chilcot inquiry into the 2003 war in Iraq there will also be similar questions and inevitable recriminations. What is beyond dispute, is that the long suffering of people of Iraq is, as we saw in the weekend terrorist outrage in a shopping mall in Bagdad is still far from over, and true peace remains elusive.

I was recently invited to the formal unveiling of a beautifully illustrated short prayer included in prayers said before the start of formal proceedings in the Lords. It reminds Parliamentarian, of a responsibility to put 'all selfish interests and partial affections' to one side in all our deliberations. It is remarkably similar to the Sikh daily prayer the Ardas, that concludes Sikh services in gurdwaras, and closes with the words 'sarbat ka bhala' – a pledge to work for the greater good of all. Such sentiments should be central to all debate and political decision making, in helping us to reflect objectively on the past, and work together towards a better future.

13 July 2016

Indarjit's Law

The seventeenth century poet John Dryden, reflecting on democracy wrote:

*'Nor is the people's judgement always true,
The Most may err* as *grossly* as *the Few'.*

Many on the 'remain' side of the referendum may feel this speaks to them. While both sides agree that the democratic decision must be respected no matter how close the result. The incoming Prime Minister Theresa May has already pledged to respect the decision to leave as she begins the task of steering the country through uncertainty, as for the first time in many years we are now forced to look afresh at basic questions of identity, sovereignty and aspirations, in our relations with Europe and the rest of the world.

It's a sad aspect of human nature that sometimes the easiest way in getting someone on our side in discussion or debate is to find someone else we can blame for all our problems. In the '50s and '60s it was people from the Commonwealth. In recent debate we have heard unhelpful nasty language about immigrants and refugees which has led to a rise in hate crimes. It all reminds me of what I call Indarjit's law:

that when two or more people can find sufficient in common to call themselves 'us', they will immediately look for a *'them' to look down on; to strengthen their new-found unity.*

We see it in rivalry between football fans but in its extreme form, it can lead to horrors like the holocaust and more recent genocides.

In the India of the fifteenth century, Guru Nanak witnessed unnecessary divisions in the religions around him and stressed the importance of recognizing common beliefs and aspirations. Guru Arjan, the fifth Guru, took this emphasis on commonalities further by incorporating some verses of Hindu and Muslim saints into our scriptures, the Guru Granth Sahib, to emphasize common ethical teachings, while the ninth Guru, Guru Tegh Bahadur gave his life defending the right of all people to freedom of belief.

My hope is that later today when Theresa May assumes office as Prime Minister, she will similarly use her considerable experience to focus on commonalities like the pursuit of social justice and respect for the rights and beliefs of others, as she leads the country to a new future.

21 March 2017

An Insensitive Ruling

Last week's ruling by the European Court of Justice that employers have a right to set dress codes (that can exclude religious symbols and dress), came as a shock to turban wearing Sikhs, Muslim women who wear a head scarf, and many Christians and Jews. Despite assurances from the government, legal experts and the European Court of Human Rights stating that faith communities in the UK would continue to be free to both practice and manifest their religious belief, postings on internet discussion groups, suggest some people still feel the ruling might be used to their disadvantage.

Some European politicians, playing to growing populism, welcomed the ruling. For me it was all deja vu. In the early '80s, I spent a day and a half in court as an expert witness for the then Commission for Racial Equality, in a case against a school that said its uniform rules did not allow a Sikh boy the right to wear a turban in school. The case, that went all the way to the House of Lords, finally established the right of Sikhs to wear the symbols of their faith.

During my cross-examination, I was asked: 'Would you be equally offended if you were told you could not enter a church or a school?'

I replied: 'No, because for a Sikh it is not necessary to go to a church. But it is necessary to be educated. A Sikh child would be placed at a severe disadvantage, especially when, to add to the hurt, he is told, "we are doing this in the interest of the racial harmony".

I honestly thought that we had now finally moved on from earlier insensitivity, to 'those not like us', but populism, which can open the door to racism, seems to be gaining ground in much of the world, with its unstated message that those 'not like us', are responsible for all our problems.

Guru Gobind Singh, the last of the Sikh Gurus, directly challenged such prejudiced thinking. He taught:

Though some see only difference,
We are all of *one race in all the world.*
We all have the same form, compounded
Of *the same elements The one Lord made us all.*

I believe the Gurus words are a timely warning against the growing allure of populism, now all too evident in much of the world.

18 July 2017

Understanding terrorism

Met. Police Commissioner Cressida Dicks' weekend statement that police had prevented as many as five near imminent terrorist attacks over the last few months, reminds us that we still have much to do to understand and combat the roots of such terrorism.

The seeming paradox behind increasing terrorist outrages and much of the violence in the world today, is how can religious teachings designed to help us be better human beings, be manipulated to lead to the deliberate killing of innocents?

Sikh teachings remind us that what generally passes for religion, is, in reality, a complex mix of superstition, rituals, culture, group history and uplifting ethical teachings. No religion, including my own is immune from followers going against its ethical teachings which are easy to state, but difficult to live by, and in practice, greater emphasis is often placed on culture and rituals, and sometimes, a perversely unifying belief, that God favors our faith over that of others.

Guru Nanak, looking at conflict between religions in the India of his day, reminded us: 'the one God of us all is not the least bit interested in our different religious labels but in what we do for others'. It's a perversion to believe that God condones killing and murder in His name, and to horrendous crimes and savagery not only between faiths but within the same faith.

Today, despite many years of earnest effort for interfaith understanding, there is virtually no dialogue between faiths to explore and understand their different religions. Religious leaders come together, deplore the violence in the world, share tea and samosas, and then, often go back to their congregations to preach exclusivity.

There is an urgent need to look at the environment in which the cancer of terrorism thrives. We need legitimate discussion of questionable attitudes and practices, beginning with those that discriminate against women, gay people and others. Prime Minister Theresa May was right when she recently spoke of the need for difficult conversations about religion. A bold, but courteous, questioning of seemingly divisive practices will help make religion, what it was always intended to be, an active player in working for the common good of all.

25 July 2017

Commendable Courage of Humanitarian Workers

The weekend post brought its usual appeals for donations to help in alleviating suffering in Syria, Iraq and other areas of the Middle East. The scale of suffering, wrought by internecine political, religious and ethnic conflict, is truly devastating and it is important that we support such appeals and help those risking their lives to help the victims of war and violence.

Next month representatives of different faiths and secular society will meet at a service at Westminster Abbey for Humanitarian Aid workers killed in conflict. At the inaugural meeting, four years ago, I referred to the extraordinary dedication and concern for others of an American woman, twenty-six-year-old Kayla Mueller, captured by ISIS and reportedly killed in a Jordanian air strike. In a letter smuggled to her family, she wrote:

If I have suffered at all throughout this experience, it is only in knowing how much suffering I have put you through… The thought of your pain is the source of my own.

No self-pity; no harsh word about her captors. Only a concern for others. There are many others like Kayla, and they all deserve our prayers and support. The reality however is their dedication and international aid efforts alone, cannot cope with the suffering of those caught up in the fighting, and in the huge displacement of people we have witnessed, which just goes on and on.

I believe it is important to look more closely at the causes of such suffering. True, that violence begins with local rivalries, but unfortunately, these are magnified and made more horrific by larger factional rivalry between the great powers, supporting rival factions with ever-more sophisticated means of killing in pursuit of strategic interest. The Sikh Guru, Guru Amar Dass, looking at the dubious alliances fracturing the society of his day wrote:

I am of *God's Faction. All other factional alliances are subject to death and decay.*

Speaking from a Sikh perspective, if we wish to avoid the seemingly endless man-made suffering of innocents, I believe we must continually remind all in power to look beyond, solely, their own self-interest, to what Sikhs call 'Sarbat ka Bhalla', a single-minded resolve to secure the well-being of all.

9 January 2018

Dangers of Populism

At the start of a New Year, we all look to our concerns and hopes for the year to come. For me, a major concern is the potential for populism rooted in xenophobia that looks only to economic prosperity for 'me and my'.

Last weekend, Sikhs throughout the world celebrated the birthday of Guru Gobind Singh, who through his life and work, taught us to look beyond narrow sectarian interests and work for the wellbeing of wider society.

Guru Gobind Singh was the last of the founding Gurus of Sikhism whose role was to show that the teachings of Guru Nanak stressing the equality of all, including gender equality and a willingness to put others before self, were not impracticable ideals, but a necessary, though demanding, blueprint for a fairer and more peaceful society.

The task of Guru Nanak's successor Gurus wasn't easy, and two were martyred for stressing the need for tolerance and freedom of worship at a time of intense religious bigotry. A similar fate was suffered by many of the early Sikhs, but despite such persecution, the resilience of the infant Sikh community continued to grow to such an extent that Guru Gobind Singh decided he could now end the line of living Gurus and ask Sikhs to commit themselves to following the teachings of his predecessors, contained in the Sikh holy book, the Guru Granth Sahib, as they would a living Guru.

The Sikh Gurus were not the only ones who taught that ethical living, with concern and compassion for those around us, was the way to true contentment. Centuries earlier, Jesus Christ had taught much the same in parables like the Sermon on the Mount, and the story of the Good Samaritan. It is important that we recognize the common thrust for more responsible living found in our different faiths and work together to make these central to life.

Today's populism can lead to such imperatives being ignored, encouraging a drive to self-interest. Rather, I would suggest an alternative movement rooted in common ethical teachings across faith traditions and secular society. While acknowledging and respecting differences between cultures and religions. But we need to look beyond mere lip service and begin to walk the talk if we want to move from the bigotry of 2017 to a better 2018.

16 January 2018

Outsourcing Personal Responsibility

Outsourcing is clearly a growth industry. If we make a call to any service provider, it might well be answered by someone in Mumbai or Bangalore. It's something we all face every day. As we juggle our complex personal lives, we understandably find ourselves entrusting the care of our children to childminders we sometimes scarcely know.

This outsourcing of responsibility goes much wider. Questions to ministers in Parliament, are often couched in terms of: 'what is the government going to do about the care of the elderly, the grooming of vulnerable children, hate crime, knife crime, obesity, alcoholism, the dangers of the social media and much else.

Over the weekend we had dentists calling for the government to act over an alarming rise in tooth decay in young children often caused by too many sugary drinks. These are complex social issues which can never have a single answer. With the best will in the world, government policy cannot simply make up for the neglect of personal responsibility.

Escaping personal responsibility is nothing new. In the India of Guru Nanak's day, people would sometimes leave their families to wander in the wilderness in a search for God. The Guru criticised this abandonment of social responsibility and suggested that they go back home and look to the care of their families and wider society.

I was reminded of this while attending the official opening of a new, Sikh ethos school in Leeds recently. Running through the school's DNA is an underlying ethos, common to many faiths and beliefs, of commitment to personal responsibility and service to those around us.

I was given a tour of the school with the Lord Mayor of Leeds, Councilor Jane Dowson. Brightly colored posters on the walls, and writing in exercise books, emphasised what I think of as the often missing other 3 Rs: Right, Wrong and Responsibility.

The Lord Mayor looked at the list of British Values prominently displayed on one wall, and then at the summary of the essential ethos of Sikh teachings on another, and said they are one and the same! She continued, 'if only we could get adults to live by such values. Not easy. But a little less outsourcing of personal responsibility, can have huge benefits for us all.

11 June 2018

Resetting the Tone of Public Debate

My computer and I are not the best of friends. It frequently accuses me of being a robot, or not even knowing my own date of birth! Fortunately, when it is in one of its really ratty moods, I can usually reset it, back to a date when it was working properly, or make it behave itself, by closing it, and restarting.

It's far more difficult to see what we can do about an increasing human 'rattiness' in discussion and behaviour towards those who do not share our opinions or prejudices on Brexit, immigration or anything else. A little resetting of the tone of debate towards respecting the sincerely held beliefs and opinions of others is clearly needed.

I believe, religion in its true essence, is supposed to help us to do just this, and help us develop more tolerant attitudes to those who may not share our views. But unfortunately, over the centuries, religions themselves, have displayed intolerance and violence, not only to others, but even to members of their own faith.

This week Sikhs are commemorating the martyrdom of Guru Arjan, the fifth Guru of Sikhs, who literally gave his life trying to end fractious in-fighting between religions, by building bridges of understanding and respect between them. Guru Arjan was the founder of the famous Golden Temple in Amritsar. To emphasize Sikh respect for the followers of Islam, he asked a Muslim saint, Mia Mir to lay the foundation stone. The Guru was a prolific poet and scholar and the main compiler of the Sikh holy scriptures, the Guru Granth Sahib. In it he also added verses of Hindu and Muslim saints to emphasize important commonalities.

Guru Arjan was well aware of the dangers of emphasizing tolerance and respect in an age of bigotry. He was arrested by the country's rulers and tortured to death in the searing heat of an Indian June. In traditional commemoration of Guru's martyrdom, and in the spirit of his teachings, Sikhs make no show of anger or bitterness. Instead, sweetened cold drinks are served to all who pass by Sikh homes or gurdwaras.

Guru Arjan gave his life for interfaith understanding, and tolerance and respect for the sincerely held beliefs of others. His life serves as an inspiration not only to Sikhs, but for all seeking to nudge society in a less fractious direction.

19 June 2018

Sport and the Dignity of Difference

The excitement and *wall to* wall press coverage of the football World Cup, has temporarily diverted our attention away from appalling suffering in Yemen, Syria and much of the Middle East. Former Liverpool manager Bill Shankly's famous saying that football is more important than life or death, has a ring of momentary truth for many.

It is much easier to lose ourselves in the excitement of England's last night's thrilling victory over Tunisia with Captain Harry Kane's winning goal in injury time, or Cristiano Ronaldo's hat-trick in Portugal's earlier match against Spain, and other highlights of the tournament, than come to terms with the continuing suffering in the Middle East, made worse by Saudi Arabia's attack on the Houthi rebel port of Hodeida, now mostly under Saudi control. Peace imposed by force, simply tilts things in favour of one of the combatants, and can even add to suffering and a heightened sense of injustice.

Guru Nanak, reflecting on similar suffering in fifteenth century India, courageously declared that: 'the one God of us all, looks beyond supposed superiority of birth or creed; that we all belong to the same one human family of equals, all deserving the same rights'. God, he taught, is not interested in religious or other labels, but in what we do for our fellow beings.

Following the suffering of the second world war, the UN Declaration of Human Rights carried similar sentiments. The Security Council was created to ensure such rights were respected. The tragedy of politics today, is those charged with keeping us to norms of civilized behaviour, without taking sides, the referees of political foul play, are often active offenders, sometimes taking sides to further their own self-interest. It is worth reflecting that much of the weaponry fueling conflicts across the world is supplied by members of this peacekeeping body.

Football may at times be fractious, and has its own share of problems, but in football and sport generally, there is genuine respect for different teams, as well as for members of different faiths within teams. The world of sport readily accepts, what the former Chief Rabbi, Lord Sacks called: the 'dignity of difference' and has a lot to teach the world of politics.

22 November 2018

Continuing Intolerance

This weekend, Sikhs will be celebrating the birth anniversary of Guru Nanak, founder of the Sikh faith. He lived at a time of conflict between the two main religions of the subcontinent, Hinduism and Islam, with each claiming superiority of belief. An important thrust of his teaching was to show that despite superficial differences, both faiths recognized common ethical values of truth, justice and responsibility. He also emphasised the oneness of our human family and the dignity and full equality of women.

Guru Nanak, born in Punjab, taught that the one God of all people is not in the least bit interested in our different religious labels, but in what we do for wider society. Yet five and a half centuries on, in the same Punjab, the nine-year incarceration on death row of a Christian, Asia Bibi, and in Myanmar the appalling persecution of the Rohingya remind us that religious bigotry is still very much with us.

We claim to live in more enlightened times and yet in many parts of the world, religious bigotry continues to grow at an alarming rate, often leading to horrendous conflicts and the death of innocent people; a situation made worse by the ready availability of guns and the trade in arms.

Religious bigotry will not go away by itself. It has to be challenged by the adherents of all faith and by wider society. Faiths that seek to teach us how to live must be open to question and criticism. This was the approach adopted by Guru Nanak when religious rituals and superstitious practices had virtually obscured ethical teachings that are the essence of true religion. Importantly, he did not rubbish cultural practices that attach themselves to, or distort religious teaching, but in a manner reminiscent of the sermons of Jesus Christ, questioned their relevance.

When I speak to young people in a gurdwara, I say that if something said by a priest in a gurdwara defies common-sense, question it. Religious texts referring to challenges faced by a community thousands of years ago, need to be placed in the context of today's times if they are not to be misused. Only then can religion become a true force for good in our troubled world.

28 November 2018

Sikhism on Freedom of Belief

Last weekend was, for Sikhs, a bit like Christmas and Easter rolled into one. Celebration of the birth anniversary of Guru Nanak who taught the need for responsible living centred on the rights and concerns of others, was followed next day by the commemoration of the martyrdom of the nineth Guru, Guru Tegh Bahadur who in 1675 gave his life in the defence of human rights.

The Mughal ruler Aurangzeb, in his determination to extend Islam to the whole of the sub-continent, was forcibly converting large numbers of Hindus in Kashmir. In desperation the Hindu leaders asked Guru Tegh Bahadur to intercede on their behalf. They said, we know that you and earlier Sikh Gurus have always stood up for the rights of all people, will you appeal to the Mughal Emperor to stop this forced conversion?

The Guru knew that such an appeal would almost certainly cost him his life. But true to Sikh teachings on freedom of belief he set off for Delhi. The Emperor refused to change his policy and instead offered rich gifts to the Guru to convert to Islam. When Guru Tegh Bahadur refused, he was publicly beheaded in the centre of Delhi. His crime, defending the right to freedom of belief of those of a different religion to his own.

The universal right to freedom of belief is emphasised in the UN Declaration of Human Rights, written in the aftermath of the Second World War. We all applaud its lofty sentiments, but all too often put these below trade and economic interest. For example, questions have been recently asked about the selling of arms to Saudi Arabia in the light of the killing of the prominent journalist Jamal Khashoggi and the on-going conflict in Yemen.

Guru Tegh Bahadur set the bar high when on a cold winter's day, he gave his life in the defence of human rights and gave stark reality to Voltaire's, famous words: 'I may not believe in what you say but will defend to the death your right to say it'. Yet, in the Sikh view, fundamental human rights will continue to be ignored unless those in power and authority are prepared to put these rights well above the false lure of short-term economic gain.

NOTE

The BBC tried to dissuade me from broadcasting the talk on the grounds that it criticised a Muslim tyrant, and my decision to leave the slot soon after led to an editorial in The Times critical of the BBC. Curiously, the offending producer later referred to my talk as an example of standing up for the religious freedom of others.

1 May 2019

Looking in From the Outside

I've been watching a fascinating You Tube interview with Kapil Dev, a former Indian Test captain, feared pace bowler and record wicket taker. Kapil Dev, a Punjabi Hindu, said he had many Sikh friends and had visited gurdwaras in India and around the world. He was saddened by the complacency with which Sikhs took the Gurus' teaching on equality, service to others and respect for the teachings of other faiths; treating them simply as background, rather than placing them to the fore in all they did.

He saw Sikh teachings as unifying principles of responsible living that could benefit all humanity. He felt so strongly about this that, instead of writing his own cricketing memoirs, he got his friends to help him write a beautiful, illustrated book about Sikhs and Sikhism to promote a better understanding of Guru Nanak's teachings, not only in the outside world, but importantly among Sikhs themselves who did not seem to understand their true worth. Though himself a Hindu, he called the book 'We the Sikhs'.

Kapil Dev's outsider's view of the true worth of Sikh teachings, simply taken as a background by many Sikhs themselves, reminds me about the story of an art dealer, who when visiting the house of a friend, was struck by the beauty of a painting hanging on the wall. He pointed out to his astonished friend that the painting was a masterpiece, worth thousands.

Our view of our own religion is often distorted by a parallel immersion in culture and customs that are easily mistaken for religion. The outsider looking in can often see things in a clearer perspective. As an outsider to Christianity, I sometimes feel, that some of my Christian friends do not fully appreciate the power of the uplifting teachings of Jesus Christ in his sermon on the Mount to move us to more responsible living, or the importance of the parable of the Good Samaritan in reminding us of the good in other people.

Over the centuries, we have erected barriers of exclusivity between our different faiths. I believe that the outsider looking in, can help us understand that what seem like barriers, are simply gateways to a greater understanding and enrichment of life. We will also find that seeming areas of difference, are much smaller than that which we share in common.

8 May 2019

Persecution of Christians

A Report commissioned by the Foreign Secretary Jeremy Hunt has found that the persecution of Christians in many parts of the world amounts to what some see as near genocide. Millions of Christians have been uprooted from their homes, and many have been killed, kidnapped, imprisoned and discriminated against.

Sadly, the experience of Christians is mirrored in the experience of other faiths. Whilst there are restrictions on Christian freedom of worship in Saudi Arabia, Sikhs are prohibited from opening a gurdwara there. In Afghanistan, a prosperous Sikh population of more than 20,000 has been reduced to a few hundred. Similarly, once thriving Sikh communities in Tehran and other cities in Iran have almost disappeared without trace. Regular reports of the All Parliamentary Group for Freedom of Religion and Belief and other agencies, remind us of similar suffering of religious communities across the world.

A follow up report to examine the response of the Foreign and Commonwealth Office to growing religious persecution will be published later this summer. I do hope that this will lead to positive initiatives to counter world-wide abuse of UN Universal Declaration of the Right to Freedom of Religion and Belief.

I feel part of the problem is a failure of religious leaders to interpret religious texts in the context of today's very different times. Candlelit vigils and expressions of religious solidarity following an atrocity are fine, but in the Sikh view such sentiments must also be carried to our different places of worship, to counter centuries of easily exploited bigotry and misunderstanding, with due emphasis on respect and tolerance of other beliefs.

Two of the Sikh Gurus gave their lives stressing the importance of interfaith understanding. Sikhs believe that our different faiths are like paths up a mountain towards an understanding of God through pursuing truth, equity and justice in our daily lives. The further we go, the greater the similarity of the view ahead. Guru Arjan, our fifth Guru, included some writings of Hindu and Muslim saints in our holy scripture the Guru Granth Sahib, to emphasize that no one faith has a monopoly of truth. Recognition of this essential truth will help us counter the increasing manipulation of religion for grossly irreligious ends.

A Closing Reflection on Pause for Though on BBC Radio 2

For a number of years, I also had the pleasure of presenting 'Pause for Thought' (PFT) with the late and much missed Sir Terry Wogan. Terry was a highly intelligent man with an impish sense of humour which blended well with my own sense of the ridiculous. The following talk, given at a time of much discussion on suggestions on toning down the celebration of Christmas to avoid giving offence to other religious communities, drew a record postbag of appreciation.

Pause for Thought BBC Radio 2 December-07

Terry, your comments yesterday on Christmas meanies remind me of the curious correlation between the switching on of Xmas lights and the speed with which scrooges come out of town hall woodwork and look for excuses to ban Christmas celebrations of any sort. Climbing a ladder to put up Christmas lights is, in their view, a health and safety hazard! They pompously argue that the power used by the lights is a waste of precious, diminishing resources. They even suggest that the word Christmas might offend people of other faiths, and, after chopping down more trees for inter-departmental memos, come up with absurd alternatives. Where will all this end? I know it sounds a bit over the top, but soon they'll even start suggesting that there is no such person as Father Christmas!

It's all great for the media who in their love of controversy, suggest that these misguided do-gooders have the support of people of other faiths. Every year I am asked, 'do I object to the celebration of Christmas?' It's an absurd question. For Sikhs the more excuses for a party, the better.

It's easy to sum up Sikh attitudes to other faiths. It is total respect.

Because of this, I'm delighted that this year the new Commission for Equality and Human Rights is issuing its own Christmas card which I will be happy to sign along with people of other faiths.

As ever, my family and I will send out our Christmas cards to our Christian friends and others. In the spirit of Christmas, we in the Singh family will, as usual, force ourselves to have extra turkey, Christmas pudding and mince pies, the lot – all in the cause of inter-faith harmony. No one can say Sikhs don't go the extra mile!